Teaching Information Fluency

How to Teach Students to Be Efficient, Ethical, and Critical Information Consumers

Carl Heine
Dennis O'Connor

THE SCARECROW PRESS, INC.
Lanham • Toronto • Plymouth, UK
2014

Published by Scarecrow Press, Inc.
A wholly owned subsidary of The Rowman & Littlefield Publishing Group, Inc.
4501 Forbes Boulevard, Suite 200, Lanham, Maryland 20706
www.rowman.com

10 Thornbury Road, Plymouth PL6 7PP, United Kingdom

British Library Cataloguing in Publication Information Available

Library of Congress Cataloging-in-Publication Data
Heine, Carl, 1951–
  Teaching information fluency : how to teach students to be efficient, ethical, and critical
information consumers / Carl Heine, Dennis O'Connor.
    pages ; cm
  Includes bibliographical references and index.
  ISBN 978-0-8108-9062-6 (pbk : alk. paper) – ISBN 978-0-8108-9063-3 (ebook)
  1. Information Literacy – study and teaching 2. Computer literacy – study and teaching
2013021294

♾™ The paper used in this publication meets the minimum requirements of
American National Standard for Information Sciences—Permanence of Paper
for Printed Library Materials, ANSI/NISO Z39.48-1992.

Printed in the United States of America.

Contents

Part IV: Ethical and Fair Use

Part V: Instructional Applications

Figures

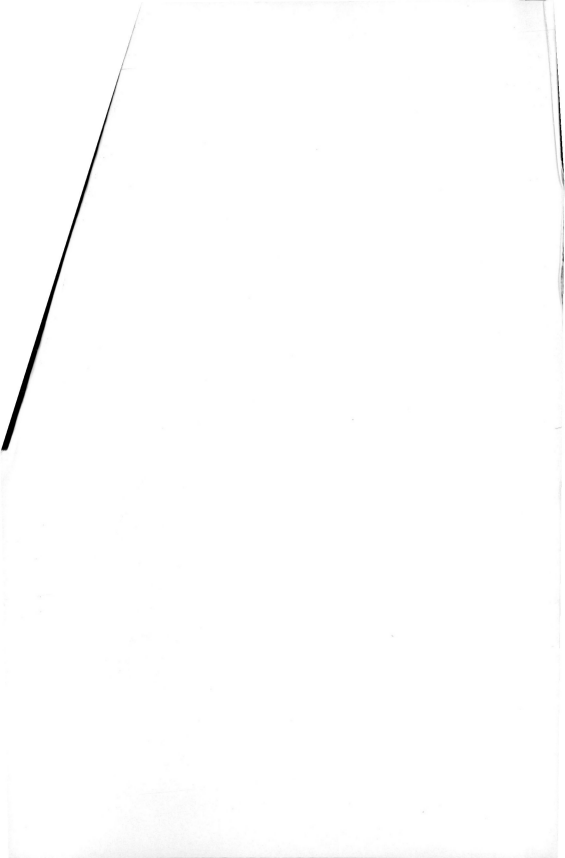

Tables

Foreword

We don't have to look very far these days to see the dramatic changes brought to our lives by the wealth of digital information available today. We are surrounded by it. Virtually every aspect of our lives is being impacted in some way, large or small. Familiar phrases, such as "information explosion" and "information age," coined in the latter half of the twentieth century, hardly seem to do justice to the rapidity and magnitude of the changes taking place every day.

The rise and proliferation of digital information formats and tools has brought with it significant challenges as well as apparently endless opportunities. As with any new resource or tool, realizing its potential requires understanding its inherent strengths and weaknesses, acquiring the skills to use it well rather than badly, and adopting the attitudes needed to ensure we make the most of its possibilities. But these essential skills don't always come easily, even for a generation that has grown up in an increasingly digital world.

Digital information fluency, as described in this book, is a set of knowledge, skills, and attitudes essential to using this newfound wealth of information to make a difference in our world. Some of these proficiencies are included in what is known as information literacy. But the terms *digital* and *fluency* are intended to focus attention on the expanded and less familiar aspects of these new proficiencies.

Perhaps an analogy will help. Digital photography, which has virtually replaced film-based photography in recent years, has much in common with traditional photography. The skills of selecting what to include in a picture, adjusting the exposure for different lighting conditions, focusing the lens so the key figures or objects are clear, and similar skills are fundamental to creating any good photograph. But anyone who has used a digital camera knows that learning to use this new tool involves sometimes challenging adjustments to our familiar habits. We find ourselves looking at the picture not through a viewfinder but in a small screen on the back of the camera. Changing settings doesn't involve buttons but rather electronic menus that must be navigated using unfamiliar and sometimes counterintuitive strategies. We can see the pictures immediately after we take them, if (and only if) we know which sequence of steps to take. We can print our own glossy-paper pictures—if we have learned to download the pictures, find the right paper, and operate the printer properly. Pictures can be sent instantaneously to friends and family without waiting for them to be developed—if we have the interest and the patience to learn how to attach them to an e-mail.

Using these powerful and time-saving new features successfully requires us to add to the fundamental skills of photography a number of new ones that are unique to the new equipment and the new contexts in which we use them. In other words, having film-based photography skills doesn't guarantee success using a *digital* camera, particularly if we mean taking advantage of the new applications for which they were created. In addition, the ability to put digital photography skills to use in the circumstances in which we often take candid pictures can be demanding. When we see a photographic opportunity, we often have to grab the camera, make composition decisions, alter the camera's settings, and take the picture before the window of opportunity passes. Success at this task requires not just a passing familiarity with how to use these new skills but a practiced habit that enables us to perform the activity quickly and seamlessly. This is what is we mean by *fluency*. In real work situations, it is often crucial to be able to apply digital information skills effectively *and* efficiently.

Digital information fluency competencies are much more complex and much more powerful than those needed to use a digital camera well. As the term *fluency* implies, they are more akin to language skills that are prerequisites to and enablers of many other kinds of learning. And like language skills, they are versatile—applicable to a wide range of problem-solving activities from planning a vacation or buying birthday presents to diagnosing complex diseases or delving into the secrets of the atom.

On the basis of my own observations as well as data cited elsewhere in this book, it is clear that the knowledge, skills, and attitudes of digital information fluency are not typically learned during a student's formal educational experience. National educational standards, such as the Common Core State Standards and the National Educational Technology Standards, include these proficiencies in their recommendations, but they have yet to be fully adopted and implemented in a systematic way. Additional challenges are posed by the fact that many students overestimate their proficiencies in this area. Both these trends, documented elsewhere in the book, highlight the importance of providing students and adults alike with learning experiences that will enable them to acquire these essential proficiencies.

The following chapters provide readers with both a deep theoretical understanding of digital information fluency and a wealth of practical strategies for helping learners of all ages acquire what are becoming critical real-world skills that will enable them not just to survive but to thrive in an increasing digital world.

D. David Barr
Illinois Mathematics and Science
Academy, Emeritus

Acknowledgments

This book would not have been possible without the contributions and support of numerous individuals and organizations over the years. Foremost, we wish to recognize David Barr for his mentorship and partnership in developing the information fluency model around which this book and approach to information fluency is built. As principal investigator on the Department of Education grant that gave birth to the 21st Century Information Fluency Project (21CIF) in the early 2000s, David is personally responsible for many of the fundamental concepts articulated in this book. Without his pioneering leadership, the focus of the research and much of the philosophy and content of this book would never have been pursued or come to light.

We are deeply indebted to Laura Kaisler, Chris Kolar, Bob Houston, Dan Balzer, Gautam Saha, Jane St. Pierre, Jane Yoder, and Mary McNabb, members of the 21CIF team over the course of its development. Each contributed uniquely to the research from which information fluency is derived, the 21CIF Web presence, and the reputation of this project in educational circles, starting in Illinois and ultimately extending around the world. We also wish to credit Paula Garrett, director of the Information Resource Center, who was instrumental in arranging and running training sessions with faculty and students at the Illinois Mathematics and Science Academy. Paula also introduced 21CIF and our research to the world by submitting a paper and presenting it at the Australian Library and Information Association in Perth, Australia.

The support of the Illinois Mathematics and Science Academy, known as IMSA, made all this possible. IMSA was the birthplace and home of information fluency from 2001 to 2007. The IMSA brand was invaluable in promoting our work to thousands of educators and students across schools and libraries in Illinois, Wisconsin, and neighboring states, lending significant credibility to our efforts. By releasing its interest in the project to its creators, IMSA ensured the resources of the project would remain available to all.

Our partnership with the Center for Talent Development at Northwestern University in bringing information fluency training to its students is also gratefully acknowledged. In particular, we wish to thank Susan Corwith and Randee Blair for their proactive leadership in promoting a vision of information fluency for gifted students and helping us tell the story at national conferences.

Finally, we simply could not have written this without the unwavering support of our wives and dearest partners, Patricia Heine and Janice O'Connor, who graciously allowed us time and space to create this book.

Prologue

The greatest redistribution of global wealth, estimated at up to a trillion dollars annually,[1] is happening online today. Some of it is taken by force (hacking), but much of it is given away willingly in response to information that, on the surface, seems trustworthy. The victims are individuals, their corporations, and their countries. Unwitting consumers of information fall prey to a variety of misinformation online: offers that sound too good to be true or too real not to be true. Sadly, much of this loss could be avoided if people were better prepared.

One fake tweet about explosions at the White House can send Wall Street into a dive, as it did when @AP was hacked. It took only a few minutes for the market to reverse its course following a statement from AP that its message was not true. What the world saw was a country, hypersensitive to terrorism, react involuntarily. News on Twitter tends to break first from eyewitnesses and then is picked up by news services. Had anyone stopped to look for the original tweet on the story, AP's would have been the source—a red flag to a careful information consumer. Instead, less careful people by the thousands ate this up.

The failure to investigate digital information before acting on it is a hallmark of Internet usage today. It starts young and persists into adulthood. Finding information online seems so easy. Sometimes, thanks to personalization, it finds us. The Internet has a way of making believers out of normally savvy searchers. At some point, one's guard comes down, along comes an opportunity and a searcher turns into a consumer at a cost that is more than the opportunity is worth.

This trend can be altered with training and practice. Informed searching does not occur automatically. It happens by design. Of all the ways to search for information online, some are more productive and efficient than others. Curiously, individuals struggle to become proficient searchers and careful consumers of information without help. One might think the hands-on, trial-and-error experience of online activity would be more self-instructive than it is. Without guided help, learners tend to remain unaware the search tactics they employ are ineffective and inefficient, the information they find is inaccurate or out-of-date and how they use what they find is unethical.

At the same time, becoming information fluent isn't difficult. It can be learned in minutes. Searching with purpose, fact checking results and putting findings ethically to use requires no extraordinary talent. Everyone is capable of fluency.

Even though the Internet has emerged as a staple of learning, helping students to search more productively and efficiently remains largely overlooked. The inclusion of online research competencies in the Common Core standards signals a move to address this, but it is not likely to produce change given pervasive emphasis on schools to produce students capable of reading, writing, and doing math. Compared to these more highly prized objectives, search skills will continue to languish in the background. For this reason, the approach taken in this book is to provide educators models for integrating information fluency instruction into existing coursework as systematic support for informational reading and writing. The main thrust is not to create separate units or courses to promote information fluency—although that could be effective—but rather to weave into courses that require research strategies and techniques for locating, evaluating, and ethically using information.

While the book has primarily an educational flavor, readers interested in searching but not education, will find practical lifetime benefits: becoming information fluent saves time locating information that may be trusted, fosters independent learning, and strengthens critical thinking prior to consumption. In short, disciplined searching supports informed decision making, which, for many has great potential for saving time as well as money.

NOTE

1. Peter Maass and Megha Rajagopalan, "Does Cybercrime Really Cost $1 Trillion?" *ProPublica.org*, last modified August 1, 2012, http://www.propublica.org/article/does-cybercrime -really-cost-1-trillion.

I

DIGITAL
INFORMATION FLUENCY

1

Digital Information Fluency in an Age of Information Consumption

Searching is becoming easier than thinking. Enter a query in a search engine, and the searcher is instantly flooded with results. Information has never been easier to retrieve and consume. At the same time, determining the quality of the results remains a daunting task. Despite the attempts to make search tools "brain dead easy"[1] to use, searching that reduces the need to think invites problems. Machines cannot reliably predict what each individual is hunting for, machines cannot determine what is credible, yet that is the direction search engine development is headed.

One sign that searching takes less thought is seen in changes to a browser's address bar, now known as the omnibox. A common mistake ten years ago was to type a query in the address bar of a browser rather than the search box of a search engine. Back in the Netscape and Alta Vista heydays, unless the query was also a URL, typing a query in the address bar would yield a "404 page not found" error. This result became an opportunity for a little trial and error learning—why didn't that work? Today one can type a query in the omnibox and specify which search engine results to display for that query. This is a clear accommodation to general patterns of user behavior (and a preference that may be edited). Typing in the wrong box is a thing of the past, a problem overcome by making the address bar more inclusive. As a result, searching is easier; there is no longer a need to think about where to type a query.

Another consumer accommodation involves the query itself. Predictive services offered by Google, Bing, Yahoo!, and others display alternate queries based on user input. For example, if *assessment* is typed in the address bar, many suggestions appear: assessment test, assessment for learning, assessment and taxation, a Wikipedia article on assessment, and a Web page on the characteristics of twenty-first century learners, among others. These suggested queries may or may not be relevant to the user's need, but there's a good chance the user did not have these specific alternatives in mind when embarking on the search. These automated suggestions could take the search in directions the user did not initially have in mind.

It is certain that search technology will continue to evolve, requiring less effort from the searcher to locate information. However, this does not diminish the need for competent, thoughtful searching and careful consumption, which requires training and deliberation. Instant and predictive results do not diminish the need for strategic searching. Interestingly, solo trial-and-error searching does not result in effective strategies.[2] If the purpose of improved tools is to reduce error, it also diminishes the possibility of learning from one's mistakes through trial-and-error practice. Determining whether instant and predictive results are accurate or objective is optimally a skill learned by practice, not an automated process. Tools may become easier to use, but there is no substitute for instruction and collaboration where searching is involved. Skilled searching is not brain-dead easy.

The short definition of digital information fluency (DIF) is the "ability to find, evaluate and use digital information effectively, efficiently and ethically."[3] Most definitions of information literacy cover the same ground. Take, for example, the competencies described by the American Library Association (ALA):

- Determine the extent of information needed
- Access the needed information effectively and efficiently
- Evaluate information and its sources critically
- Incorporate selected information into one's knowledge base
- Use information effectively to accomplish a specific purpose
- Understand the economic, legal, and social issues surrounding the use of information, and access and use information ethically and legally[4]

The real difference between information literacy and fluency lies not in what searchers or consumers do but how they do it. Fluent individuals have more experience, know more about the "language" they use, and can accomplish what needs to be done more easily using multiple pathways. The emphasis with information fluency is to equip users with sufficient strategies and methods to overcome most retrieval challenges. A fluent searcher knows how digital and print information differs, quickly learns specialized tools for finding digital information, and engages effectively in a digital information environment. The sections that follow provide a framework for understanding these competencies and the dispositions necessary for developing fluency.

SPECULATIVE AND INVESTIGATIVE SEARCHING

Viewed from the highest perspective, information fluency is part of a research process that encompasses two types of searching: speculative and investigative searching. Together, these are part of a larger process that starts with speculation and extends beyond investigation. One view of the larger picture is the Big Six. The process outlined by the Big Six starts with (1) task definition, followed by (2) information-seeking strategies, (3) location and access, (4) use of information, and (5) synthesis, and ends with (6) evaluation of the product and process.[5] In information fluency terms, the first three steps in the Big Six involve speculation, and the fourth step (use of information) is where investigation occurs when students extract information that is relevant and of quality. The process does not have to be linear, though in practice it tends to start with (1) task definition and end with (6) product and process evaluation. Taken together, mastery of the elements equals information literacy.

Speculation and investigation together do not result in a finished research paper. Each is a different type of research that involves different competencies. The ultimate outcome could be a research paper, but it could also be locating a good-quality TV for the best price, fact checking claims made during an election, or hiring a reputable contractor for a household project. No matter the outcome, the combined objective of speculation and investigation is to locate information that can be trusted. To this end, speculation relies on prediction and guesswork; investigation does not. Understanding the differences between them—as well as the applications of each—is crucial to effective digital research.

Speculative searching is far more common than its investigative counterpart. Everyone who looks for information online is familiar with speculation. Speculative searching is how the search process begins. For many, it is synonymous with querying and browsing. Speculation starts with a question, proceeds to a results page, and moves on to a clicked link. Faced with an inexhaustible supply of information and a limited amount of time, searchers must make calculated guesses about which word(s) to query, which search engine(s) to use, and which result(s) to follow in order to find answers not already known.

Sometimes guessing is unnecessary, for example, using a mobile device to find simple facts like the current temperature or the spices that go into a curry. But even the easiest searches may require guesswork the first time. First-time searches require thinking about which words to search with and where to use them. Consider this example: "Find the top speed of earth's fastest animal." The words to use in such a search include one or more of those that appear in quotation marks as well as additional terms (and operators) yet to be discovered in the process. Many words and combinations are possible. Will the query *top speed of earth's fastest animal* work? Or is *fastest animal* better? Does it make a difference?

It's hard to answer these questions without entering keywords into a search engine and checking results. Before jumping to a conclusion, which search engine should be used? Google's search engine is by far the most common default choice.[6] But is Google guaranteed to work in this case? Will a different search engine yield a different answer? To be sure, the same query must be tried in multiple search engines. Google is a great general-purpose search engine, but it is not the only one. Other choices include Yahoo!, Bing, Ask, AOL, MyWebSearch, Dogpile, WebCrawler, and Hakia. There are also many choices that retrieve content stored in databases unavailable to Google: EBSCO,

JSTOR, Grolier, PubMed, Whois, WayBackMachine, and so on. Selecting Google is a speculative choice; it's one option among many.

The query *fastest animal* entered into Google produces around eight hundred results. The results page states there are over five million results, but the accessible list ends well before that. (For Google, efficiency is more important than depth; it would take more than a few seconds to load up several million records.) A mere ten results on the first page satisfies an average searcher's needs, so trimming the results to only 0.016 percent of what's available to Google for this query remains quite reasonable.

In fact, there is a surplus of information in the top ten results. These animals are mentioned or pictured in the context of *fastest animal*:

- Peregrine falcon (2)
- cheetah (3)
- sailfish (2)
- pronghorn antelope
- wildebeest
- lion
- Thompson's gazelle
- quarter horse
- man

Which is the correct answer? If the top answer (from Wikipedia) is accepted, the answer is the Peregrine falcon. Or should the most frequent answer, cheetah, be accepted? The situation doesn't improve if *top speed of earth's fastest animal* is substituted. Now the top ten results include:

- Peregrine falcon (2)
- man
- greyhound
- cheetah
- cow dropped out of a helicopter

Determining the best answer takes more than looking at the results page snippets (also known as abstracts). Opening and scanning each of the top ten results shows that three sites claim the fastest animal is the Peregrine falcon, while three other sites identify the cheetah. This is a classic student dilemma: Which source is right? Upon closer reading, the results describe the falcon as the fastest *bird*, the cheetah as the fastest *land animal*, and the sailfish as the fastest *fish*. Since the original question merely asked for *animal*, the falcon ought to win hands down. But is Peregrine falcon the best answer? If the falcon beats the cheetah by virtue of gravity, a cow dropped from a sufficient height could break the sound barrier and plummet past the falcon in a flash. A 1960s-space-program chimpanzee or a present-day astronaut orbiting the earth might actually be the record holder, but was that the intent of the question?

Knowing what question to answer makes a crucial difference in recognizing an appropriate answer. Interpreting the question becomes part of the speculative process. What exactly is being sought? Whether the question is given as an assignment or arises out of a personal need, speculation may be involved. Searches fail when information is sought to answer the wrong question. The first question one searches for is often not the right question. Clearly articulating what information is being sought is the first step in the information fluency model and helps eliminate a lot of aimless speculation.

Digital searching consists of five sets of competencies.[7] Three of these apply to speculative searching:

- The first, as indicated, is being able to understand the question in order to translate it into a query.
- The second is to know which database to search—and how to find and use an unfamiliar database.
- The third is to figure out how to home in on information through iterative searching, browsing, skimming, and scanning.

Students experience problems with each of these competencies. A fourth problem area—evaluating the results—encompasses the domain of investigative searching, discussed later. The fifth area students find difficult is how to use or consume the findings, which in the context of research means avoiding plagiarism and not violating guidelines of fair use, both matters of ethical use. These five competency sets, along with dispositions, make up the Information Fluency Model.

INVESTIGATIVE SEARCHING

Investigation involves evaluating results by searching with finely honed keywords and specific search engines. Investigative searching requires a skeptical mindset and the perseverance to look well beyond the first page of results. The chief purpose of investigative searching is fact checking: Do the facts or claims found by speculation stand up to scrutiny? Is the content accurate, fresh, and credible? Is the author sufficiently knowledgeable and experienced? Is the publisher reputable and unbiased?

The persistent problem encountered with investigative searching is the failure to do it. Most students—adults, too—accept the face validity of initial results and typically forego investigation,[8] even though in many respects it is easier than speculation. Virtually no guesswork is involved with investigative searching. Using the *fastest animal* example, an investigative search uses *given* keywords and *known* databases to fact check either the source, the content, or both.

Starting with content, a good query is *Peregrine falcon* along with *speed OR fastest animal*. All are keywords found in the assignment and initial results. The purpose of fact checking is to establish how fast the falcon travels. At least two additional sources should be located. Triangulation, comparing three or more sources when fact checking, is an essential tactic for investigation. If several credible, unrelated sites agree, the information appears to be more reliable. If several unrelated sites disagree, then it is wise to remain skeptical and continue the investigation.

Here are the top three results for the query *Peregrine falcon fastest speed:*

- wikipedia.com: 322 km/h (200 mph)
- topspeed.com: easily eclipsing 200 mph
- extremescience.com: 160–440 km/h (99–273 mph)

This information may be found by clicking search results for three different sites, then locating the word *speed* (with the "Find" command, Ctrl+F) on the respective pages. The most conservative speed is faster than any known cheetah. Several sources claim the falcon, thanks to gravity and aerodynamics, can attain such speeds.

So what's to prevent a cow dropped from a helicopter or an orbiting astronaut from being an acceptable answer? It immediately becomes apparent that attempting to answer one's own question by speculative and investigative searching reveals ambiguities or incompleteness in the wording of questions. For educators it's always a good idea to test initial questions by searching online to discover what students are likely to find. Doing so leads to better questions that lead to better results (and fewer sarcastic answers). Poor searching starts with ill-defined questions that fail to be improved by iterative querying. This is why most models, the Big Six and ALA included, start with determining the information needed.

The differences between speculative and investigative searching frame how the search may be understood. The types of questions that guide research activity and the training received will help learners grasp where they are in the process and how to proceed fluently. Speculation and investigation form the two halves of the Digital Information Fluency Model (see figure 1.1). One without the other is an incomplete search. The following five sections introduce the competencies that comprise the whole of information fluency.

Digital Information Fluency Model

Figure 1.1.   Digital Information Fluency Model

WHAT AM I LOOKING FOR?

The Information Fluency Model is based on five questions that occur throughout the search process. What am I looking for? Where will I find the information? How will I get there? Is the information any good? How will I use the information ethically? Like the Big Six, these tend to start with the first question and end with the last, but in between the order is not necessarily linear. In practice, the order is often iterative. As information is retrieved, the speculative question is refined, different sources are consulted, and better keywords are substituted until relevant information is found. As a result of investigation, a decision to revise or accept the information is made. If revised—known as the revision decision—the process may restart with a better speculative question. Without exception, a search is conceived when an individual acknowledges a need for information. In the context of digital searching, no computer is needed at this moment. The "I need information step" happens in the head of the searcher.

How the question arises may alter only slightly what happens next. If the need for information arises from immediate need or, more formally, from a teacher, the process is limited to words in the user's memory, the environment, or the assignment. The words available to the searcher are what matter most. A person with an average vocabulary may be at disadvantage compared to one with an extensive knowledge of words. Why? Because the words taken from memory or the environment may not be the words necessary to locate the information needed. The more words one knows, the better one's chances of matching words used by an online author. Nonetheless, a subject matter expert may use professional vocabulary that is unfamiliar or seldom used by a general audience. Predictive search suggestions may level the playing field somewhat. The words used in assignments may also help. From observation, it is uncommon for students to use keywords in a search other than those given in an assignment. Knowing this, a teacher may introduce words that serve as useful clues. Carefully worded assignments can take a lot of guesswork out of speculative searching. But not all assignments are carefully worded, and self-initiated searches generally start with words—and questions—that need to be improved.

It doesn't take much digging to unearth a complex set of competencies around the question "What am I looking for?" Some of these are bedrock competencies, like memory and the ability to read, both of which are beyond the scope of this book. Others are more application oriented or operational. In this regard the ability to turn a question into a query is the core competency. Knowing how to transform a question into a query involves understanding parts of speech, knowing the meaning of words, and recognizing which words make powerful search terms. Choosing the best words at hand is an effective way to distill the essence of what is being sought.

"Keyword Challenge"[9] on the 21st Century Information Fluency site is designed to help users think about words, their meanings, and how to create effective queries. Users are directed to sort the words in a question into four categories: words that are effective "as is," words that are important but probably not effective as is, words that are unimportant, and "stop" words. Sifting a sentence to identify the good as-is terms and the terms that could be better often distills the meaning of the question in as few words as possible. Discarding terms that add nothing results in a more powerful query. Students tend to adopt the words given them, so taking this approach makes sense.

To illustrate, take the question "Who first claimed that China's Great Wall could be identified from space?" Sort all the words into one of these categories:

- Good as is: Great, Wall, space
- Important, but there's probably a better word: claimed, identified
- Unimportant (and stop words): who, first, that, China's, can, be, from

As-is words are usually nouns. Objects, in particular proper nouns and numbers, tend to make better search terms than verbs. A verb may be important, but there is often a better word for it. Unimportant words are small parts of speech: pronouns, prepositions, and modifiers. The proper noun *China* is unimportant here because it is redundant. Because the Great Wall is in China, *China* adds nothing.

Keeping the first query to the fewest terms possible, the user must remember one important detail from the question now missing from the query: who. The answer to the question is going to be a person's name. Competence depends on more than choosing what goes in the first query. An effective query retrieves only a collection of relevant information. From this the information consumer must make a selection using terms that may not have been part of the first query. This is an important point. Trying to include everything necessary in a query is not how to get the most value out of a search engine. The user who filters the first round of returns using what could be called an invisible query finds the best results. The searcher scans for terms never entered in the search box but that are important nonetheless. This is another example of how searching is not brain-dead easy. The search engine rarely receives all the speculative information, and if it does, the overloaded search suffers. More about search-box strategies is found in chapters 3 and 4.

WHERE WILL I FIND THE INFORMATION?

The first core competency is coupled with a second: knowing where to search. Once again, this step is speculative and has no active role for a computer.

Where does a search happen? There are chiefly two places to start: a search engine interface or a Web page. A third option, infrequently used, starts with a URL and involves truncating that URL to access directories on a Web site. The user must start somewhere. A competent user bases the decision on a prediction: Which starting point and path will be most effective? The informed user is already thinking ahead to step 3: How will I get there?

Experience, training, or both inform the decision. The experienced user knows that browsing may involve a hard path to follow. Compared to querying or truncation, browsing requires luck and a high degree of sensitivity to hyperlinked words and contextual clues. Browsing can quickly devolve into a hollow game of clicking links. Hoping for the best, the searcher is quickly sidetracked or lost. This approach can be pleasurable, such as surfing the Web, but trying to do research this way produces frustration. Curiously, browsing seems to be students' default search method. It doesn't take much thought to click a link. It takes a high degree of discipline and persistence to click the right one (and to click the back button when the search goes awry).

A more straightforward approach may be to ask someone knowledgeable. While going to a teacher or librarian may be the shortest path to information, it depends on who is available at the time. Needless to say, this option must be weighed alongside the digital alternatives. So, how does one decide whether to consult a person or turn to a digital resource?

Returning to the Great Wall of China example, a strategic step-2 question to ask is "Who would know this information?" Maybe the searcher knows someone who has been talking about this topic. If not, this is going to involve a lot of guesswork and hunches. Deductive reasoning and imagination may be involved in this competency. Because the topic pertains to space, someone from an organization like NASA might know about it. But who could that be? Someone who's been in space, like an astronaut, might know if the wall is visible or not, but would they know who was the first to claim the Great Wall could be seen from space? That's the real question. Maybe a historian would know best.

Without specific knowledge of this subject matter, deciding whom the expert is—let alone trying to find such a person—is a guessing game. The simple fact that it's hard to imagine someone specific who might know the answer excludes all but one starting point. Starting on a Web page or truncating a URL doesn't make sense because there's no Web page or URL to start with. The appropriate starting place is a standard query.

The Information Fluency Model defines this set of competencies as "learners effectively and efficiently select digital collections based on their characteristics."[10] If the best starting point is a digital collection, competent searchers should understand how digital information is organized and that different collections have different characteristics. A digital collection is a database. Digital information is saved in databases that can be retrieved by searching. Google searches its database when a query is sent through its engine. Yahoo!'s database is separate from Google's, although much of the same information may be found in both, aggregated from public pages on a myriad of sites. NASA's database is different than Google's and Yahoo!'s and contains, potentially, a vastly different collection. Some of NASA's content is proprietary and off limits to other search engines. This is what makes NASA's collection part of the Deep Web: It's only available by going to NASA's site. No other search engine can retrieve it—although Google, Yahoo!, and others index some parts of it. Using the reasoning outlined earlier, a search might start by querying NASA rather than one of the large aggregated databases.

HOW WILL I GET THERE?

Once a question comes to mind and a place to start is determined, it's customary to go to a computer. Numerous competencies cluster around the process of homing in on information. If a direct query is the preferred method, a search engine page is brought up. If a different starting point is identified, other skills come into play. Each of these and the associated competencies is introduced in turn.

Two sets of competencies go hand in hand to "get there": querying and browsing. For querying, tools consist of a search engine, all the features that come with it, and a results page. Browsing mainly involves scanning Web pages and trying hyperlinks.

Starting with query, the software behind the search box provides powerful functionality, part of which is standard no matter what search engine is used. Other specialized tools are specific to a particular engine. Search algorithms may be proprietary and secret, giving a company a competitive advantage over its rivals. It's not possible to know everything about the tool at the code level, and that's not the searcher's goal anyway. However, a key competency is the ability to use a search engine effectively, which means the fluent user must be able to *learn* to use an unfamiliar engine. This implies a strategic approach to search-engine use on several levels: first-time use, basic search, and advanced search. Information on teaching these strategies is addressed in chapter 3.

As search algorithms advance, the search engine will learn by feeding on queries and provide automated query suggestions, giving the fluent searcher more to think about. If queries are being assessed in order to provide the user with more personalized results, other information must be filtered out. The specter of the filter bubble[11] signals a level of control that may blind the searcher and eventual consumer of information to some results based on incremental data submitted by other searchers pursuing similar results. Implementing ways to overcome the filter bubble is an emerging competency, discussed in chapters 5 and 9.

Competent searchers know that the number and order of terms in a query makes a difference. The more keywords combined, the fewer the results. This may be a good strategy for the end of a search but not its beginning. The most effective first attempt is to use two to five keywords and see what happens. Homing in on information is likely to involve finding better keywords that the user did not start with. To locate these words, it is best to start by searching with just a few terms in the query.

Fluent searchers also understand concepts of linguistic granularity, known as hyponyms and hypernyms. While the terms may sound technical, the ideas are not: Many words have synonyms that are more general (hypernyms) and other synonyms that are more specific (hyponyms). The ability to adjust the specificity of a term can be crucial to querying. For the keyword *automobile*, *vehicle* is a hypernym and *Chrysler* a hyponym. The importance of choosing the right grain-size term depends on the number of results retrieved by a query. Faced with too few results, a hypernym will broaden the search as well as the results. A hyponym will narrow the range of results.

Search operators are additional tools the competent searcher can use. Improvements to search-engine algorithms have reduced the need for operators but not removed them entirely. Many search engines built on older code still require Boolean operators, so it is in the fluent searcher's best interests to know about operators. In brief, operators may be classified as simple or advanced. Simple operators are AND

(+), OR (|), NOT (-), and "ALL," where "ALL" is replaced by a search string or phrase. Most search engines have eliminated the need for AND (+) by making it the space-bar function. The purpose and application of these and advanced operators, such as "link:" and "site:," are examined later in this book (chapter 5).

Returning to the earlier example, if the query *great wall space* with no operators is entered into Google, a page of snippets is displayed filled with relevant-looking information and even a possible answer. Something that happens just before the results are delivered should not be overlooked. Google suggests adding the term *myth*. Apparently other searchers associate the term *myth* with this query. This is an immediate red flag and implies something may be amiss with the claim that the wall can be seen from space.

As soon as the query comes back, homing in switches from querying to browsing. Browsing includes skimming or reading results snippets, scanning for specific terms, clicking on links, and reading the URL. Skimming, the more general reading skill, involves quickly reading the content of a page to get a sense of its meaning. Scanning is more targeted: looking for specific terms, names, or images on a page. It is possible for homing in to stop once the first snippets are obtained, however this is not a good decision. The name *Jake Garn* is found by skimming the contents of the first ten results without having to click through to any other content. This is a speculative answer (and incorrect). A user who fails to investigate if astronaut Jake Garn is the first person to make this claim has performed only half a search.

Typically, the process of homing in is more complicated. For example, in this case the first snippet is from an article on NASA's site. Because NASA could be a credible source on the topic, this article seems worth browsing (skimming the content or reading more closely). The article claims the wall is difficult, if not impossible, to detect with the naked eye from close-earth orbit. Halfway down the page is this statement: "The theory that the wall could be seen from the Moon dates back to at least 1938. It was repeated and grew until astronauts landed on the lunar surface."[12] While it doesn't mention who theorized the visibility of the wall, the article contains an important clue: 1938. This date is a very specific hyponym for *when*. The competent searcher now has an improved query: *great wall space 1938*. This second query is very likely to retrieve the same NASA article in addition to other articles that may actually name the "who" in question.

Browsing the results, the first snippet for the improved query now contains a new name: Richard Halliburton. The second snippet, snopes.com, also names the same person, found by reading the article. Using the "Find" command to locate *1938* on the page, Snopes states that while the original source is unknown, Halliburton's book *Second Book of Marvels: The Orient* attributes the claim to astronomers.[13] Several other snippets lead to information naming Halliburton as at least a catalyst for spreading the idea. Jake Garn, whose mission did not launch until forty-two years later, certainly was not the first person to make this claim.

The same Snopes article refers to Henry Norman, whose 1904 book *The People and Politics of the Far East* talks about the wall being visible from the Moon. This predates Halliburton and the space program and thus far is the earliest known reference to the theory. There may be no definitive answer to the question; in fact, the question could now be improved. A little searching has provided two names and two dates for information published long before anyone could substantiate it.

Homing in, as this illustrates, may involve alternating between querying and browsing. Browsing often leads to more specific keywords and stronger queries in an iterative process. But there are other ways that rely predominantly on an alternation of hyperlink clicking and page skimming. Like surfing the Web, this involves clicking through an indeterminate number of pages until the user discovers something interesting or useful. Hyperlinks and their surroundings are the critical tools at the searcher's disposal. A great deal of information is located this way and is exactly how most searches end. Like public transportation, a query is good at getting one close to a destination. Browsing is like having to walk the remaining distance. Here's where the analogy differs: Unlike walking the rest of the way home, the location of home may or may not be close, and there is no map.

Even when "home" is only two clicks away, it is possible to get hopelessly lost when searching for digital information. As part of an assessment of the search skills program developed by the 21st Century Information Fluency Project for the Center for Talent Development at Northwestern University, participants were directed to find information about members of the Actroid robotics team on a company website.[14] This turned out to be one of the hardest challenges in the assessment, despite the information being just two clicks away. A considerable number of students got frustrated and consulted their parents. Their parents got lost.

The task is completed by using a search engine to get close and browsing the rest of the way. A search for *Actroid* on the company site results in two links. (A query is unable to find the required page.) With hindsight and a map, it doesn't seem overly complicated:

- First click: "Intelligent Systems Research Institute"—This snippet includes a literal reference to Actroid Group Members.
- Second click: "Group HP"
- Information located

But these are not the only links that could be clicked. Thinking of it as a path, the first junction is a fork with two choices: "Intelligent Systems Research Institute" or a link/snippet written in Japanese. Taking the first choice leads to a page of information and another junction: "Group Members" and "Group HP." The first link seems more likely but doesn't match the specific information in the directions. "Group HP" does that, but to get to that link, the user might need to back up. Besides being sensitive to terms (What is the closest match?) and context (Am I getting closer?), the user must be able to retrace steps (Where was I before this when things made more sense?).

Browsing without a map is like playing the children's game "Hot and Cold": The closer one is to the information, the warmer one becomes, except here the user is never explicitly told what to do. The context must be interpreted to determine if the search is headed in the right direction. Even when the user has a one-in-four chance of clicking on the right links, browsing can be a challenge.

Related both to querying and browsing is truncation, another way to home in. As it applies to keywords, truncation involves removing the end of a word to make it less specific, converting it to a hypernym. For example, *instructor* or *instruction* may be truncated to *instruct** (the * is a wildcard operator), telling the search engine to find words that start with *instruct* but may end with anything else. This may yield a wider range of results, a sound strategy to expand a search.

Truncating a URL removes tailing sections of a Web address divided by slashes. For example: https://21cif.com/tutorials is a truncated version of https://21cif.com/tutorials/micro. This is a quick way to navigate to directories or other pages of a site. Sometimes access is forbidden; many times it is not, and the user gets to see the contents of a directory or an index page. Truncation may be useful to home in on information, however it is more commonly used as an investigative technique to find information about an author, a publication date, or other content.

In order to locate information, a fluent searcher must understand effective ways to construct a query, then use browsing either to locate information or, more frequently, find better keywords from which to build more powerful queries. A fluent searcher:

- depends heavily on language skills,
- has the ability to learn how to use a search engine,
- knows how to overcome the filtering effects of a search engine,
- edits queries to broaden or narrow their focus,
- knows how to use operators,
- finds better keywords in snippets and articles,
- navigates through hyperlinks,
- truncates keywords and URLs, and
- strategically knows when to use the methods that make the most sense.

EVALUATION

Most people recognize "If it's on the Internet, it must be true" is meant as a joke. The phrase has been popularized in posters, cartoons, and television commercials. Despite this, it's not uncommon to fall victim to erroneous information online. Among information's many qualities are accuracy, objectivity, and freshness. To the fluent evaluator/consumer, each one of these qualities is important. The ability to detect inaccuracies, bias, and outdated information is essential. Otherwise, the outcome is hardly different than believing everything online is true.

Information online can be inaccurate due to a variety of causes. Misinformation can occur because of unintended mistakes, like typos, or more deliberate attempts to deceive, like scams. Some misinformation is harmless, even fun; some is malignant and may properly be labeled malinformation.[15] The fluent evaluator aims to find credible, consumable information for research and seeks neither to be misinformed nor malinformed.

This is accomplished through investigative searching. Like speculative searching, this involves querying, browsing, reading, and thinking. The main difference is that the searcher starts with information from "homing in" to be evaluated. Evaluation encompasses the first three questions but with far less speculation. For example, instead of *great wall china*, an investigative query might read *jake garn great wall*. Here the evaluator is gathering evidence about Mr. Garn: Who is Jake Garn? Did he say this? When? Why? Was he the first? If the user stopped after just one query and turned to investigate a single clue (Jake Garn), it would take no time to see that, while this material is accurate, it fails to answer the question, and needless consumption of the wrong information would be avoided.

Knowing what clues to investigate is half the competency. The other half is actually doing it. The difficulty with information fluency is having the dispositions to practice strategies and methods that are not difficult to use. Developing confidence, persistence, curiosity, open-mindedness, and flexibility is, arguably, more challenging than learning how to identify a good keyword to investigate. Yet lacking sufficient dispositions, all but the easiest searches become exercises in incompetence. Getting students to *use* sound search strategies is harder than teaching them how to do it.

Unfortunately, the Internet provides plenty of opportunities for information consumers to be fooled. It takes constant vigilance to avoid Internet hoaxes and scams. The way to avoid being fooled is through investigation. Investigating a Web site or an author's claim can be a rewarding experience on several levels. First, there's the joy of discovering that something that sounds good is not what it seems (or vice versa). There's also the intrinsic enjoyment of the problem-solving process, which can be very motivating. For students, the process is stalking clues like a detective. Investigation can become gamelike. There is almost always something to be discovered.

Evaluation starts by examining a search result to determine its usefulness. Does it address the natural language question? If not, how can the search be revised to produce a more accurate result? This is the revision decision that leads to selecting other search results or changing the query based on the results. If information passes the initial "sniff test," it is time to evaluate either the reliability of the source or the accuracy of the content.

Whether source or content is selected first depends on what looks more suspicious. If a fact or claim seems implausible, then triangulating that information is a good first step. If something about a Web site or author (e.g., of a blog) seems unusual, then investigating the source is a good place to start. In either case, the fluent searcher must be able to detect red flags in information that looks suspicious, out of place, tampered with, or just not right.

What makes digital information appear "not right" is hard to define and varies from one person to the next, but a skeptical searcher knows it when he or she sees it.

Red flags may include typos, misplaced or misused words, graphics that don't look right or are out of place, claims that seem outrageous or too good to be true, facts that are missing, advertisements, popups, personalizations, other evidence of profit seeking, and viruses that are downloaded. The ability to detect red flags includes having a gut feeling something is just not right without being able to put one's finger on it. Masahiro Mori coined the term *uncanny valley* to describe the creepy feeling people get when confronted with robotics that are too lifelike.[16] People are increasingly put off the more a robot looks human. Something in what they see raises a red flag. Even though the robot's nonhuman characteristics are minimal, on some level of awareness, they are perceptible. Information that may be just a little off can have the same unsettling effect. When that happens, it's usually a good idea to follow one's instincts and investigate the content, the source, or both.

Content evaluation takes two forms: internal accuracy and external validation. It's more of a task to determine the accuracy of contents than to check external sources for validation. Internal accuracy revolves around what the author wrote and how and when the author said it. In some cases content may be inaccurate because it doesn't coincide with or support other facts in the text. Crucial details may be omitted or extraneous information may be included to cover up facts that are missing. At other times, information will be inaccurate simply because it was mistyped or written so long ago that it is no longer current. Is the information fresh or outdated? Determining the date information was written or published is an essential competency.

Author bias is also a factor that may contribute to inaccuracy. Bias, or subjective viewpoint, potentially skews content and communicates information about the objectivity of the author. Information passed through the lens of personal perspective may become distorted, exaggerated, or cloaked. This happens to authors and readers alike. Detecting internal inaccuracies and bias depends on careful, objective, even slow reading, something hurried searchers tend to gloss over. The connection between careful reading and evaluative searching should not be taken lightly. Without sufficient language skills, searchers will be blind to internal inconsistencies or information that should be there and isn't. Without self-awareness, searchers will be blind to the bias they bring to their reading. This has direct implications for reading levels and when the time is right to teach information fluency in schools (chapter 2).

External validation is, in many respects, easier to determine. It requires plugging a found fact like *peregrine falcon* or *jake garn* into a query along with one or two given details. Competent searchers can extract a fact from a page. Oftentimes these facts are proper nouns or numbers, as previously discussed. Other times, the fact may be a string, in which case it may be good to use it with the quotes operator. For example, to check the external validity of the phrase, "If it's on the Internet, it must be true," the entire phrase could be pasted in a query as is. Results will be all the instances that match the phrase exactly (if quotes are used) or come close (if quotes are not used). Google reports over 800,000 instances of the exact phrase in its database of digital information. Obviously, it's a very popular phrase and not one the present author can claim to have originated. If that were the claim, it would be easy to determine its external reliability by including the name *Carl Heine* with the string. There is only one relevant result for that query, and it is the author's blog.[17] No site supports the claim. However, if the claim to be evaluated is whether this phrase occurs in posters, cartoons, and television commercials, external results unequivocally support that claim.

Source evaluation takes into account the credentials and point of view of the author and/or publisher. Where did the information come from? Who is responsible? Identifying the author and publisher is one aspect of this competency. Another is fact checking their credentials. What qualifies them as an expert source? What education have they had? What is their relevant experience? What else have they written or published? On what basis do they select information to be published? Questions that are answered by fact checking, supported by careful reading, matter greatly in evaluating source credibility.

Content that passes the red-flag test reduces the need to evaluate source credibility. There's no reason to check one's credentials unless the content is important and the author's reputation is unknown. Credential fact checking makes sense before acting on an unknown or alleged source's recommendation (e.g., to avoid scams). It also makes sense before including an unknown source in a research paper (e.g., no one has ever cited this person before). The fluent searcher knows when to check the source.

Thinking back on the Great Wall example, would Snopes need to be fact checked? Not really. The site is a popular source for checking urban legends and other claims. However, if the user had never heard of Snopes before, it would be wise to see who links to Snopes. If no one links to the snopes.com site, then the user has a reason to be skeptical, at least initially. To discover who links to the site, the searcher must know how to use the "link:" operator or perform a domain name check or both. The result of a "link:" query for snopes.com provides a long list of sites that bolster the face validity of Snopes: "Directories, Calendars, Research Guides, Encyclopedias and Hoaxes,"[18] the English Department of St. Columba's College,[19] Pasadena City College,[20] and many more. More about external link checking—also known as backlinks—and domain ownership is found in chapter 5, "Investigative Searching."

Many factors can go under the microscope in order to evaluate source credibility. In addition to what may be normally found on an author's resume, how the author says something can reveal something personal about beliefs and values. This can supplement what is provided in a resume. Therefore, bias detection is not only a valuable part of content evaluation; it offers potential insights about an information source. Many books have been written on bias,[21] so this one is not going to add anything new to understanding this topic. Most of the time, competent bias detection will correctly recognize propaganda techniques, stereotypes, language, and images that exaggerate (hyperbole), as well as underemphasize and omit details. Bias detection, often challenging to teach, should be done in the context of content and source evaluation. With so many authors uploading digital information, there has never been a greater opportunity—and need—to evaluate bias.

ETHICAL USE

Ethical use is the ultimate destination of the search process. The question "How will I ethically use the information?" lies at the heart of the matter. Once the decision is made that the information is good enough to be used, the task becomes how to incorporate digital resources as part of one's work. In an ideal world, researchers and writers always cite the source of the information they use. However, students do not always practice ethical use: copying and pasting, remixing and recycling other authors' insights and facts without citation.[22] Acknowledging the origin of ideas while contributing unique insights is what thinking, learning, communication, and education is all about in an Internet-connected world.

Educators know that students fail to cite digital materials, and when they do, the citations can be so weak that it is difficult or impossible to verify their sources. This is a persistent problem rooted in student inclinations to accept the first results returned by a search and to copy those results blindly without citation into their research work. According to a survey of educators by turnitin.com, copying and pasting is the most common form of plagiarism, followed by paraphrasing someone else's work.[23] When confronted about plagiarism, students may plead ignorance, but some openly admit that this type of cheating is a shortcut that saves them time.[24] Teachers who think that students should arrive in their classrooms understanding citation and plagiarism believe it is someone else's job to teach these skills. Assuming plagiarism instruction is someone else's responsibility is not a good instructional strategy, nor does it help students become ethical researchers or consumers of information. Teaching the nuances of proper citation and paraphrasing takes preparation. Ways to teach plagiarism avoidance and proper citation are detailed in chapter 7, "Ethical Consumption."

Ethical use begins when a searcher decides to integrate digital information into the research task. Fluent searchers know proper ways to use quotations or paraphrase and then accurately cite the source. The use/not use decision depends on the quality of the information and its relationship to the search task. Information that is deemed useful will likely find its way into the research project. How that information is managed is critically important. For example, information gathered during the search may need to be bookmarked and perhaps marked up with annotations and notes. This helps greatly when it comes time to quote and cite the materials. This can be accomplished with specialized tools like Diigo[25] or Evernote,[26] which may need to be learned on one's own.

Deciding how to attribute text and media resources is based on knowledge of copyright law and fair-use guidelines. In casual blog writing, a hyperlink may function as an informal citation because it can take the reader directly to the source. If a writer is working from a blog or curated platform, hyperlinking an author's name back to a source and proper use of quotations is sufficient citation to insure ethical use of the information. Most writing does not require a formal citation described by the American Psychological Association (APA), Modern Language Association

(MLA), or Chicago Manual of Style (CMS), to name a few. Proper citation (and style) is most important in academic writing and journalism. In these circumstances, citation alone is not enough. The writer must accurately cite the source even when the source has been paraphrased. For technical and academic work, footnotes may be required for both direct quotation and paraphrased writing. The literary ability to quote, paraphrase, and cite sources properly is essential for ethical use.

Developing a formal citation is a demanding task when working with online resources. Unlike print materials, online resources do not always present the author, date, and copyright information in a manner that is easy to find. This means the searcher must use investigative search techniques described earlier in this chapter to ferret out the information required to create a formal citation. Tracking down details for a citation is much the same process involved in finding the author and publisher when investigating credibility and bias. With this in mind, citation may be seen as one aspect of the detective game of investigative searching. Indeed, investigative searching is necessary before a writer selects a source in the first place. Investigative searching combined with the intent to cite and the ability to organize online sources using social bookmarking or cloud-based research tools defines a fluent researcher's skill set.

Students may think of citation as a highly demanding formatting experience where the order of author's names or the proper placement of a comma or use of italics are the most important elements of the process. This focus on form over function diverts attention from critical thinking and the investigative nature of the process. Online citation generation systems like the 21CIF Citation Wizard[27] provide templates that insure proper academic formatting so searchers can concentrate on investigation.

An understanding of fair use is also part of a fluent searcher's competencies. Using materials ethically means knowing how much of copyrighted work to quote or what percentage of a video to show. The Four Factors test helps navigate the gray areas of ethical use. Skilled searchers will understand the importance of the purpose and character of the use, the nature of the copyrighted work, the amount and substance of the portion taken, and the effect of the use upon the potential market.

When it comes to actual use of online writing, video, or audio, there are limitations as to how much of the materials can be used. These limitations vary based on the purpose of the writing and the copyright restrictions of the materials. Fair use is addressed more fully in chapter 7. To be an ethical user, the fluent searcher must have a deep understanding of:

- intellectual property,
- paraphrasing versus copying,
- educational fair use,
- citation of sources, and
- writing conventions of research.

Ultimately, the disposition of the fluent searcher is to use technology to organize the digital information found in a way that ensures citation and attribution. When researching a topic, the fluent searcher aims for transparency, creating an archive of bookmarks, often including annotations and notes stored in a cloud-based repository. When the information task is complete, the writer creates a document that allows the (online) reader easily to click through to the original sources or, in the case of print, turn to footnotes, endnotes, or a bibliographic reference. Using information-fluency skills in this way honors copyright and safeguards the fair use of intellectual property.

TEACHING INFORMATION FLUENCY

The model of information fluency presented in this book includes many practical applications for teaching and learning. While this book is not explicitly a curriculum, it contains many curricular resources, starting with discreet competencies, such as converting natural-language questions into queries, and culminating in research strategies. For example, chapter 6 offers four mini-lessons in investigative searching. Chapter 8 demonstrates three ways to embed information-fluency instruction into existing lessons. Finally, chapter 9 presents a vision for engaging students as curators of information that synthesizes all the steps in the Information Fluency Model. The appendix conveniently groups the model lessons into one table.

There is no national curriculum for information fluency, nor is one likely to emerge any time soon. Not many schools allow time for courses or even units of instruction dedicated to this discipline. Consequently, educators who wish to help students become fluent must be inventive with the model resources provided.

The reader is advised not to treat the examples as ready-to-use lesson plans but as a vision for what is possible. The recommended approach is to embed learning opportunities into existing courses where students are expected to conduct digital research: language arts, social studies, and science. Ascertain students' strengths and weaknesses by giving them a challenge and watching them search. Then provide specific instruction and practice. While this work would best be coordinated at a district or building level, the efforts of individual librarians and teachers working alone nevertheless makes a difference in helping students achieve fluency.

SUMMARY

Although tools continue to improve, there is no indication that searching will ever become brain-dead easy. Finding information is not enough. Without evaluation there is no information fluency; having to investigate results makes thinking imperative. The highly skilled searcher outlined in this chapter is the exemplar of fluency. The searcher is in control of the tools, not the other way around. The filter bubble is no hindrance; the fluent searcher is not limited to what personalized search engines are programmed to retrieve. From an array of strategies and methods, optimal approaches are selected to meet the demands of each search challenge. If one approach doesn't work, another one is available. The fluent searcher locates information efficiently, evaluates it effectively, and uses it ethically.

To become fluent takes training and practice. There are some individuals the authors have observed who have all the right natural inclinations. But this is not the norm. More common, even among gifted populations, is the student who is effective about half the time. Being right only 50 percent of the time is unacceptable performance in most educational activities. With just a few hours training, the same students improve to being right two out of three times; many exceed that mark. With repeated exposure to good strategies and practice, students continue to improve, as the next chapter illustrates.

NOTES

1. Matt Richtel, "A Silicon Valley School That Doesn't Compute," *New York Times*, last modified October 22, 2011, http://www.nytimes.com/2011/10/23/technology/at-waldorf-school-in-silicon-valley-technology-can-wait.html.

2. Carl Heine and Dennis O'Connor, "Final Report for the Center for Talent Development" (unpublished report, Chicago, IL, 2010), 2.

3. David Barr, Bob Houston, Carl Heine, Dennis O'Connor, and Dan Balzer, "Digital Information Fluency Model," *21st Century Information Fluency*, last modified January 1, 2013, https://21cif.com/resources/difcore/index.html.

4. "Information Literacy Competency Standards for Higher Education," *American Library Association*, accessed December 15, 2012, http://www.ala.org/acrl/standards/informationliteracycompetency.

5. Mike Eisenberg and Bob Berkowitz, "Introducing the Big6," *The Big6*, last modified January 28, 2012, http://big6.com/pages/lessons/presentations/big6-overview-2011.php.

6. Kristen Purcell, Lee Rainie, Alan Heaps, Judy Buchanan, Linda Friedrich, Amanda Jacklin, Clara Chen, and Kathryn Zickuhr, *How Teens Do Research in the Digital World* (Washington, DC: Pew Research Center, November 1, 2012), http://www.pewinternet.org/~/media/Files/Reports/2012/PIP_TeacherSurveyReportWithMethodology110112.pdf.

7. Carl Heine, "Five Things Today's Digital Generation Cannot Do," *21st Century Information Fluency*, last modified January 1, 2013, https://21cif.com/resources/features/fivethings_directory.html.

8. Eszter Hargittai, Lindsay Fullerton, Ericka Menchen-Trevino, and Kristin Yates Thomas, "Trust Online: Young Adults' Evaluation of Web Content," *International Journal of Communication*, 4 (2010): 468–94.

9. Carl Heine, "Keyword Challenge," *21st Century Information Fluency*, accessed January 20, 2013, https://21cif.com/rkitp/challenge/v1n3/Keyword_Challenge/KeywordChallenge.swf.

10. See note 3.

11. Eli Pariser, "Filter Bubbles, Meet Upworthy," *The Filter Bubble*, March 26, 2012, http://www.thefilterbubble.com.

12. "China's Wall Less Great in View from Space," *NASA*, last modified November 30, 2007, http://www.nasa.gov/vision/space/workinginspace/great_wall.html.

13. "Great Walls of Liar," *Snopes.com*, last updated September 6, 2010, http://www.snopes.com/science/greatwall.asp.

14. Carl Heine and Dennis O'Connor, "Final Report for the Center for Talent Development" (unpublished report, Chicago, IL, 2012).

15. SchemeHater, "Malinformation," *Urban Dictionary*, last modified April 20, 2009, http://www.urbandictionary.com/define.php?term=Malinformation.

16. Masahiro Mori, "The Uncanny Valley," *Energy*, 7, no. 4 (1970): 33–35. Translated by Karl F. MacDorman and Takashi Minato, *Android Science*, last modified September 19, 2005, http://www.androidscience.com/theuncannyvalley/proceedings2005/uncannyvalley.html.

17. Carl Heine, "Tips from Google: What's Missing?" *Internet Search Challenge*, last modified July 3, 2012, http://internetsearchchallenge.blogspot.com/2012/07/tips-from-google-whats-missing.html.

18. "Directories, Calendars, Research Guides, Encyclopedias and Hoaxes," *Online Public Relations*, last modified December 22, 2012, http://www.online-pr.com/directory.htm.

19. "SCC English," *The English Department of St. Columba's College*, accessed January 20, 2013, http://www.sccenglish.ie.

20. "Useful Links," *Pasadena City College*, accessed January 20, 2013, http://www.pasadena.edu/studentservices/lac/links.cfm.

21. For example, Thomas Kida, *Don't Believe Everything You Think: The 6 Basic Mistakes We Make in Thinking* (Amherst, NY: Prometheus, 2006).

22. "White Paper: The Plagiarism Spectrum: Instructor Insights into the 10 Types of Plagiarism," *Turnitin.com*, accessed January 21, 2013, http://pages.turnitin.com/rs/iparadigms/images/Turnitin_WhitePaper_PlagiarismSpectrum.pdf.

23. See note 22.

24. Kathy Slobogin, "Survey: Many Students Say Cheating's OK," *CNN.com*, last modified April 5, 2002, http://articles.cnn.com/2002-04-05/us/highschool.cheating_1_plagiarism-cheating-students.

25. https://www.diigo.com.

26. https://evernote.com.

27. Carl Heine, "Citation Wizard," *21st Century Information Fluency*, last modified February 12, 2012, https://21cif.com/tools/cite.

2

Information Fluency, Achievement, and the Common Core

Without instruction in searching, students resort to trial and error, inventing their own methods. They manage to get by until challenges come along that test their abilities to find information efficiently, determine its credibility, and use it ethically. When challenged, they are wrong as often as they are right. Once the same students are introduced to efficient, effective, and ethical methods, they become more capable searchers and critical consumers of information.

Beginning in 2009, the Center for Talent Development (CTD) at Northwestern University and the 21st Century Information Fluency Project partnered to offer gifted students in grades 6 through 12 training in digital searching, evaluation, and ethical use. This partnership involves more than one thousand students a year enrolled in Spectrum (middle school) and Equinox (high school) summer programs and online courses provided by the Gifted Learning Links program. The objective is to help students improve their abilities to do digital research, strengthening skills not formally taught in many schools nor picked up through trial-and-error practice.

A performance baseline measure was designed to assess information skills found to be lacking in middle school and high school:

- querying an unfamiliar database,
- browsing to find information,
- truncating a URL to find information for evaluation,
- determining bias,
- locating proof of ownership,
- fact checking,
- finding and interpreting authoritative secondary references, and
- determining the date of publication.

Constructed around ten search challenges, the pretest requires students to use appropriate methods to locate information, check facts, and evaluate findings. Instead of prescribed multiple-choice items, the staple of most information literacy assessments, this is a performance evaluation that requires young researchers to input text, revealing their speculative and investigative strategies as well as methods correctly and incorrectly applied.

Young people, including those who normally do very well on achievement tests, struggle with the information fluency assessment prior to training. Students in Northwestern's CTD programs are all academically gifted, having passed above-grade-level tests, such as the SAT (e.g., minimum critical reading, 470) or ACT (e.g., reading, 22 or higher). These students are not used to doing poorly on tests, so when middle-schoolers earn forty-four points out of one hundred (on average) and high-schoolers score fifty points on average, eyebrows are raised.[1] Could they really be that incompetent, or is the test too hard?

The argument for being too hard maintains that the challenges are not appropriate tasks. In other words, they fail because the tasks are not something young people should be able to do. That view loses traction when one considers how educational standards, such as the Common Core State Standards, now adopted by most states, define expectations for student performance:

- "Use text features and search tools (e.g., keywords, sidebars, hyperlinks) to locate information relevant to a given topic efficiently." (RI-5, grade 3)[2]
- "Gather relevant information from multiple print and digital sources, using search terms effectively; assess the credibility and accuracy of each source; and quote or paraphrase the data and conclusions of others while avoiding plagiarism and following a standard format for citation." (W.7.8, WHST.7.8, grade 7)[3]
- "Gather relevant information from multiple authoritative print and digital sources, using advanced searches effectively; assess the strengths and limitations of each source in terms of the specific task, purpose, and audience; integrate information into the text selectively to maintain the flow of ideas, avoiding plagiarism and overreliance on any one source and following a standard format for citation." (W.11–12.8, grades 11–12)[4]

What these statements lack are explicit strategies and skills students must use to satisfy the standards. Information fluency competencies and performance-assessed, self-paced learning experiences, like those described previously, help fill in the missing details. How does one use "search terms effectively"? Answer: Distill a question into a query, retaining two or more nouns, keeping in mind other important ideas for which there are likely better terms. If performing that operation demonstrates using search terms effectively, which it does, then it is a task students should be expected to do in middle school and higher. If they can't gather relevant information, use advanced searches, and so on, young people, despite many other talents, must either not have the skills or are attempting to search in less-effective ways. It's this harsh realization voiced by teachers that prompted leaders of CTD programs to seek training for the high-performing students enrolled in their programs.[5]

In chapter 1, an example was shared of inefficient searching, how students got lost browsing when they had a one-in-four chance of clicking the right links. Where students really come up short is when asked to assess the credibility of a source, clearly a Common Core standard. Credibility assessment is no simple task. It takes effort, effective methods, and a disposition to look beyond immediate results to establish the facts. A good way to build this skill is to search for information about an unknown author and use that to determine if the author's experience and training add up to authority. As is often the case with Web pages, blogs, and tweets, if the author's name cannot be found, the first task is to locate the name. For a large percentage of untrained students, this proves to be impossible.

Following is a task from the 2010 CTD pretest that caused students to struggle. A link to a URL was provided with these instructions:

> http://greenrgy.org/innovations/futurefuels/humanpower/bodyheat-power.html. Use truncation to find the name of the author of this article. Copy and paste the name of the author in the answer box.

Designed by the authors as an *assessment playground*, the entire greenrgy.org site exists for the purpose of assessing discrete skills. The only way to find the author's name in this case is to truncate the URL back to the "humanpower" directory, where the name Malcom Verndahl appears with a link to the target URL of the article in question. Other techniques may be tried, such as browsing, but that leads to a page of names not associated in any way with the article. Because of the input they submit, it is possible to know how students arrived at their answers. On this task, 53 percent of middle-schoolers (Spectrum) and 69 percent of high-school (Equinox) students successfully truncated the URL to find the author's name.

Having to find a missing author's name this way is by no means an isolated incident on the Internet. Truncation can be a highly efficient way to piece together information located on different pages. Finding the name this way is only half the investigative task. The student must also ask, Is this author an expert? Malcom Verndahl is a fabrication. Searching for him in Google matches zero documents, however to discover that, students need to fact check.

Fact checking depends on querying keywords (e.g., the author's name) from the information found. When it comes to this type of task, students are less prone to success. On average, 39 percent of Spectrum and 49 percent of Equinox students come to accurate conclusions using fact checking in this type of challenge. Reading and interpreting the results is the obstacle, not creating the query. But few students take time to create a fact-checking query. Teachers and librarians report how common it is for young people to take the first result they find as an authoritative source.[6] The hopeful news is fact checking becomes easier with training and practice.

In addition to the pretest, online self-paced training exercises and a posttest are bundled in the CTD experience. The most recent version, entitled Information Researcher,[7] is built around typical research tasks students might encounter. All together, the pretest, tutorials, and posttest are expected to take students three hours to complete. Some spend considerably more time than that. In the first year of the program, the plan was to provide eight hours of self-paced instruction. This time demand, in addition to their other coursework, proved burdensome for participants.

Consequently, in 2011 the training was compressed into a much shorter time frame. The big question was what would happen to student performance given such a drastic reduction in training and practice? The gains realized during eight hours (2010) were impressive: Spectrum students improved from a pretest score of thirty-seven points to a posttest score of fifty-two points, an average increase of more than 40 percent. Equinox students also gained significant ground, going from a pretest score of 45 points to a posttest score of 60 points, an average increase of more than 33 percent. Concerns were eased when results of the shortened training were tabulated. With less than half the investment of time, Spectrum students gained 42 percent (pretest: 45, posttest: 64), and Equinox students gained 19 percent, with their highest posttest scores to date (pretest: 57, posttest: 68).[8] Even larger gains were obtained in 2012 (see figure 2.1).[9]

The fact of the matter is that with minimal training students improve. It could be the case that students with average abilities take longer to understand and apply effective search methods. Three hours of instruction once a year is not likely to suffice for the average individual. Regardless, the message is clear: Without training, even the best learners struggle to search in a manner that meets Common Core standards. When appropriate training is provided, their performance improves significantly. Information fluency skills can be taught effectively in just a few sessions a year.

Information fluency maps well to the Common Core and offers sufficient task definition to guide instructors whose responsibility it is to translate standards into practice. By design, the standards are global statements of intent and do not presume to prescribe how these results may be achieved.[10] To obtain the outcomes they define, intermediate steps must be taken. That is how information fluency strategies and methods function in light of the Common Core.

Information fluency and Common Core standards align in multiple ways. The following approach pairs up references to information fluency in the Common Core with the Digital Information Fluency (DIF) Model.[11] Common Core standards

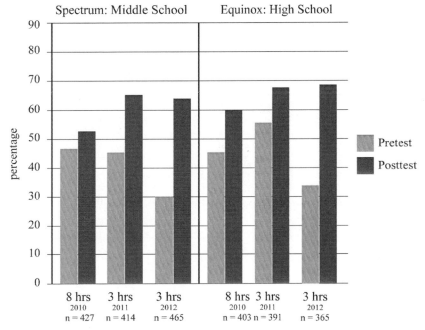

Subjects: Students enrolled at the Center for Talent Development

Figure 2.1. Students' Information Fluency before and after Instruction

encompass English language arts (ELA), as well as history/social studies, science, and technical subjects. These are also the subjects in which information fluency is best taught. The standards specify the literacies and understandings for college and career readiness. The same may be said of information fluency, which aims to prepare students for college-level research.

The Common Core ELA is divided into four strands: reading, writing, speaking and listening, and language. Information fluency intersects explicitly with the first two, specifically reading informational text (RI); writing (W); reading literacy in history/social studies (RH); reading literacy in science and technical subjects (RST); and writing literacy in history/social studies, science, and technical subjects (WHST).

Information fluency is most closely tied to literacies defined for RI, RST, and RH. Taken together, reading and writing standards consist of clusters of interrelated literacies/fluencies spanning grades 3 through 12 that intersect with speculative and investigative searching as well as ethical use. Table 2.1 groups the Common Core literacies into three clusters that correspond with DIFs.

COMPARISON OF COMMON CORE STATE
STANDARDS AND DIGITAL INFORMATION FLUENCY

This overarching view serves as a reference and a map for the remaining chapters of this book. Table 2.1 captures all the essential elements of information fluency through the lens of the Common Core. There are redundancies in the table due mainly to grade-level differences; no attempt has been made to identify literacies that grow more complex from grade to grade. Grade-level differences are brought into the discussion where they belong in terms of curriculum and instruction. In

Table 2.1.   Comparison of Common Core Literacies and Digital Information Fluencies

Digital Information Fluencies[12]	*Common Core Literacies*
Search	**Reading**
Learners use *search* strategies and techniques related to querying and browsing:	Locate relevant information efficiently—using text features and search tools such as keywords and hyperlinks. (RI-5)
"Identify key concepts in a research question; translate a natural language question into a search query; identify terms that are likely to be effective 'as is'; identify terms for which more effective vocabulary is likely to be required." (DIF I.A)	Integrate and evaluate multiple sources of information presented in diverse formats and media (e.g., visually, quantitatively, as well as in words) in order to address a question or solve a problem. (RH-7)
"Create effective and efficient search queries; develop and apply vocabulary building strategies effectively to conduct a digital information search—seek out more specific terms (hyponyms) to narrow a search or more general terms (hypernyms) to broaden a search; effectively act on informed decisions to revise their search queries based on search results/feedback; interpret evidence that results are relevant and significant." (DIF I.B)	**Writing**
	Conduct short research projects (as well as more sustained research projects) to answer a question (including a self-generated question), drawing on several sources; refocus the inquiry when appropriate; generate additional related, focused questions that allow for multiple avenues of exploration. (W-7, WHST-7)
"Understand the organization of digital information; select visible Web collections (and sub-collections) based on their characteristics; select Deep Web (invisible Web) collections (and sub-collections) based on their characteristics; select other digital collections (and sub-collections) based on their characteristics." (DIF I.C)	Conduct short research projects to answer a question drawing on several sources and gather relevant information from (multiple) print and digital sources. (W-8)
	Use advanced searches effectively; assess the usefulness of each source in answering the research question. (W-8, WHST-8)

"Select features of a variety of digital search tools based on the probability of effectiveness and efficiency." (DIF I.D)

"Select and apply appropriate search strategies effectively and efficiently to locate reliable digital information related to their academic learning goal(s); navigate hyperlinks, employing browsing strategies; use subject directory strategies; use search engine strategies." (DIF I.E)

Evaluation

Learners *evaluate* the quality of a search result to:

"Determine its usefulness in the search process; determine whether or not the digital information addresses the natural language question; decide whether or not the digital information suggests revisions to search queries (revision decision). (DIF II.A)

"Determine the reliability of its content; investigate internal content reliability (accuracy); investigate external validation of information." (DIF II.B)

"Determine the reliability of its source; investigate author/publisher reliability (authority, bias); investigate external validation of author/publisher (references). (DIF II.C)

Reading

Evaluate textual arguments and claims on the basis of reasoning that is sound and evidence that is relevant. (RI-8)

Analyze how different authors write about a topic, emphasize different evidence and advance different or conflicting interpretations of facts. (RI-9)

Distinguish among facts, opinions, and reasoned judgment based on research findings and speculation in a text. (RH-8)

Evaluate the hypotheses, data, analysis, and conclusions in a science or technical text, verifying the data when possible and corroborating or challenging conclusions with other sources of information. (RST-8)

Assess the extent to which the reasoning and evidence in a text support the author's claim or a recommendation for solving a scientific or technical problem. (RST-8)

Writing

Assess the credibility of each source. (W-8)

Gather relevant information from multiple authoritative print and digital sources, using advanced searches effectively; assess the strengths and limitations of each source in terms of the specific task, purpose, and audience. (W-8, WHST-8)

Ethical Use

Learners *ethically use* digital information to:

"Decide whether or not to integrate digital information related to a specific information task; cite the source and/or

Reading

Integrate visual information with other information in print and digital texts— charts, graphs, photographs, videos and maps. (RH-7)

(continued)

Table 2.1.   *(Continued)*

Digital Information Fluencies[12]	Common Core Literacies
author for the selected digital information." (DIF III.A)	**Writing** Quote or paraphrase the data and conclusions of others while avoiding plagiarism and providing basic bibliographic information for sources. (W-8, WHST-8)

For grade-specific mapping of Common Core and Information Fluency, see the appendix.

general, however, introducing information fluency in third grade supports the Common Core, as does continuing to expand it through middle school and high school.

Relative to searching, where Common Core calls for locating print and digital information for the purpose of research projects, information fluency provides the means to the end. Strategies for choosing querying or browsing, methods to turn a question into a query by use of semantics, and, if necessary, transforming a poor question into a better one are practical ways to locate digital information. As the standards make clear, digital information includes interacting with images, audio, video, formatting, and layouts in addition to text. Information fluency relies on methods for finding, evaluating, and using multimedia appropriately. Visual fluency is increasingly important because images can be manipulated (and forged) almost as easily as text. Another element specified by the standards, advanced searching, depends on skills for learning and using multiple digital collections, including the Deep Web and unfamiliar databases. Every search strategy and technique involved in information fluency supports the Common Core standards for finding digital information.

Returning to a theme introduced earlier, finding information is becoming less demanding than determining whether the information retrieved is credible. Information issued by highly trusted sources may greatly reduce the need for evaluation; however, this actually contributes to the evaluation problem. When some information can trusted—arguably the majority of information presented in schools—students can have a hard time identifying information that *needs* to be evaluated. Safe searches within a walled garden of professionally selected resources can lull searchers into a false sense of security. When a search isn't safe, can students tell?

The emphasis on evaluation in the Common Core may serve as its most important feature. The standards aim to foster careful reading and critical thinking. Students must determine if evidence is relevant and claims are supported by facts. They must see how different sources compare. In this way, students will be able to evaluate information retrieved from the Internet. At the same time, evaluation can appear to be overwhelming. Having to vet every piece of information is as impractical as it is tiring. The Digital Information Fluency Model lessens this problem by providing a limited number of practical, direct avenues to travel in pursuit of credibility investigation.

Three types of information are helpful in determining credibility, which may be stated as questions:

- What can I discover about the source?
- What can I determine about the content?
- What can I learn from others who found this information before me?

Each of these elements is present in the Common Core. Relative to the source, it is helpful to investigate the author and/or publisher. Several well-defined methods not directly addressed in the Common Core can also be useful: fact checking, Deep Web queries for domain ownership, and tracing backlinks to see what others say about the author(s) or publisher.

When it comes to evaluating content, the standards clearly move students toward detecting bias and checking accuracy by comparing multiple sources (triangulation). Another facet that must be addressed in the context of the Internet is the freshness of the information. How old is it? Has the information outlived its usefulness? The Digital Information Fluency Model describes the technical means, in addition to critical reading, to streamline the task of content evaluation: right-clicking for more information, checking Web page properties and metadata, and using special commands to locate information efficiently are easy to teach and empower the searcher. Methods such as these are too fine grained to include in global standards; nevertheless, they are keys to achieving the standards and constitute a major part of this book.

The third Common Core cluster pertains to integration and plagiarism and how to avoid the latter by citing all information brought into one's work. Unless information about the author, publisher, title, or date of publication is missing, citation is not a difficult information fluency to achieve. Once students know what needs to be cited, including paraphrased material, they have tools to cite it. Proper integration, aside from citation, is more about writing mechanics and is not considered here.

In theory, the three clusters should add up to information fluency. In practice, they do not. Foremost is that these clusters comprise only part of the Common Core and may be viewed as less important than other literacies. For example, RI-2 states, "Determine two or more main ideas of a text and explain how they are supported by key details; summarize the text."[13] This standard is bound to receive more attention. It's just the way it is.

How important are the information fluency skills in the Common Core compared to other skills in reading, writing, and mathematics? According to educators attending a recent school library conference,[14] when asked if other standards, which are subject to testing, take precedence, they answered without hesitation: "Absolutely!" In practice, it's hard to find time to work on RI-5, RI-8, W-7, W-8, and the others like them. The best hope is to embed the overlooked standards in their competition: fundamental reading and writing instruction.

Still, even if time has been set aside for information fluency instruction and practice, something critical may be missing. Standards, including the Common Core, focus on measurable behaviors. They bypass personal dispositions that are integral to fluent searching, investigation, and ethical use. The Digital Information Fluency Model attempts to capture these essential dispositions of a fluent searcher:

- confidence
- persistence
- attentiveness
- open-mindedness
- curiosity
- metacognitive thinking

Lacking these personal disciplines, a searcher may easily walk away from a challenging search frustrated and vulnerable to taking uninformed action. From a motivational perspective, confidence, persistence, and the like develop in tandem with search skills. An individual with more skills is more likely to withstand frustration and enjoy the search experience more than a novice.[15] This relationship between ability and intrinsic motivation, sometimes known as flow, helps to explain the importance of dispositions in searching and how to strengthen them: through supported practice. On exactly the same task, one searcher can be completely frustrated while another finds the activity rewarding in itself. Level of search experience helps to explain the difference. Giving students practice with simple search skills at first and progressively increasing the difficulty is one way to develop dispositions. Doing so in the context of games and intriguing self-paced challenges can be powerful, time-efficient instructional strategies.

Being aligned to standards is an essential starting point, but achieving those ends requires means not found in the Common Core or other state standards.[16] What is missing is how to put the skills described by the standards into practice. This depends on an array of specialized strategies and techniques, such as those found in the highly effective, small-dose CTD tutorials.

NOTES

1. Carl Heine and Dennis O'Connor, "Final Report for the Center for Talent Development" (unpublished report, Chicago, IL, 2010), p. 2.

2. *Common Core State Standards for English Language Arts and Literacy in History/Social Studies, Science, and Technical Subjects* (Washington, DC: National Governors Association Center for Best Practices and the Council of Chief State School Officers, 2012). http://www .corestandards.org/assets/CCSSI_ELA%20Standards.pdf, p. 14.

3. See note 2, p. 44.

4. See note 2, p. 46.

5. Susan Corwith and Carl Heine, "Improving 21st Century Information Fluency Skills" (presentation, Annual Convention of the National Association for Gifted Children, New Orleans, LA, November 3–5, 2011).

6. Jacqui Cheng, "Students Trust High Google Search Ranking Too Much," *Ars Technica*, accessed January 16, 2013, http://arstechnica.com/science/2010/07/alt-title-students-place-too.

7. Carl Heine, "Information Researcher," *21st Century Information Fluency*, last modified May 30, 2012, http://searchwhys.com.

8. Carl Heine and Dennis O'Connor, "Final Report for the Center for Talent Development" (unpublished report, Chicago, IL, 2011).

9. Carl Heine and Dennis O'Connor, "Final Report for the Center for Talent Development" (unpublished report, Chicago, IL, 2012).

10. See note 2, p. 4.

11. Carl Heine, "DIF to CCSS Comparison," last modified October 15, 2012, https://21cif.com/resources/difcore/DIF-to-CCSS-Comparison.pdf.

12. Carl Heine, "Common Core State Standards Mapped to the Information Fluency Model," *21st Century Information Fluency*, last modified January 1, 2013, https://21cif.com/resources/difcore/ccss-dif.html.

13. See note 2, p. 14.

14. Carl Heine, "College Ready Research Skills" (presentation, Illinois School Library and Media Association. Annual Conference, St. Charles, IL, October 18–20, 2012).

15. Mihaly Csikszentmihalyi, *Finding Flow* (New York: Basic Books, 1998).

16. Dick Carlson, "State Goal 5: Use the Language Arts to Acquire, Assess and Communicate Information," *Illinois State Board of Education*, last modified October 10, 2007, http://www.isbe.net/ils/ela/pdf/goal5.pdf.

II

SPECULATIVE SEARCHING

3

Self-Taught Search-Box Strategies

Google Intuitive Search Answers Are SO Weird . . .[1] is an interesting group on Facebook. The small community's sole purpose seems to be screenshot captures of how Google Instant autocompletes queries. Take, for example, the query *google will*:

- eat itself
- take over the world
- not load
- not open
- you marry me
- not search for chuck norris
- pay you

The answers are diverse but not nearly as random or weird as they may appear. The first one, for example, links to a Web site (gwei.org) that merits this description: "Google Will Eat Itself (GWEI) is an art/economics project/prank/criminal enterprise that uses a network of hidden sites that register fraudulent clicks on Google Ads."[2] Google Will Eat Itself is not a random result; it earned its position in the list of query suggestions by being popular. Thinking of it as weird is an example of an inaccurate assumption that can happen when information is seen without regard to the way things work in a digital world.

Understanding how to find information develops naturally. When young children want something, they ask someone they trust. Seeking a trusted source, an authority, becomes ingrained. However, when this strategy is brought into a digital world without thinking about it, complications can ensue. If most students are self-taught searchers, as evidence suggests,[3] they can easily fall into the trap of "if it works for me here, it will work for me there."

Students quickly figure out that a search box is a good way to find information. Search engine use among young people is so commonplace and automatic that it could be considered an implicit or native digital research strategy. Native, as used here, does not refer to the "digital native" sometimes used to describe a generation that has grown up with digital devices.[4] Instead, it signifies a naturally occurring, self-taught strategy. To the user such strategies are implicit, and like intuitions or assumptions, they seem so right if they work. Nothing is wrong with a native strategy, unless it doesn't actually work the way the searcher thinks it does.

According to the Pew Internet and American Life Project, almost all teachers surveyed (94 percent) say their students turn to Google or similar search engines when asked to do research—as opposed to online databases, news sites, printed books, or reference librarians.[5] A student's go-to choice when looking for information is a search box, Google's in particular.[6] That statement really should be amended because when students can't find what they want using a search box, they tend to abandon that strategy in favor of another approach. According to Thomas Scott and Michael O'Sullivan, students who get frustrated resort to browsing, surfing from page to page.[7] The present authors have observed this repeatedly, often enough to claim that browsing qualifies as the fallback native search strategy.[8]

If the Internet is viewed as a haystack of galactic proportions, search engines are the only practical way to retrieve the needle. Without search engines, most information on the World Wide Web (estimated at over 13 billion pages[9]) would be hopelessly out of reach by browsing. Whether students know it or not, using a search box is a strategic choice, one that vastly improves their chances of finding a vast array of information. At the same time, other viable means of searching can be overlooked. In many cases it is quicker to consult someone who knows the answer or knows how to find it. The information one needs may be just one librarian, teacher, parent, friend, reference book, phone call, e-mail, or text message away. The choice of the search box without considering the alternatives can be a strategic misstep just in terms of efficiency.

Nevertheless, a self-taught strategy can have even more severe consequences when the information found lacks credibility and the user doesn't know it. As children come online, seeking a trusted source is transferred to the Internet, where finding trustworthy information involves an unfamiliar process not easily discovered by doing. Using Google quickly becomes second nature; evaluating the results does not. Consequently, evaluation is routinely overlooked. Even in the broader population, it is by no means common to question what search engines have to do with evaluation. If it was, Google would autocomplete this query: *google will . . . (not) evaluate search results.* Of course, that suggestion is nowhere to be found.

Problems arise when it is assumed the search engine can be trusted.[10] In all fairness, that assumption is not the search engine's fault. The user is to blame for assuming an implicit strategy works in a digital space where it has serious shortcomings. But in fairness to the user, that assumption is understandably naive. Seasoned digital researchers, in particular those who've been tricked or scammed by trusting and consuming bad information, learn this lesson the hard way—unless someone warns them (and that doesn't even work all the time). Educators and others who know better share some of the blame if they neglect to inform young people that 1) the "rules" for trusting authority are different online, and 2) under few circumstances is a search engine an authority. While Google, Yahoo!, Bing, and other search engines have inherent authority as brands and sources of data *about* searching (e.g., Google Analytics[11]), they have no responsibility for the information they retrieve from external sources. "I found it in Google" has no connection to credibility, a fact that young searchers need help understanding.

The assumption that students believe anything they find online is verified by Donald Leu's investigation of middle school students and the Pacific Northwest Tree Octopus.[12] The tree octopus site is packed with tall tales about octopi living in trees in a republic known as Cascadia. As far-fetched as it sounds, when shown the site, all twenty-five seventh-graders in the study succumbed to the hoax. All but one student rated the site as "very credible."[13] To quote Professor Leu, who directs the New Literacies Research Lab at the University of Connecticut, the majority of students "simply have very little in the way of critical evaluation skills. . . . They may tell you they don't believe everything they read on the Internet, but they do."[14] As reported in chapter 2, when gifted students in Northwestern University's program score in the 50th percentile or lower in terms of evaluation skills, it's not hard to believe what Leu says. Students poorly equipped to evaluate are persons at risk in a world of information consumption.

NATURAL LANGUAGE STRATEGY

A less troublesome native strategy shared by younger learners is the inclination to use natural-word queries. Once a real stumbling block, natural-language queries can be effectively interpreted by search engines with semantic capabilities. Submitting whole sentences or literal strings as queries makes perfect sense to novice searchers; after all, why ask it any other way than normal? Natural language is not the norm online, however. Search engines operate as literal matching machines. They come up short on results trying to match too many words. To illustrate, try the query *what is the top speed of earth's fastest animal,* and then follow that with a shorter query, *speed fastest animal.* Tabulate—better yet, have students tabulate—the results from a selection of search engines (see table 3.1).

While there are obvious exceptions, students can see that the more words in the query, the fewer the results. Have older students figure out why Yahoo! is so different. Yahoo! is an outlier because it includes all the matches for all the separate keywords found in the full-sentence query (placing OR between terms instead of AND would have a similar effect). In this case, one doesn't have to dig far into Yahoo!'s results to find matches that are completely irrelevant to the question. Hakia,[15] on the other hand, is a semantic search engine that parses the query for meaning before execut-

Table 3.1. Number of Results from Search Engines Using Full-Sentence and Three-Word Queries

	Full-Sentence Query	*Three-Word Query*
Google	727,000	1,610,000
Yahoo!	289,000,000	879,000
Bing	111,000	801,000
Search.com	330,000	785,000
Wikipedia	150	659
Ask	320	390
Hakia	50	50

ing literal matching. Its viewable results are capped at fifty, perhaps to save processing time or the fact that few people need many relevant results. Like Hakia, Ask's number is the number of matches that are viewable, obtained by counting pages of results. Neither Hakia nor Ask reports the number of records they match. For the larger commercial engines, the number of viewable matches is always a fraction of what is reportedly matched. Google displays only 661 results for the long query and 770 results for the short query even though it claims to match millions.

Because of the inability of some engines to process natural-language queries, accommodations must be made, either in one's search-box strategy or in the choice of search engine. Altering the natural-language strategy to render it more effective includes paring down the question to its most important parts, using two or more words (but not too many) and keeping other words in mind that are important to use in filtering results (invisible query). Searchers may discover this without help by trying different combinations of words in queries, but a quicker and surer way is to show them.

QUERY OPTIMIZATION

The "Query Checklist" is an instructional method developed to help students craft better queries.[16] In its original form, this was a series of nine steps that, if followed, would help students turn a natural-language question into a more effective query. Because of semantic capabilities of some search engines, some of the steps have been collapsed. Here is the current version of the checklist:

1. What essential words (key concepts) are found in the question? (Eliminate unimportant and redundant terms and stop words.)
2. How many essential keywords will I put in a query?
3. What essential keywords are probably effective "as is?"
4. For which ineffective "as-is" keywords (e.g., words with multiple or vague meanings) are more effective keywords needed?

5. Can hyponyms or professional language be substituted for any of the less effective words?
6. Did I spell the keywords correctly?
7. Did I put the words in a meaningful order?

A good way to introduce the checklist is to compare the results of two queries, one natural language and another following the steps outlined above. Ideally, the search topic is taken from coursework that requires students to engage in online research. For the purpose of demonstrating a "think-aloud" instructional approach, imagine a social studies course where the assignment is to find five different points of view on the causes of poverty in the United States today. A possible natural-language question could be *How do five different groups of people in the United States view the causes of poverty today?* Have students try the query in a couple of different search engines. Examine the results. Are the results relevant to the question? One of the snippets looks promising and does address the views of two groups: sociologists and feminists. If there are other points of view, they are missing. Scanning the snippets for the matched keywords (in bold), most abstracts refer to people in poverty and identify causes of poverty, such as unemployment. The results are partly relevant but do not completely answer the question. The connection between *views* and *causes* has been marginally realized.

Now analyze the question using the checklist. With the full question written out, have students identify the keywords that represent the main concepts. For younger students this could be a group activity at the board. For older grades, it could be independent work. The intersection with language arts is immediately apparent in terms of vocabulary acquisition and use (Common Core L.4.b). Students are engaged in defining the parts of speech that carry significant meaning or define the purpose of the sentence. In this case, important concepts are *people, United States, view, causes, poverty,* and *today.* Crossing out the small parts of speech, any redundancies (e.g., *different* people) and stop words (e.g., *of, in, the*) isolates the main ideas. Language arts teachers will see that building optimal queries reinforces reading and writing competencies. Queries and language instruction are a good pairing.

The second step in query optimization is to determine how many of these ideas are necessary for the search. All six seem important, but two to four concepts are often better than six for reasons noted earlier pertaining to query length. The query *people United States poverty view causes today* returns information about people living in poverty in the United States, offering statistics about poverty rates but with little relevance to how people view causes of poverty. Skimming the abstracts, the search seems to be headed in the right direction but has a ways to go. Shortening the query is a good next step.

If the query is conducted from the United States, including the keywords *United States* may be redundant. By default, Google knows the location of the computer that submits the query.[17] If one wants information on poverty in a specific country other than the United States, that requires additional help from special operators, a topic addressed later in this chapter. In order to keep the query as short as possible, *United States*, a perfectly good search term, may be omitted. If so, it becomes part of the invisible query because it remains critical in addressing the question. Likewise, publication date, represented by *today*, and *five*, the number of views to collect, can be part of the invisible query.

The keywords *people* and *view* lack the kind of power *United States*, *causes*, and *poverty* have. In light of the third step, only *United States* and *poverty* are probably all right "as is." Determining what constitutes an optimal keyword involves less guesswork than calculating the number of keywords to use. One way to think about this is to consider meanings. How many meanings does each keyword have? Proper nouns and terms with precise meanings are hard to improve upon. In the context of the topic, *causes* is fairly clear and there may be no way to improve it. The word *people* has few meanings, but the information retrieved focuses on people who are impoverished, not their viewpoints. Therefore a different keyword may be better. *View* has multiple meanings. Steps 3, 4, and 5 work hand in hand: *people* and *view* are likely not good enough; more specific terms—hyponyms— should be substituted. An online thesaurus may suggest more powerful synonyms for *people*, such as *populace* or *public*; *view* may be replaced by *opinion*, *perspective*, or *point of view*.[18] The abstracts from the previous search actually contain some of these terms, so it is not always necessary to turn to a thesaurus or wait for better words to spring from memory.

Until spell checking was added to search algorithms, searchers who couldn't spell faced additional difficulties. For example, if the query contained *povrety*, only matching misspelled instances would be returned. That is not good if the goal is authoritative information, as experts are exacting with words. If *povrety* is entered into Google, the search engine ignores the misspelling and matches 33 million results for *poverty*. Google can be forced to search for the exact match (Google provides a link: "search instead for *povrety*"), in which case 126,000 results, all mis- spelled by their authors, are matched. Typos or misspellings in a query no longer stop a Google, Yahoo!, or Bing search from looking for the closest-matching term, but other machines lack this capability. Spelling still matters if the search is con- ducted in PubMed, JSTOR, Wikipedia, and the like. Capitalization doesn't matter, and punctuation is ignored.

Finally, word order can be important, but that does not prevent relevant results from being matched. Inserting *States United* rather than *United States* could be an issue, but in this case it makes no difference. As a general recommendation, Google advises putting words in the order they would normally be used.[19] Arranging words in order of importance has little effect.

Fortunately, the checklist approach takes less time to implement than this de- scription takes to read. By now, the query has been reduced, and a number of new possibilities are ready to be entered in the search box. A good search-box strategy is iterative: reduce the query, submit it, skim the results, and decide if they are "getting warmer." In terms of the information fluency model, homing in on the information describes step 3: "How will I get there?" If the results are not promising, the process returns to the beginning: "What am I searching for?" If a particular search engine is not producing the results expected, another one may be tried (step 2): "Where will I find the information?"

Now consider the results. *Public perspective causes poverty* produces articles on poverty and public opinion as well as polls on the perceived causes of poverty: for example, a page on "Public Opinion and Attitudes" published by the Stanford Center on Poverty and Inequality.[20] The query is interesting in its own right because, if it were a sentence, it suggests public perspectives cause poverty. That is not how a search engine would process it. *Public perception causes poverty* produces an abstract that points to an article titled, "Rags, Riches, and Bootstraps: Beliefs about the Causes of Wealth and Poverty" from *The Sociological Quarterly*.[21] Keeping in mind the invisible query, its publication date of 1989 definitely does not satisfy the condition *today*, however the article could contain valuable search terms.

The returns for both these queries should be scanned, keeping in mind the rest of the invisible query, *United States*, as many articles (especially on the second page) pertain to other countries. The longer string *public perception causes poverty United States* retrieves relevant results with a focus on the United States, so the strategy to keep the query as short as possible is unnecessary in this case. In fact, it's a good search-box strategy to experiment with several versions of a query to collect a wider array of sources. Coming up with the "perfect query" (*sic*) in speculative searching requires experimentation. That being said, no query is perfect. It is really a matter of sufficiency: More queries are better than one.

The longer query that includes *United States* brings to the top a result not found using shorter queries: "Many See Those in 'Poverty' as Not So Poor."[22] This references another article, "Understanding Poverty in the United States: Surprising Facts about America's Poor."[23] Browsing, then skimming the contents, confirms the article is current. Furthermore, the text is loaded with potential keywords: *Poverty Pulse Poll, survey, American, population, households, mainstream, activists, public understanding of poverty, Republicans, Democrats, advocacy groups, liberals*—and the list goes on. The report provides evidence that poverty may look different if you are in the mainstream public or an activist, a Republican or a Democrat. This addresses the original question, *How do different groups of people in the United States view the causes of poverty?* The question, on its own, was unable to retrieve a relevant result; it had to be turned into several effective queries.

The instructional technique just described, when shared with others, is known as a "think-aloud."[24] Students seldom have an opportunity to observe what a skilled searcher does, let alone thinks. Sharing the thought process explicitly can help less experienced searchers see new ways of understanding search strategy. As a result, they may start to examine their own implicit strategies.

Another way to learn query optimization incorporates search simulation in a game-like format. "Keyword Challenge" games[25] were created by the 21st Century Information Fluency Project as a way for learners to experiment with the "Query Checklist."

Each short game provides a natural-language research challenge, for example, "What toy utilizes a construction design that reduces damage from earthquakes?"[26] Players are directed to drag and drop keywords into search boxes. Immediate feedback is provided about the effectiveness of their choices: Is the keyword good "as is"? Is there a better word to use? Should this word be excluded? Keyword effectiveness is based on actual search results. An optimal score is 80 percent or higher, which means an answer to the challenge can be found online using the selected "as-is" keywords and important concepts (for which there are better keywords). Individuals or groups may play the games. As shown in figure 3.1, a player has sorted all the keywords from the original question into the four boxes. If the query *earthquake toy design reduces construction* is entered in Google, an answer to the question will be found. Ironically, the top answer, provided by Answers.com,[27] is incorrect. This underscores the need for online fact checking.

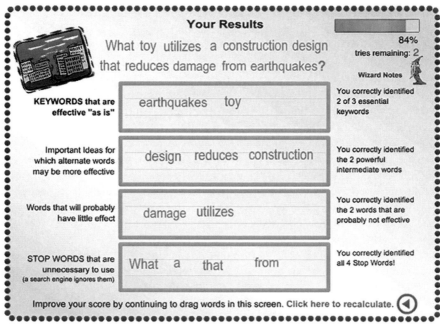

Figure 3.1. Earthquake Search Challenge

SEMANTIC SEARCHING

Managing keywords is no longer the only way to obtain good search results. Relevant results may be obtained by using a semantic search engine, one that interprets word meaning. For example, the semantic engine Hakia processes full, unaltered questions and produces comparable results to using optimized queries in Google. One of the top returns in Hakia is the article cited earlier, "Understanding Poverty in the United States: Surprising Facts about America's Poor." A semantic engine allows users to skip straight from the question to relevant results without doing anything to the query or having to browse.

Commercial engines like Google increasingly have this semantic capacity, but the majority does not. Consequently, users of semantic engines must keep in mind other engines' natural-language limitations. The drawback with Hakia, like every other search engine, is that it does not index everything. Other search engines will always be needed. As demonstrated with a complex natural-language query, not even Google produced relevant results, but at least it had results. The same query produces nothing in JSTOR, a good source of information for this question. JSTOR appears to have zero results, which is definitely not the case because one of the articles Google retrieved came from JSTOR. The real issue is that not all engines process natural language. The technology is improving, and an increasing number of engines will develop semantic capabilities, but until then the limitations of the natural-language search-box strategy still matter.

SEARCH-BOX OPERATOR STRATEGIES

Search operators add functionality to keywords. Most of the time, operators are not needed. Words are enough. The most common operator, the AND function (e.g., search for *perception AND poverty*), is added between terms using a spacebar press. This eliminates the need to insert *AND* (or the + sign) at all. This user-friendly search-box accommodation may be overridden with another operator, but users generally don't pick this up on their own without help. Native search-box strategies start with natural language. Operators are added later.

To differentiate operators from normal language (the words *and, or, not, all*), special conventions were invented: *AND* (+), *OR* (|), *NOT* (-), and "quotes." Known as Boolean operators, the first three each has its own strategic search-box application; quotes does as well.

AND directs the search engine to return information that includes as many of the keywords as possible.

OR (|), the pipe symbol, when used between two terms instructs the engine to match one or the other. This is useful when alternative terms are present, such as *perspective OR perception OR opinion*. Using *OR* keeps the query short, like submitting three queries in one.

NOT, or the minus sign, may be used to eliminate a term from the search results. The effect is that fewer results are produced. The query *poverty −war* excludes all references to war (e.g., war on poverty), which might be beneficial if those results are not relevant. One must be careful when using *NOT* because desirable information may be excluded if *war* appears somewhere in the source.

Quotes around words may be the most useful operator besides default *AND*. Quotes tells the search engine to match a literal string, for example, "poverty plus poll" will only return matches for the whole string. When quotes are used, the spaces between words are no longer automatically filled with *AND*. Quotes is a powerful method to create very specific search strings.

Recalling the query, *public perspective causes poverty*, only *AND* was needed. *OR* could have been useful for creating multiple queries with a single submission. There was no reason to eliminate terms using *NOT*, nor was there a reason to put words in quotes. As a search-box strategy, using quotes and *NOT* greatly reduces search flexibility to home in on information. Comparatively, *AND* as well as *OR* enhances flexibility to broaden the search. Therefore, operators have definite strategic applications. If too few results are obtained, quotes and *NOT* should be avoided. Conversely, to trim down a large number of unwanted results, quotes and *NOT* can be very effective. Knowing how and when to use operators appropriately adds significant power to searching. Not to use them properly or in the right circumstances impairs the search. Searchwise, it's better to leave operators alone than to inadvertently misuse them.

JSTOR ADVANCED SEARCH STUDY

As an example of what happens when students run afoul of operators, members of the 21st Century Information Fluency team collaborated with a librarian and teacher at the Illinois Mathematics and Science Academy (IMSA) in assessing students' research skills. IMSA students are highly gifted and used to challenging instruction. In preparation for a research assignment on World War II, 59 sophomores in three sections of American Studies participated in an introduction to library research. As part of the orientation, students were introduced to JSTOR's advanced search features that include operators and several proprietary filters. No instruction on how to use operators or filters was offered, although many students claimed to be familiar with operators and their use. A survey was given to participants to inquire about their understanding of digital searching. They were also given a search challenge to be conducted using JSTOR: *Find an article published in December 1946 that focuses on the topic of isolationism in WWII in the middle west.*[28] More than 200 student queries were captured using a simulated JSTOR interface backed by a database.

A number of search box–related strategies emerged from the data. Six out of seven students searched only with keywords that were provided in the challenge. This practice is observed so often that the authors deliberately insert ineffective terms in the challenges, such as *view* and *middle west*. Other words are more effective. Whether students lack imagination or prefer to stick with the terms of the assignment, a "do not experiment with different words" strategy confounds a search. Because searches do not start with well-defined questions or all the right words, finding better keywords while searching is essential. How often can the average person accurately predict the words an unknown author uses in an article? Some estimate the odds of being able to predict the word another person uses averages to one in five.[29] Whatever the odds, on the basis of literal matching alone, a significant percentage of queries will falter on their first attempt.

From the survey, 63 percent of students misunderstood that search engines literally match terms. Taking this into consideration, it is surprising only one in three queries contained stop words, for example. In the years since the study, JSTOR has improved its ability to parse queries, so the limitations that faced the IMSA students are no longer as relevant. To be sure, the importance of literal matching has not changed. The difference is what a search engine does to a query *before* literally matching terms. JSTOR ignores stop words and checks the proximity of keywords. Going a step further, Google checks spelling and adds synonyms in an effort to discern the meaning.

What the majority of students did right in terms of keywords was largely lost by what they did to them with operators.[30] In 60 percent of queries that included *OR*, the operator was inserted between the wrong pairs of words. To illustrate, *isolationism WWII OR "World War II" middle west* is a good use of the operator. A single query does the work of two, looking for either *WWII* or *World War II* in combination with the other keywords. Incredibly, students did something like this: *isolationism OR WWII OR middle OR west*. They may have thought they were creating a more robust query, but what they did, in effect, was create four independent queries with no connection between any words. What's worse is that they would not be able to recognize this mistake without taking a hard look at the results: only one word is matched in every abstract. This is one way the misuse of an operator can quietly creep into a search strategy.

Another example of silent misuse involves the use of quotes. A small number of students put quotes around phrases that aren't phrases at all. *"Isolationism WWII"* will return very few, if any, articles in JSTOR. The exact string must be matched. Despite its obvious relevance, an article containing the text *isolationism during WWII* would go unmatched. Again, students remain oblivious to this mistake unless they remove the quotes and try it again. In both cases it would have been better to ignore OR and quotes completely. Students need to be shown the right way to use operators.

Placing quotes around a single term (e.g., *"isolationism"*) does nothing, yet that is how quotes were used 75 percent of the time. The quoted string and the word are the same. On the positive side, no harm is done to the search. What is noteworthy is that students thought they were doing something effective. The noneffect would be impossible to discern from the results, so students might never realize the pointlessness of quoting single words, an illustration of how a useless method becomes part of a search-box strategy.

A similar problem involves the *AND* operator, evident in one out of five student queries. Like quoting a single word, explicitly adding *AND* does no harm (although the spacebar uses two less keystrokes and has the same effect). What could be a concern is that JSTOR offers *AND* as part of "Advanced Search" and shows how the operator is used in the query: *(((((isolationism) AND (WWII)) OR (World War II)) AND (middle west))*. The impression is given that *AND* is necessary (for the engine, it is) when the user experience no longer requires it. Not long ago, *AND* *had* to be inserted between words. Times have changed. Now its demonstration may serve to confuse a generation raised on Google who encounter it here, possibly for the first time. For a segment of students in the study, single-word quotes as well as *AND* represent search-box strategies to be unlearned.

A final example involves the *NOT* operator. Only a handful of students tried it. Those who did used it correctly—if they had been searching in Google. Unfortunately, JSTOR requires a different method, a proprietary filter to cull results. As a consequence, these queries did not produce the predicted outcomes.

The IMSA study revealed detailed problems of the students' own making, problems created by taking advantage of JSTOR's search features in unintended ways. Some misuse could be considered harmless (e.g., quoting single terms). On the other hand, using quotes indiscriminately with multiple terms and inserting *OR* between nonequivalent pairs caused queries to fail. Would students overcome these errors on their own? It seems unlikely because tracing problems back to operators is difficult merely by looking at search results. Search-box results do not explicitly warn the user that something is amiss with the query, at least not yet.

Operator misunderstanding has the potential to become embedded in a student's search-box strategy. Operators do not become part of a search strategy the same way natural language does. The latter simply transforms into natural-language queries. Operators have the potential to be absorbed into the fabric of a natural-language strategy as an add-on. When operators get in the way of searching, as they did for the students using JSTOR, it is hard for the user to identify operators as the cause. The only immediate solution is a knowledgeable person who can evaluate queries. The correct use of operators can be achieved through trial and error, analyzing results, and reading up on their use, but that takes time and the drive to do it. A faster alternative would be to help students evaluate queries, showing them better ways to search and how best to take advantage of at least one unfamiliar search engine.

Fortunately, there are many paths to information online. In only 10 percent of the cases did students truly become stuck, due to misunderstanding the assignment. There is no remedy for focusing on the *middle east* instead of the *middle west* or *World War I* instead of *World War II*. Except for these cases, students overcame poor word choice and operator mistakes with repeated effort. An informed search-box strategy would make the task considerably easier.

LIBRARY INTERVENTION

The question guiding the study was "How can we assess database research skills while engaging students and delivering data to drive library instruction development?"[31]

The study succeeded in meeting that objective. Armed with data from the search-challenge queries, the librarian and a member of the information fluency project engaged students in a 55-minute library training session (one for each section of the course). Instead of providing the usual broad overview of how to use the library for digital research, the pretest revealed three knowledge gaps to address: keyword selection, operators, and JSTOR advanced filters.

Three learning activities were selected for each training session. The first was a type of group query triage that featured screenshots of anonymous, problematic queries submitted the day before by the students. Each query was displayed one at a time for all to see. The leaders introduced the activity by explaining that these queries, without identifying their authors, contained characteristic errors. In an open discussion, students were invited to talk about the errors and what could be done to fix them. In the free exchange of this learning activity, students learned from one another. The leaders merely had to ask questions. The discussion was followed by a worksheet activity in which students returned to the original search challenge and each transformed it into a query according to the "Query Checklist."[32] Following a think-aloud, the librarian then demonstrated how these queries are properly entered with operators and proprietary filters (e.g., date range, periodical type) into several of the library's databases: JSTOR, Opposing Viewpoints, Newsbank, and CQ Researcher.

During a third class session, students completed another set of search challenges similar to the pretest. The results helped to determine if students were better able to search as a consequence of the library instruction. Figure 3.2 compares students'

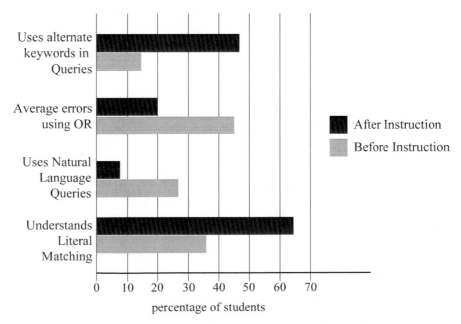

Subjects: Students enrolled at the Illinois Mathematics and Science Academy, n = 59

Figure 3.2. Tenth Graders' Search Box Skills before and after Instruction

performance on the pretest and posttest. The percentage of students who understood that search engines perform literal matching almost doubled. Queries containing natural language dropped markedly from 27 to 8 percent. The average number of errors using the *OR* operator declined more than half, from 45 to 20 percent. The frequency of queries containing new keywords (i.e., not provided in the search challenge) increased threefold, from 14 to 47 percent. All these changes, with the exception of the *OR* operator, due to the small sample size, were statistically significant and attributable to feedback provided in the library training.

One-off sessions like this can have a significant impact, but young learners need additional assistance. Ongoing, just-in-time learning opportunities make more sense. The posttest analysis in their possession, the librarian and teacher were now positioned to address resistant, ineffective search-box strategies if they chose to.

On the topic of testing, the importance of formative assessment is paramount. Information fluency is not a constellation of strategies and skills measured by high-stakes standardized tests. This is probably a good thing. Localized, informal testing for the purpose of designing instruction that targets students' faulty search assumptions seems more appropriate and, as shown, can make a real difference. Persistent formative assessment could contribute to even bigger, lasting gains. The tests need not be complex or time consuming; they may be as simple as examining samples of students' queries or having students complete online tutorials and checking their progress. Likewise, interventions do not require multiple class periods or even whole classes. Layering information fluency training and assessment over regular coursework or embedding it can be an effective combination. Intervention need not usurp much time away from other learning activities; in fact, it can complement it if done right. To accomplish this is best done by understanding problems students are experiencing not only with search-box strategies, as was the focus in the IMSA study, but extending as well to evaluation skills and ethical use.

SUMMARY

An effective approach to teaching information fluency is based on the premise that students are largely self-taught and unaware of efficient digital research practices. This applies to search-box strategy, browsing, skimming snippets, and locating information on pages.

When a person needs information, a strategic choice is made that determines how the search will start. That choice may be implicit or explicit. A considerable part of being fluent is becoming aware of the decisions one makes to locate information. As young people look for information online, implicit strategies are developed mainly by trial and error, sometimes with help from a parent or a friend, sometimes with help from school. Self-taught strategies learned through trial and error are commonly based on the following assumptions:

- A search box is the go-to choice for finding information online;
- Search engines are able to retrieve results based on natural-language queries;

- Words given in an assignment or that first come to mind should be able to retrieve the information that is needed;
- The first page of results contains relevant and trustworthy information;
- One query should be sufficient;
- If the search engine doesn't deliver what is needed, it is better to click links and browse pages.

When strategies like these produce meaningful results, as they do with big commercial engines like Google, Bing, and others, it is possible to develop disproportionate confidence in contrast to one's actual abilities. Assumptions about how searching works can lead to using a search box in ways it was not intended.

Explicit instruction helps make users aware of inefficient, ineffective strategies. The failure to grow beyond inferior self-taught strategies severely limits searchers in their ability to find more challenging information and evaluate its credibility. Unchallenged searchers can easily miss an indispensable search-box strategy: finding better keywords while searching. Easy searches often yield results that are relevant on the first try; hard searches—more common in higher education—often yield irrelevant results with the first query. Poor results are frequently improved by finding more specific keywords as the search progresses. Other times, operators may be needed to filter out unwanted information or to broaden the search. Conscious strategies are invaluable, placing a variety of methods at one's fingertips and informing the best choice for the task at hand.

All search-box strategies involve keywords; some involve operators or other filters. One way to make students more aware of how keywords function in information retrieval is to use a query checklist, as demonstrated in this chapter. Various teaching techniques, including a think-aloud, screenshots of queries, and interactive "Keyword Challenge" games, provide opportunities for discussion and discovery of better keywords. Operators may be learned in similar fashion. At the heart of each of these learning activities is a significant, speculative search task. Challenging search tasks can put pressure on learners and test their skills. Done correctly, learners who don't know what else to do can engage in self-evaluation of present practices or become more receptive to offers of help. As described in the chapter that follows, challenges may be simulated or real. What matters most is a degree of inherent complexity and that feedback is immediate; otherwise frustration may be counterproductive.

NOTES

1. "Google Intuitive Search Answers Are SO Weird . . . ," *Facebook*, accessed January 23, 2013, https://www.facebook.com/pages/Google-Intuitive-Search-Answers-are-SO-weird/204484611531.

2. Cory Doctorow, "Using Clickfraud on Google Ads to Amass Shares of Google," *Boing Boing*, last modified June 7, 2011, http://boingboing.net/2011/06/07/using-clickfraud-on.html.

3. Melissa Gross and Don Latham, "Undergraduate Perceptions of Information Literacy: Defining, Attaining and Self-Assessing Skills," *College and Research Libraries*, 70, no. 4 (July 2009): 336–50, http://eduscapes.com/instruction/articles/gross.pdf.

4. Marc Prensky, "Digital Natives, Digital Immigrants," from *On the Horizon*, 2001, http://www.marcprensky.com/writing/prensky%20-%20digital%20natives,%20digital%20 immigrants%20-%20part1.pdf.

5. Kristen Purcell, Lee Rainie, Alan Heaps, Judy Buchanan, Linda Friedrich, Amanda Jacklin, Clara Chen, and Kathryn Zickuhr, "How Teens Do Research in the Digital World," *Pew Internet*, November 1, 2012, http://www.pewinternet.org/~/media//Files/Reports/2012/ PIP_TeacherSurveyReportWithMethodology110112.pdf.

6. Kristen Purcell, Joanna Brenner, and Lee Rainie, "Search Engine Use 2012," *Pew Internet*, last modified March 9, 2012, http://pewinternet.org/Reports/2012/Search-Engine -Use-2012/Main-findings/Search-engine-use-over-time.aspx. This study states that "Google is far and away the most popular search engine," preferred by 84 percent of users. What segment of all users is students isn't clear, but research by the 21st Century Information Fluency Project several years ago found that more than 55 percent of students turned to Google 90 percent of the time. See note 28.

7. Thomas Scott and Michael O'Sullivan, "Analyzing Student Search Strategies: Making a Case for Integrating Information Literacy Skills into the Curriculum," *Teacher Librarian*, *33*, no. 1 (October 2005): 21.

8. Carl Heine, "Teaching Research Skills Using the Internet" (presentation to the Illinois School Library Media Association Annual Conference, Arlington Heights, IL, October 5–6, 2005).

9. "The Size of the World Wide Web," accessed January 24, 2013, http://www.world widewebsize.com.

10. Paul Barron, "How Google Works: Are Search Engines Really Dumb and Why Should Educators Care?" *Internet@Schools*, last modified January 1, 2011, http://www.inter netatschools.com/Articles/PrintArticle.aspx?ArticleID=73090.

11. "Google Analytics," *Google*, accessed January 25, 2013, http://www.google.com/analyt ics.

12. "Help Save the Endangered Pacific Northwest Tree Octopus from Extinction!" *Zapato Productions Intradimensional*, accessed January 26, 2013, http://zapatopi.net/treeoctopus.

13. Beth Krane, "Researchers Find Kids Need Better Online Academic Skills," *University of Connecticut*, last modified November 13, 2006, http://advance.uconn .edu/2006/061113/06111308.htm.

14. "Media Advisory: Schools Facing Learning Crisis Spawned by Internet," *PRWeb*, last modified January 28, 2011, http://www.prweb.com/releases/2011/01/prweb5010934.htm.

15. *Hakia*, accessed January 31, 2013, http://hakia.com.

16. Carl Heine, "Optimal Query Checklist," *21st Century Information Fluency*, last modi- fied January 1, 2013, https://21cif.com/resources/curriculum/querychecklist.html.

17. "Privacy and My Location," *Google*, accessed January 31, 2013, http://support.google .com/maps/bin/answer.py?hl=en&answer=153807.

18. "View," *Thesaurus.com*, accessed January 30, 2013, http://thesaurus.com/browse/view.

19. Jon Alcibar, "Notes on 'Power Searching with Google' Course, July 2012," *Google*, ac- cessed January 30, 2013, https://docs.google.com/document/d/1DShfXSPP3GjDIAiSnOPqf CTUzc3l11FsT8voM65i2kI/edit.

20. "Public Opinion and Attitudes," *The Stanford Center on Poverty and Inequality*, accessed January 31, 2013, https://www.stanford.edu/group/scspi/issue_public_opinion_ attitudes.html.

21. Kevin Smith and Lorene Stone, "Rags, Riches, and Bootstraps: Beliefs about the Causes of Wealth and Poverty," *The Sociological Quarterly*, *30*, no. 1 (Spring 1989): 93–107.

22. "Many See Those in 'Poverty' as Not So Poor," *Rasmussen Reports*, last modified August 19, 2011, http://www.rasmussenreports.com/public_content/lifestyle/general_lifestyle/august_2011/many_see_those_in_poverty_as_not_so_poor.

23. Robert Rector and Rachel Sheffield, "Understanding Poverty in the United States: Surprising Facts about America's Poor", *The Heritage Foundation*, last modified September 13, 2011, http://www.heritage.org/research/reports/2011/09/understanding-poverty-in-the-united-states-surprising-facts-about-americas-poor.

24. Carl Heine, "Evaluating Digital Information," *21st Century Information Fluency*, last modified February 12, 2012, https://21cif.com/rkitp/features/v1n4/leadarticle_v1_n4.html.

25. Carl Heine, "Action Zone User's Guide to Keyword Challenges," *21st Century Information Fluency Project*, last modified January 28, 2009, http://21cif.com/rkitp/curriculum/v1n3/use_flash_applications_v1n3.html.

26. Carl Heine, "Earthquake Challenge," *21st Century Information Fluency Project*, last modified June 26, 2007, http://21cif.com/rkitp/challenge/v1n3/SC_earthquaketoy/SC_012.swf.

27. "Which Toy Demonstrates a Construction Principle That Can Reduce Damage from an Earthquake?" *Answers*, accessed February 15, 2013, http://wiki.answers.com/Q/Which_toy_demonstrates_a_construction_principle_that_can_reduce_damage_from_an_earthquake.

28. David Barr, Paula Garrett, Dan Balzer, Carl Heine, and Bob Houston, "Search Challenges as Assessment Tools: A Collaboration between the Library and the 21st Century Information Fluency Project in Illinois" (paper presented at the Australia Library and Information Association Biennial Conference, Perth, Australia, 2006), http://conferences.alia.org.au/alia2006/Papers/David_Barr_and_Paula_Garrett.pdf.

29. Carl Heine, "Speculative and Investigative Searching," *21st Century Information Fluency*, last modified January 28, 2009, https://21cif.com/rkitp/newRkit/gettingstarted/searchtypes.html.

30. Carl Heine, "Taking Advantage of Operators," *21st Century Information Fluency*, last modified January 20, 2010, https://21cif.com/rkitp/features/v1n7/leadarticle_v1n7.html.

31. Paula Garrett, "Search Challenges as Assessment Tools" (PowerPoint presentation for the Australian Library and Information Association Biennial Convention, Perth, Australia, September 19–22, 2006, slide 6).

32. See note 16.

4

Internet Search Challenges

Optimal queries, operators, and numerous other time-saving search methods help to improve performance in speculation as well as investigation. The difficulty is how to convince students of that fact. Self-taught strategies, provided they work, can form barriers to information fluency. The worst-case scenario for information fluency involves individuals using native strategies founded on bad assumptions that go unchecked. Without deliberate intervention, this can easily happen. The self-taught novice researcher almost always retrieves results regardless of how imperfect the search-box strategy. Poor searching can develop a click at a time and last for years when there doesn't seem to be an obvious problem. The result can be underchallenged, overconfident searchers.

Students not only insist they don't believe everything they find online, but they also claim they are good searchers.[1] Teens aren't the only ones who think too highly of their skills. Postsecondary students have been found to rate themselves higher than their actual abilities.[2] Nine out of ten adults in the 2012 Pew Internet report on search-engine use claimed they "always or most of the time find the information they are seeking when they use search engines."[3] With such a high incidence of perceived success, it isn't surprising that adults attribute success to personal ability: 56 percent of the adults felt very confident, and another 37 percent felt somewhat confident about their search-engine abilities. Only a handful of adults (6 percent) surveyed admitted a lack of confidence. These are very strong confidence ratings but not as strong compared to teachers surveyed the same year. Only 1 percent of teachers admitted they did not feel confident, the rest reporting high levels of confidence (73 percent) and some confidence (26 percent).[4] Younger teachers felt better about their abilities than older colleagues.

Ask teachers to rate their students' abilities, as the Pew Internet researchers did, and the indexes are markedly lower. In terms of search-box ability, teachers felt only 62 percent of students were good to excellent, the rest being poor to fair. In response to the question whether students know how search results are generated, the numbers dipped more: 53 percent have good to excellent knowledge; 47 percent fell short of that.

Stepping back to reflect, it is likely the numbers provided by students and teachers have less to do with actual search ability than self-serving bias and fundamental attribution error. Asking people to rate themselves is, of course, highly subjective. Given a track record of searches that do not end in failure, it makes sense for people to attribute it to their ability.[5] When considering the actions of their students, teachers rate students' skills lower. It is just as possible that students' failure is the result of teacher errors, like providing students with inadequate keywords and assigning unfamiliar databases without training.

What if personal ratings of ability were a function of easy searches both in and out of school? Not all academic searches are easy. Some may be exceptionally demanding: establishing the date of a Web page, tracking down the identity of an author or publisher, or fact checking the accuracy of a claim. An educational objective, therefore, could be for students to perform challenging searches in order to test the worth of their self-taught strategies. Internet search challenges can reveal strategic and tactical shortcomings. Making users aware of their shortcomings is only half the battle, however. The rest involves providing better ways to search combined with realistic opportunities for practice.

PUTTING TEACHERS TO THE TEST

A good way to challenge overconfidence is to present individuals with searches that are harder than normal. This strategy has consistently proven effective with educators and students alike. Teachers and librarians enrolled at the University of Wisconsin–Stout, as part of their online coursework, are assigned "Information Researcher" modules. These constitute a stress test for searching. The same online assessment is given to students in Northwestern University's Center for Talent Development programs. For a majority of the teachers, search confidence quickly erodes when they must locate evidence to evaluate the accuracy of Web pages. Two sample challenges from "Information Researcher," one a simulation and the other a live challenge, are explored in detail later in the chapter.

Reading through comments posted in online forums, it's not unusual for educators to characterize their experience as "frustrating," "wrong," and "arghhhhhhh!"[6] These graduate students seemed to grasp the underlying problem and not just fault the test:

> "I swear I am an illiterate librarian sometimes! I was so confused when I couldn't find the guy's Twitter name. Then it occurred to me that maybe I should read the question again (and again and again) and, yup, it helps to read AND pay attention."
> "I didn't put in the time I should have. I found the first thing that popped up and I used it. Not always right, I might add. I was oftentimes rushing through it, and that caused a lot of wrong answers. Once I stopped and took my time, I actually got some good digging in. It was a real eye opener for me, and now I understand a bit more why many students could find it difficult to search responsibly."

"While it had some frustration involved, in every case it was with myself for missing details or not reading carefully."

When individuals confront challenging searches, they start to question their abilities. It becomes an eye-opening experience. Frustrated teachers start to identify how
they can improve and gain empathy for their less-experienced students. The assessment challenges prove to be more difficult than most searches teachers are used to,
but few doubt the skills required are essential:

"I thought I had pretty good research skills, but I was surprised at what I didn't
know. To the question: Is Information Fluency part of your curriculum? Should
it be? I would answer with a resounding yes (that it should be, though it is not
currently)!"

Self-confidence, when it comes to searching, matters little if individuals cannot
find essential information. Teachers and librarians, if anyone, should be able to locate
authors, publication dates, and accurate information even when those facts are not
easy to find.

TOWARD MORE REALISTIC PERCEPTIONS OF ABILITY

Students in the Center for Talent Development programs who complete the "Information Researcher" modules fill out end-of-course surveys each summer. The results
show what happens to self-perceptions when search skills are rigorously challenged.
Key indicators in regard to information fluency stem from this question: "How
would you rate your Web fluency skills (in general) prior to and after participating
in the modules?"[7] Ratings are made using hindsight, so there is a good chance the
numbers (see "Before" in figure 4.1) are lower than if the respondents had been asked
this question before tackling challenges. Regardless of before or after, these teens appear nowhere near as confident as adults in the Pew Internet survey of search-engine
usage. If more than half of adults feel very confident about their digital information
skills, it is a dramatic reversal to discover that four out of five gifted teens—not a
group typically short on confidence—rate their own skills average to poor. Similar
results have been obtained over the course of four consecutive years.

The gains in perceived ability match gains in performance. Findings such as these
support assigning learners nontrivial search challenges. When challenged and given
feedback about their performance, students start to think more realistically about
their abilities; they admit their weaknesses. Frustration may occur along the way, but
concurrent with this can come the recognition that improvement is needed. Search
challenges help raise student awareness that self-taught strategies are inadequate
when confronted with college-ready research and evaluation of credibility.

Search challenges are considered integral to information fluency instruction, giving students opportunities to demonstrate what they know about search boxes and
searching and, in most cases, helping them see they don't know enough. This chapter

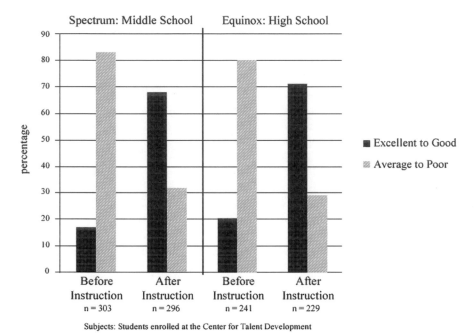

Figure 4.1. Student Self-Perceptions of Search Ability before and after Instruction

examines the use and design of challenges in and out of classrooms. Two types of challenges are considered: simulations and live searching. Gamelike simulations are ideal for targeting specific search competencies and informing learners in an instant how well they performed. Coupled with step-by-step solutions, learners can grasp new strategies quickly. Live search challenges—opening a browser, going to a search engine, and retrieving relevant information from a database—are also powerful experiences if done with adequate support, for example, in a group where answers can be compared anonymously and methods discussed. Live searching can be unpredictable, but the adventure can be used to challenge self-taught strategies and open eyes to more powerful search alternatives.

SIMULATED SEARCHES

The rationale behind simulations is to reduce the number of search variables to a manageable number and still retain a degree of realism. With simulations it is possible to isolate skills to determine searchers' competencies. Table 4.1 is a partial list of simulations on the 21st Century Information Fluency site that concentrate on discrete skills. It helps to know some programming to design a computer simulation; otherwise it either has no interactive hands-on elements or turns into live searching.

Table 4.1. Competencies Incorporated in Simulations

Information Fluency Competency/Skill	Free Simulations[8]
Keyword selection	Keyword Challenge
Search-engine selection	Archery Challenges
Browsing	Directory Challenge
Boolean operators	Pirates and Piranhas
Skimming challenges	Gold Rush Games
Finding better keywords in snippets	Snippet Sleuth
	Snowsport Challenges I–III
	Soccer Challenge
Evaluating sources	Author Challenges
	Publisher Challenges
Evaluating content	Bias Challenges
Evaluating references	Link-to Challenges
Web Site evaluation	Evaluation Wizard
	Use It or Lose It
	Bad Apple
Proper citation	Citation Wizard
Avoiding plagiarism	Plagiarism I and II

Most of the examples listed in table 4.1 were built in Flash and are gradually being converted to an iPad-friendly format. However, it is just as possible to design simulations using PowerPoint or another graphics editor that achieve some of the same effects without needing input text boxes, buttons, and automated feedback. Game creation software programs could be a viable option to coding.

"SNOWSPORT NYM" CHALLENGES

"Snowsport I, II, and III"[9] are games that introduce students to optimal queries and finding better keywords in snippets and provide practice using hyponyms and hypernyms. Two or more teams in a class or after-school program can play this game. The first challenge introduces the idea that expert searchers know how to select nyms (synonyms, hypernyms, and hyponyms) in order to improve their search results. Nyms may be professional language used by experts in a particular field. In this game, the field is snowboarding; a professional term might be *fakie*. The following question from the simulation could be projected: *What competitive winter sport is considered a variation of motocross on snow?* Teams of students could be asked to confer and choose only the important search words or ideas in the question. Each team writes their choices on a sheet of paper to hold up, not unlike contestants on one of the old television shows like *Match Game*. One point is awarded for every correct answer. Depending on the experience level of the students, one point could be deducted for every incorrect answer. Students may actually have more fun playing this activity in a group setting than online. As a group game, there is the added bonus of helping one another. Online games are not necessarily better than live games—a game with a social component is almost guaranteed to produce more laughter than an online game played by an individual.[10] Here is the challenge:

"What competitive winter sport is considered a variation of motocross on snow?"

The most important keywords in this challenge are *competitive motocross snow.* Have students talk about why these terms and not the others are considered important. Valid observations include:

- If there's *snow, winter* is unnecessary;
- *Competitive* (Google finds *competition*) takes the place of *sport*;
- *Variation* isn't an important search term—this could just as easily been phrased as *something like motocross*; and
- The remaining words add nothing.

There's always the chance for debate—which should be welcomed—if teams don't agree. Disputes may be settled by entering keywords in a search box to see if a word helps or not. As search engines continue to evolve, the most important words may start to change. Playing the game as a group without the need for Flash player or having to program boxes, buttons, and feedback adds a degree of flexibility that an online version cannot deliver.

"PIRATES" AND "PIRANHAS"

"Pirates" and "Piranhas" are both operator challenges. Developing a live search that depends on Boolean or special operators presents serious design difficulties. *OR* (|) or *NOT* (-) are especially hard to render essential. If students use Google, there is virtually no way to prevent them from finding information using words alone; operators merely represent a possible efficiency. The only way to guarantee students *not* find something is to have them look for the wrong thing from the start.

The most useful operator, when an exact phrase is known, is quotes (all the words). As search engines improve their performance, placing quotation marks around a short phrase or sentence increasingly has the same effect as leaving the phrase unquoted. Nonetheless, there are times when quotes prove necessary, even in Google. And as stated previously, many other search engines lack Google's versatility, so knowing when and how to employ operators still has value.

As operators become less essential in search engines frequented by students, simulations are better for assessment and training than live searches. With a simulation, Boolean operators can be made indispensable means to find information, which helps to clarify their appropriate use. In "Pirates" and "Piranhas," two different sets of challenges start with keyword selection, followed by considering how operators can make the queries even more effective. As described in the online user's guide,[11] a group game could kick off the session, having students identify the essential keywords in the challenge question *What island off the coast of Africa was considered a paradise for pirates in the 1800s?* Only three words are necessary: *island, pirates,* and *paradise.* A projection unit could be used to display the six word choices on a screen. Have students call out a word and click the appropriate term to get feedback. For each correct choice, the simulation adds a point; for every incorrect choice, the pirates take a point. Otherwise, the Flash version of the game keeps track of scores.

The "Pirates Challenge" is unusual in that the two proper nouns, *Africa* and *1800s,* do not help. This helps to underline a point: No "rule" for searching the Internet works all the time. There are sound practices, but they aren't always effective. This is why getting perfect scores on information fluency assessments is not an objective; 80 percent is about as good as it gets. There will be times that sound strategies fail; this is one of them. In this case, another good practice does work: Keep the query short.

Island, pirates, and *paradise* are all keywords that can be used as is. There is a better word than island, but it will be the name of the island that answers the question. The second page of the challenge prompts students to recall elements of the "Query Checklist" in order to come up with the best keywords possible. All three keywords are effective but not without an operator. Here is a case where quotes produce an effect. Unquoted, *paradise pirates* retrieves information irrelevant to the question. There are references to pirate havens not off the coast of Africa, for instance. Putting quotes around the phrase "*paradise for pirates,*" picked straight out of the question, creates a unique string that retrieves a relevant answer (the island of Sainte-Marie, near Madagascar—also a good answer). Quoting just "*paradise pirates*" matches nothing close. Inserting quotes around the three-word phrase may not be the first query a seasoned researcher tries, but it works. As stated previously, a fluent searcher will try more than one query. Are there other ways to find the name of the island? Undoubtedly, but it means coming up with keywords outside the question. Using an operator to make the most out of the keywords available saves time.

The "Pirates Challenge" had to be updated for this book, which points out an inherent drawback of Internet-based challenges. Information about piracy had changed since the challenge was first published in 2007. An effective query for the original question *What watery location is currently considered the world's paradise for pirates?* no longer includes *2006 OR 2007* (or an alternate version, *2006..2007*—a slick Google shortcut for number sequences). Besides that, Indonesian authorities have intervened to stem rampant piracy in the Malacca Straits. The Internet, like the world, is an ever-changing environment. What is fresh today could be stale tomorrow. Useful information may be replaced overnight by a "page not found" error. Many Internet search challenges have a short shelf life and need to be checked regularly to maintain freshness.

In addition to information disappearing, changes to search engines affect how well challenges work. The companion to the "Pirates Challenge" is an operator simulation known as the "Piranhas Challenge." Time has not been kind to "Piranhas," either. The original question *What fish other than piranhas is a threat to humans in the Amazon?* can now be entered word for word into a search box to retrieve relevant information. Solving the challenge no longer depends on the *NOT* (-) operator. In connection with *fish threat*, the search results now include Amazon the *river*; it is no longer necessary to remove *Amazon.com* with an operator. Amazon.com is still an immensely popular site, but it no longer dominates the results when the search algorithm determines the focus of the search is the longest river in the world.

The refreshed challenge demonstrates how the *OR* operator improves results without having to find other keywords. The search question is *Do piranhas or pacus fear butterflies?* The simulation walks learners through the steps of identifying important keywords. Following the user's guide, individuals perform the keyword activity and conclude with a group debriefing. The question contains only two potential clutter words: *do* and *or*. Because *do* and *or* are insignificant parts of speech, they neither add to nor subtract from the results. The key is to use *or* as an operator. This makes linguistic sense because of the choice between the two fearsome fish. *OR* transforms one query into two: *piranhas OR pacus fear butterflies*. Of the two, *Piranhas fear butterflies* is the one that proves effective. In the debriefing, students could be asked what makes this query ripe for the *OR* operator. By eliminating the need to match *piranhas AND pacus*, the answer page rises to the top.

The query leads to a page on Answers.com that answers the question: "(piranhas) are very afraid of butterflies, especially the pink ones with purple stripes."[12] That is one highly dubious claim waiting to be consumed:

- Does this seem like a credible answer? (maybe)
- Who can submit answers to Answers.com? (anyone)
- Can the author be identified? (no)
- Can the answer be fact checked? (yes)
- How would one do that?

Invite learners to query the claim *piranhas fear pink butterflies purple stripes* and report what they find. Outside of Answers.com, there is no information about piranhas being afraid of butterflies of any color. This finding emphasizes the need to evaluate information—it can't always be trusted even if it explicitly answers the question.

THE "*HOMELESS GUY* CHALLENGE"

A third example of a simulated challenge comes from the "Information Researcher" pretest. This is an investigative challenge to determine if searchers know how to find secondary source references to pages. The task is described as follows:

As part of a Civic Action (course) assignment, you come across the *Homeless Guy*,[13] a blog written by a (formerly) homeless person. In order to investigate the blog's credibility, you search to see if any academic institutions (.edu) link to the blog. What query would you use in Google to do that?[14]

This task requires knowing how to find backlinks (also known as inbound links) using special operators. This is relatively easy with the proper knowledge, although changes to search engines have made it harder. Two less-common operators that lo cate backlinks are *link:* and *site:* (both followed by a colon). *Link:* is used to identify pages that contain a hyperlink to a given URL, which explains why some call it the link-to operator. *Site:* limits the results to a specific domain.

In the challenge, *link:http://thehomelessguy.blogspot.com* is partly effective. There can be no space between *link:* and the URL, otherwise the *AND* operator creeps in there, and the search tries to match *link AND URL* (all punctuation is ignored). The reason the query is partly successful is that no .edu domains appear in the results. Google displays eighty-nine records, but among them are no colleges or universities. A few years ago, Google would retrieve a much larger set of linked pages in which case some educational sites would be included. Yahoo! discontinued its use of *link:* altogether. Backlink searches may be performed with specialized engines operated by search-engine optimization sites, but these tend to charge for their services. A few can be found that allow a limited number of searches per IP address per day. To find them, query *backlink search.*

Among free alternative queries is the *site:* operator, which makes for a more complicated inbound link query:

> *thehomelessguy.blogspot.com -site:thehomelessguy.blogspot.com.*

To dissect this, the first URL (http:// is optional) matches pages that contain a reference to this string. The minus (*NOT*) *-site:* operator then eliminates all the results that would come from the domain being investigated. This is done in order to re turn pages that have a link to *Homeless Guy* while ignoring all the possible internal pages of the *Homeless Guy* blog. Otherwise, most of the links would come from the blog itself. This is true for the majority of *link:thehomelessguy.blogspot.com* results in Google; the preponderance of internal (primary source) pages gets in the way of finding external (secondary source) pages.

There is a better way to find just the .edu sites, using the *site:* operator. The query *thehomelessguy.blogspot.com site:edu* returns hundreds of .edu sites that link to the site in question.

The importance of finding external pages centers on the question, Why do these secondary sources link to *Homeless Guy*? Because a large number of colleges and universities link to the *Homeless Guy* blog, they must find some value there. Exploring the contexts—how the links are used—on educational sites can help determine if those authorities believe the site has credibility.

Simulated searches are beneficial for reinforcing sound speculative and investigative searching by reducing the real-world messiness of a live database search. The applications are numerous, starting with defining the question and continuing through keyword choices, operator usage, database selection, finding better keywords, browsing, and skimming. Investigative applications also abound: evaluating authors and publishers, fact checking, detecting bias, finding publication dates, and external references. Finding ways to use simulations may be more of a challenge than designing them. If a class or extracurricular course devoted to information fluency is a possibility, coming up with a syllabus and instructional activities would not prove difficult. But that is not the reality in most schools. Instead, information fluency has to fit into existing structures and schedules, and that is no small challenge.

LIVE SEARCH CHALLENGES

The counterpart of simulation, live search challenges are unmatched for their capacity to test students' speculative search abilities in authentic conditions. Whereas discreet skills may be isolated through group and self-paced simulations, live searching cannot easily be constrained. A virtually unlimited maze of paths may be traversed to find information. Students can choose to take the long way or shorten it considerably. Some choices are better than others; a live challenge puts those decisions to the test.

Real search challenges, just like simulations, are vulnerable to the changing infoscape of the Internet. Without upkeep, they break or get stale, or they fall prey to searchers whose strategy—not necessarily a bad one—is to post challenge questions looking for crowd-sourced answers. For a majority of the challenges on 21cif.com, if one copies and pastes the challenge question into a query, a literal match is found on Answers.com. In many cases this is good because the answers supplied are often wrong, creating an opportunity to learn about evaluation. An excellent example of this is the "Broadway Challenge." The challenge question is *What is the earliest Broadway show for which both the opening and closing dates were published?*[15] Online, as of this writing, an anonymous source states that 1970 is the answer.[16] The answer to the question is not a date and is off by more than two hundred years.

The best type of challenge is a "disposable" one—intended to have a short shelf life. These are featured in assessment packages, such as "Information Researcher."[17] All challenges eventually succumb to search-engine improvements, changes to Internet content, and user-published appeals for solutions. Fragile as they are, real challenges are good for diagnostics. To demonstrate why, four different challenges are discussed: the "Broadway Challenge," the "Kermit Challenge," the "Soccer Challenge," and, from "Information Researcher," a "Citation Challenge."

THE "BROADWAY CHALLENGE"

The "Broadway Challenge" is currently in its third edition. When first issued, the task was *Find the total number of times* Funny Girl *has been performed on Broadway.*

This was a Deep-Web challenge that extracted from Google a database of Broadway shows. One of the best queries was simply *Broadway database*. This returned the *Internet Broadway Database*.[18] Searching in ibdb.com instead of Google led to the answer. Over time, other Broadway show sources posted answers that could be found merely using Google, precipitating a revision.

Today the task is to find the name of the Broadway show with the earliest known opening and closing dates. This is a moderately difficult Deep-Web challenge. Figuring out when to use a specialized database is not a normal part of a self-taught strategy. Specific information, like opening and closing dates, will either be published in an article or a list or stored in a database. It's worth trying an optimal query to find an article or list in Google just to see what happens, however deciding what that query should be is no simple task. *Broadway show opening closing* yields current show information. Adding *oldest* or *earliest* doesn't improve matters.

For nearly every topic, there exists a dedicated database or repository. Once this is known, a strategic choice is to go hunting for the database that will answer the question. For Broadway shows there is more than one.

Querying the *Internet Broadway Database* is not easy given the limited information available for the task. On the home page is a "Quick Search" link with a drop-down menu with four categories: "Show," "People/Org.," "Theater," "Season." Of these, "Season" seems the warmest choice. But what is a good keyword? The answer depends on a year. Will a year work in the search box? The only way to find out is to try one. A speculative entry for *1900* produces two results: links to lists for 1899–1900 and 1900–1901. This confirms that dates are searchable and go back over a century, but just how far back do they go? Short of trying *1898* and counting down from there, a more efficient way is to locate the "Advanced Search" page, always a good strategy when learning to drive an unfamiliar engine. A query for *advanced search* turns up nothing.

A second "warm" or relevant lead on the home page is the "Shows" tab. This opens up an advanced-search interface for shows. Eureka! Among the tools available are boxes for entering opening and closing dates. Again, experimentation is needed. Without knowing the name of the right show (which will be the answer), the only good option is to enter a year in the opening and closing date ranges. Ignore the month and day boxes; leave them blank—this can be learned by experimentation.

Because the first experimental search revealed dates as early as 1899, something earlier would be wise to try. A search for a wide opening range, 1700 to 1900, produces 865 results. That's a long list to scan, but just from the first few results, it is apparent this is exactly the type of information needed for the challenge. Rather than reduce the range from 1700 to 1800, a shortcut for finding the earliest opening date is to sort the list using the sort function provided on the page. The logical choice—sort by closing date—doesn't put the closings in chronological order. Sorting by opening day is more effective: the fifth item down the list, *King Richard III*, indicates that show opened and closed the same year, in 1750. No earlier shows have known closing dates.

Information about *King Richard III* isn't found without a fight. In sum, this search requires finding an appropriate database, experimenting with one query, browsing the site to find "Advanced Search," experimenting with a second query, sorting information (possibly a couple of ways), reading dates in a list, and determining which one was the earliest closing.

"Broadway" depends on several competencies, hence there are several ways to get off track. One way to help students determine personal shortcomings is to observe them searching. There are plenty of other ways to do this: videotape the searches, have students create a slide show of screenshots taken for each search page, or assign the challenge to pairs of students and make one a recorder, whose job it is to describe the queries, pages visited, and links clicked, either on paper or using a voice recorder. A more tech-savvy, kid-friendly way is to use software like Camtasia to record all the actions. Of course, it takes time to review the playback.

Group searching is a real-time option that involves many students and has the potential for teachable moments. Provide one computer and project the display. Ask for a volunteer to start (or choose someone). Each individual (or small group) gets to perform only one search action. Perhaps the first one wants to query Google. As a group examine the results. Is this cold or getting warmer? Call a second volunteer who may want to try another query or click through to one of the results shown. Tag-team searching like this sometimes calls for clicking the "Back" button; that counts as one action. If everyone is stuck, hints may be given, for example, finding a database of Broadway performances. This is a straightforward method for identifying points at which students make ineffective choices or get stuck. It encourages group problem solving and discovery.

An earlier version of the "Broadway Challenge" provided a timer. The goal was to find the information in eight minutes or ask for help. For most students, continuing to search beyond that amount of time is unproductive. For any staged challenge, it is better to get feedback or some help than suffer repeated failed attempts. Search challenges, when used in a group setting, benefit from a time cutoff.

Online help is especially useful for self-paced applications. For the "Broadway Challenge," as soon as a user enters an incorrect answer, a help page is available.[19] This help page includes two links: one to a training module for Deep-Web queries and the other to the answer. If the self-paced individual can't solve the challenge, at least a lesson may be gleaned from it.

THE "KERMIT CHALLENGE"

The "Kermit Challenge" is the oldest live search challenge on the 21cif.com site that still works as designed. The objective is to examine a photo to determine what keywords are needed to find information online about it. Students have a strong tendency to query only with words someone gives them. Searchers of all ages can benefit from this challenge by choosing keywords without a teacher's influence. Based on what they see in the picture, students create their own query. This challenge has become easier over the years due to a number of articles that now link to the page where Kermit the Frog is shown delivering a commencement speech at a college on Long Island. The challenge takes users to Yahoo! instead of Google for a change of pace.

Competencies needed include keyword recognition, using Yahoo!'s search box, finding relevant results from snippets, and browsing to find information that answers the challenge. The hardest part is coming up with descriptive words, for example, *Kermit frog graduation* or *Kermit cap gown*. Check to see what types of words students suggest. Are they nouns? Adjectives? Verbs? Invariably, objects make better search terms than actions. Looking at a photo, the tendency is to name objects, a sound universal strategy for keyword selection.

One route to the answer goes through a matching image of Kermit in cap and gown displayed in Yahoo!'s search results. The presence of an identical photo creates an opportunity to talk about literal matching and relevance. If students fail to find the information in this easy challenge, there are two likely causes: inability to think of object-oriented keywords or carelessness/haste in skimming results. Going too fast or not reading closely enough prevents seeing matching information in snippets.

As a social experience, the "Kermit Challenge" can be turned into a word game. Have everyone look at the picture and individually write down as many words as possible to describe the scene. After a couple of minutes, go around the room and have each student share one word. Those that share an optimal query word receive one point. Award five points for every unique word—that is, no one else thought of it. This encourages fluency in generating keywords. Try the words in search-box queries. Create a list of the effective terms for finding the information. This time award five points for each word or combination that retrieves the URL of the "Kermit" solution; add one point for all other words. Different types of vocabulary could be worth varied point values: proper nouns = 5, regular nouns = 3, adjectives = 2, verbs = 1, clutter words = 0. A point total could be recorded for several different picture searches to encourage word fluency and flexibility. Almost any interesting picture will work for such a keyword exercise. Other picture challenges on the 21st Century Information Fluency site include the "Flickr Tag Challenge" (https://21cif .com/rkitp/challenge/v1n5/SC_tagging_index.swf).

Most digital pictures may be dragged and dropped into a Google Images search box, thus avoiding keywords altogether (this doesn't work for the "Kermit Challenge" because it is Flash based). It is interesting, however, to see what keywords Google assigns to its image search. In this case Google's auto query is *Kermit the frog graduation speech*.

THE "SOCCER CHALLENGE"

Search boxes are a highly potent means of searching but are not the only means to find digital information. The "Soccer Challenge" focuses on the other: browsing.

The core competency is more than clicking a link; it involves predicting the best link. The object is to move closer to targeted information with each click, but in practice this can get messy. The "Back" button comes into play when a promising link turns out to be a dud, which is often the case. Patience and persistence—essential dispositions for a successful search—are also needed. Most searches end with browsing, having to take the last few steps by skimming or scanning and clicking. Therefore, it is an invaluable skill and takes practice.

Browsing can be notoriously difficult. The "Soccer Challenge" task involves no typing. Using only a mouse, *find the URL of a Web site that displays the results of soccer matches between international clubs prior to 1888.*[20] Instead of Google, the user is given a link to Dmoz.org, the *Open Directory Project*. This directory is curated; editors select the content and place it in categories. As the site says, there are more than 5 million sites, more than a million categories, and almost 100,000 editors.[21] There is a lot to browse. Fortunately for younger searchers, the content is, for the most part, safe (some information may be suggestive).

The only way to arrive at a URL of a site with records of soccer matches prior to 1888 is to click on one of seventy-four initial categories or subcategories. Thinking out loud here (this could be a think-aloud), what is the biggest idea? Like a "Keyword Challenge," knowing what is important means parsing the question into "as is" and important ideas for which there may be better words. *Soccer* stands out as a big idea. Fortunately, there is a matching link on the directory page—the first click. The next page appears relevant; near the center of the page are thirty-three more links, all related to soccer. The issue now is which one is closest (warmest) to the remaining big ideas being sought: *results of matches, international clubs, prior to 1888.* None of these terms appear in the list, therefore it is time to consider nyms.

There may be more than one route to take at this point. *International clubs* could be represented by one of the clickable acronyms (AFC, CAF, CONCACAF, CONMEBOL, OFC, etc.). Unless one knows more than a little about soccer, this seems like unknown territory to explore. Better not to click unpredictable links. Stay with what is warm, what is known. *Records* and *statistics* are related concepts. A nice thing about a directory is that alternatives are spelled out; the searcher doesn't have to conjure up words at all. Because *statistics* is a hyponym for *records*, it appears to be a good choice—the second click. There are fifty-eight results for *soccer*. Now using the invisible query (*international clubs* and *prior to 1888*), the list may be scanned for matching terms or even warmer information. Because the "Find" command involves typing, that won't be used here, although it could be used to save time.

Near the top of the results, some years pop out of the text: *1930–1998* and *1918–2000.* The rest of the list is examined for something closer *to 1888.* It doesn't take long to come across FootballDerbies.com, which claims to possess records between local clubs going back to 1888. Farther down the page is MyFootballFacts. com: "Football history, trivia, statistics and analysis from the first FA Cup matches in 1871–72 to today's results from around the world."[22] A third and final click takes the searcher to the site in order to verify the pre-1888 information.

An efficient methodology for browsing is extremely useful. Without an understanding of nyms and care taken to think about word meanings, much time can be wasted. A browsing challenge like this can easily be turned into a group activity. Have students vote for which link is best to click. See if crowd sourcing—tapping the wisdom of crowds—is an effective way to choose links. The group is bound to predict more accurately than the average individual. The most important thing in this exercise is the reasoning given for the choices. Use the think-aloud method to explore the group's decisions. Does the reasoning hold up? Find out by clicking.

THE "CITATION CHALLENGE"

Being able to cite sources is a standard for ethical scholarship starting in school and spanning a lifetime. There is little debate that taking credit for something created by another author is plagiarism. Citing a source is a journalistic and academic expectation. When the material being cited comes from the Internet, tracking down complete information, such as an author's name or the date of publication, can be difficult. While *Modern Language Association, American Psychological Association, Chicago Manual of Style*, and other formatting authorities make provisions for missing information, it is still a good practice to locate the missing parts, if possible. Knowing ways to find elusive information is integral to information fluency and careful consumption.

The following search challenge involves finding two missing pieces of information for a citation. It comes from the "Information Researcher" posttest:

> Complete this MLA citation by locating the missing information: *Author missing*. "Top Ten Things to Know to Start Your Career." *Web. Date missing*. http://faculty.kutztown .edu/derstine/TopTenThingsToKnowToStartYourCareer.htm.
>   Use investigative strategies to find the name of the author and the year of publication."[23]

The page under consideration offers ten tips for making the college-to-career transition. In order to cite the source or evaluate the author's credibility or even establish the date of publication, investigative techniques are needed.

Locating the name of the author starts with a simple truncation task. Removing the document string from the right end of the URL, it now ends with the "/derstine directory." Clicking the "Enter" (return) key, the resulting page offers information about Robert P. Derstine, professor of accounting. Truncation frequently works when faculty and staff have Web pages on an institutional site. Newer Web architecture—assigning space online using subdomains—prevents truncation from working. If that were the case here, the URL might look like this: http://derstine .kutztown.edu.

Should it be assumed Derstine is the author? Not necessarily. There is only one other instance of this "Top Ten" list indexed in Google, and it appears on the Villanova University site, once again in Derstine's directory. Both pages are associated with the same person, but it is still conjecture to conclude the author has been positively identified. Apart from inquiring, there's no way to be absolutely certain about authorship. Following an e-mail inquiry, Derstine claims not to be the author.[24] To the professor's knowledge, the author is unknown. Therefore, it is entirely appropriate to omit the author field in the citation.

Finding the date of publication or last modification takes some additional effort. Not all Internet browsers are designed to provide last-updated information. Firefox and Internet Explorer do; Chrome and Safari do not. This demonstrates the value in searching with more than one browser. With the page under investigation open in Firefox, the right mouse button (control+touchpad for Mac users) opens up a menu that contains "View Page Info." Clicking that, under the general information that pops up is "Modified: November 12, 2012." Something happened with this page on that date; whether the content changed or the Web site was refreshed is impossible to tell. Nonetheless, a date is now available.

If the purpose was to find out when the information was originally authored, that might require some communication with its author. Another way to proceed that may not be as precise is to search the "Way Back Machine" at archive.org. This repository of saved Web pages contains periodic updates for millions of Web pages. There's a chance this one is among them, which in fact it is. The last saved copy was added to archive.org on June 26, 2012. Comparing the current version and the last copy, there is one subtle difference: Item 3 once read "Be confident of your Villanova education."[25] It now reads "Be confident of your education."[26] Sometime after June 2012, the word *Villanova* was deleted, possibly on November 12. At any rate, the last modified date is acceptable to cite.

To reinforce citation practice, have students submit their completed citations for this challenge. Display several anonymous examples and compare them. Have students look for differences in content and format. Does everyone agree about the author and the date? Can anyone be absolutely certain Derstine is the author just because the information is on a page he created? The lesson here is that assumptions can be wrong and fact checking is the only way to have certainty.

THINKING OUT OF THE SEARCH BOX

Not only are live challenges useful for making less-fluent searchers aware of strategic shortcomings, but they also provide puzzles for all skill levels to think outside the search box. The challenges offered here are search puzzles. There is no single way to solve them; they invite divergent thinking by design. If the usual methods don't work, new ones may be invented. Fluent searchers don't stop with the strategies they already know. When pressed, they think and experiment and in the process move beyond elementary usage of the search box. The following list of search tips represents the diversity of beyond-the-box discoveries to be made on the way to becoming a better researcher:

- Think about where to look. Google is not the only database to search. Other choices are probably better if the information being sought is of a specialized nature.
- Think about the answer, not the question. Imagine how an answer may be worded to discover better keywords.
- Faced with an unfamiliar search engine, use advanced-search tools whenever possible. First, see what options are available and look for helpful suggestions. Don't unnecessarily limit a search by sticking only with the *AND* search box (the simple Google search). Other options are often available to eliminate a pesky domain (*-site:* search box) or search with synonyms (the ~ operator, which may be given its own search box). Every search engine tends to have its own set of advanced-search features.
- Browse with purpose to avoid getting lost. While not the most efficient method, browsing is indispensible. Browse with keywords and important concepts in mind. Follow links that are close matches; otherwise, follow those that hint at a match. Adopt better terms picked up along the way. Reverse course whenever a browsing search goes cold. Persist a little longer; determined searchers often locate information by browsing.
- Use a subject directory if few keywords come to mind; a subject directory is essentially a thesaurus of search terms. Apply browsing skills to subject directories: Think like an editor, not a librarian; start with known keywords; keep an eye out for more specific terms; and turn around when a trail grows cold.
- Seek advice. Success need not always depend on personal discovery. Other people may have good ideas; they may think of other keywords or sites to search. Take advantage of their experience.
- Diverge from the rules of "proper" searching. Speculative searching on the Internet boils down to managing uncertainty. Even the most fluent searchers cannot perfectly predict where information will be found or pick the best path to get there. High probability techniques don't always work. When that happens, start experimenting. Play with words. Few difficult searches are alike; what works once may not work again. Getting creative with words and tools can unlock a wealth of information.

CONFESSIONS OF A SEARCH CHALLENGE DESIGNER

The subheading refers to an article posted online several years ago by one of the authors that describes how search challenges are created.[27] For readers interested in creating challenges, even temporary ones, this how-to guide walks through the design process. Contrary to usual search practices, the design of challenges deliberately sets aside effective search-box strategies. One way to get started is to use a single-word search, a practice popular with less-experienced, or hasty, searchers. The goal of an effective keyword strategy is to combine multiple unique words, the more specific the better, to home in on results. The opposite effect is desired for an exploratory search. A single keyword is best for obtaining random and surprising results. With Google Instant, a single word produces numerous suggestions, some of which may appear intriguing and inspire a challenge.

Breaking with another common practice, the results on the first several pages are ignored. Over a decade ago, Web usability expert Jakob Nielsen reported, "Users almost never look beyond the second page of search results."[28] Evidence that this has not changed is the fierce competition among businesses vying to improve their search-engine optimization (SEO) and be listed on the first page of results. The third page, results numbered 21 to 30, is practically invisible. Page 3 to the end is a good place to mine results that may be challenging to find. Rather than click through page after page, set Google search preferences to display one hundred results at a time. That way, there are less than ten total pages of results; recall that Google displays only a fraction of the indexed results. The odds are good that the best hard-to-find information lies significantly beyond Google's last page of results. However, to find information buried that deeply takes an unknowable query.

Less challenging pages—but still hard enough—may be located without the help of a search box. Subject directory lists of words may be used as a starting point. By browsing, one can springboard to one hyponym after another until arriving at interesting material for a search challenge. Not knowing what to look for does not impede a subject directory search. Interesting information can be retrieved with minimal effort or thought. Using a subject directory can be very profitable when trying to find an unusual subject to research. The "Kermit," "Pump Price," and "Lego Builder" Challenges each started out as random browses through a subject directory.

Using either approach produces pages of snippets. These should be examined for anything intriguing that may appeal to students. If some odd bit of information catches the eye, the first thing to try is raising it to the first page of search results with an appropriate query. A selection of keywords found on the page of the "buried" Web site should do the job. If the purpose of the challenge is to require students to try alternative keywords (nyms), a variety of hypernyms and hyponyms should be tested in queries to determine how this affects the placement of the solution page. If the page persists in rising to the top, substitute other nyms until the page stays buried. Once that happens, these are the terms to place in the wording of the challenge. Repeated testing of keywords is required in designing a nym challenge. The "Earthquake," "Highest Lake," and "Piranhas" Challenges were all constructed this way.

What makes a challenge interesting? There are two ways to tackle this question. The first is to assume some understanding of what students find interesting. Current events that affect students' lives, elements from teen culture, and marketing aimed at young people are all fair possibilities. Themes that have been used successfully with gifted youth have included space colonization, green energy, and medical breakthroughs. If a topic is highly popular, however, it tends to attract a corresponding mountain of information. As a result, finding a specific bit of information can become considerably more difficult, unless the information has been replicated on many pages, in which case it is very easy to find. Challenge designers are advised to avoid the headlines and draw inspiration instead from stories that haven't made it to the front page.

A different way to think about interesting challenges is to start with personal needs. Some of the best search challenges grow out of self-initiated searches that are frustrating. Keep a notebook handy to record these. For example, here is a notebook entry for a challenge that has potential to be a good challenge for anyone who has ever tried to find replacement parts. While it takes some effort to log this information, it is valuable here as a think-aloud:

1. Today's Date: 2.18.13
2. What I was trying to find: an owner's manual for the water heater in the basement. It may be important to find out the dimensions of the metal rod in the tank. I need to replace the rod with a different type that will not react with the iron bacteria in the well water. I forgot what that rod is called, but it's a metal piece that can be removed from the top of the tank using a socket wrench.
3. How I tried to find it:
   a. Using the name and model number of the hot water tank and the keyword *manual* in Google, the first set of results were almost all ads that contained keywords from my query but no reference or obvious link to a manual. From the way these pages are built—using the product information in a title but offering no other relevant content—the primary purpose appears to be a way to drive traffic via ad clicks. Not helpful.
   b. Several results pages wanted to know if I had a manual to upload. So far, no one has uploaded the manual I need on any sites visited.
   c. Eventually, after trying other keywords, including *parts*, I went back to an Ask.com page and, scanning the page, spotted a reference to *parts and accessories* for the unit I was looking for. The link went to the home page for Richmond water heaters. I had already been on this site, thinking it was the best place to find an owner's manual but could not locate it. This time I spotted the button labeled *parts and accessories*. More careful scanning earlier could have saved me time.
   d. The link produced a second link to "Parts Catalog" that pointed off the site. Lacking other options, it was worth trying. This downloaded a 134-page PDF manual containing diagrams, model numbers, and parts numbers. The search was warming up.
4. Now, how to locate the bar for the model I needed. Using the "Find" command (Ctrl+F), there was no result for the model number. I tried to think of what else the bar might be called and tried *anodized* with no luck. Thinking what else I know about the bar, I believe I once heard it was made of *manganese*, so I searched for that and found lots of results. But the big find was the embedded keyword I couldn't think of: *anode*. Google might have suggested

that variant when I came close with *anodized*, but this was a search of a PDF, not Google.

5. "Find" and *anode* now gave me all the references in the manual, including pages with schematics. I could have picked this out by skimming the manual and spotting a reference to the anode in drawings, but that would have taken longer.

6. The model number appeared nowhere in the catalog. When this happens, it's best to try a hypernym. All I had to go on was the tank size, forty gallons. For every residential water tank, the part number for the replacement anode is always the same. While not 100 percent confident, I think I found what I was looking for: the name and number of the part and, in its description, the dimensions I was seeking.

7. Time: 20 minutes.

The information contained in this log isn't bound to become a search challenge for students, but it's worth thinking about its design in terms of next steps. This search history contains several strategic and tactical insights:

- Start with specific information, but when that doesn't work, broaden the search;
- Try to find better keywords or links by skimming results pages;
- Go to the source: Instead of querying the model number, query the manufacturer and locate the parts database (in this case a PDF)—this turned out to be the key to solving the puzzle; and
- Use the "Find" command to locate matching information quickly.

When the model number didn't work in the manufacturer search, the method of replacing a too-specific term (*6G40 36F1*) with a hypernym (*Richmond water heater*) did the trick. A challenge built on this example could focus on two things: database choice and keyword management. Information fluency competencies could include: creating effective search queries (by applying appropriate nym characteristics), selecting digital collections based on their characteristics, and, in terms of dispositions, persistence and flexibility. In this search, a user could be provided with terrific, as-is keywords and still have trouble finding information. Some experimentation is still needed searching with the term *anode* to see if relevant results are obtained more easily. The lessons learned here might come in handy next time a reference manual or replacement part must be found on a manufacturer's site.

Next, a challenge statement must be formulated. The first attempt at wording is rarely the final version. The challenge must be tested and the wording edited until the competencies identified above are the only way to find the information. In this case the statement could be *Find the length of the anodized manganese rod made for a Richmond forty-gallon water heater, model number 6G40 36F1*. Compared to many search challenges, this directive is loaded with hyponyms.

First, the entire sentence is tested and then reduced to its main parts. Pasting the full query into Hakia, Yahoo!, and Bing returns the same result from each: a Portuguese forum post in Google Groups that has no relevance. The full sentence fails to deliver any results in Google. Gradually reducing the query to *anodized manganese Richmond water heater 6G40 36F1*, Google still returns nothing. However, Bing's first snippet, Yahoo!'s second, and Hakia's fourth are the parts and accessories page at the manufacturer's Web site where the information can be found by skimming. It should be noted that *anode rod* makes an appearance in the snippets as a possible replacement for *anodized manganese rod*. Using query optimization, the answer is almost within reach. Thus far, no snippet results answer the search challenge directly.

From this point onward the search moves beyond the search box. One of the following methods will now retrieve the information:

- Scan the pages looking for *anode bar* or
- Use the "Find" command with appropriate terms (*anode* works best).

Of course, from the user's perspective, it's not yet certain this is the right site. Unless keystrokes are recorded or the search is observed, how an individual finds the dimensions of the rod at this point will be hard to determine. Therefore, this challenge may need to be limited to query optimization. The answer could be the URL of the parts and accessories page, in which case the question must be rewritten.

This provides a glimpse inside the search-challenge creation process. The procedure is iterative: refining the question, testing it as a query, evaluating the results, and going back to refine the question. The water heater example may not make a good browsing or skimming challenge if an individual has trouble finding the right keywords. Too many steps are involved. If the query proves too difficult, the individual may never reach the point of browsing. Therefore an option is to launch the challenge on the manufacturer's home page, turning this into a browsing task. Determine if the user can locate the downloadable PDF. Wrapping two major competencies (e.g., browsing then scanning) into a live search challenge makes it harder to troubleshoot what is wrong if a correct answer cannot be found. A simulated search may be better for that purpose.

SUMMARY

Inaccurate perceptions of ability can obscure the need for information fluency. This is why self-taught methods should be tested with well-designed search challenges. Simulated searches are effective in isolating specific competencies. On the other hand, live search challenges provide realistic conditions for searchers to decide which strategies will work. Challenges become most effective when combined with instruction or immediate feedback, especially because novice searchers will frequently be unable initially to solve puzzling challenges. A wide array of learning activities may be wrapped around search tasks, including group games that encourage keyword vocabulary building, query optimization, efficient browsing, fact checking, and citation formatting.

Live challenges, more than simulations, are easy victims of the changing Internet infoscape. Answers to questions unpredictably appear or disappear online, sites come and go, and semantic engines enable literal searching or, as in the case of image searching, render the traditional search box obsolete. The best solution is to create "disposable" challenges, intended to have a short shelf life.

Ultimately, students need opportunities to experiment and fail. Self-taught strategies do not always suffice; this is true for all speculative strategies, even those recommended in this book. At some point they all come up short because the Internet is not a perfect information world. Finding the way is frequently unpredictable, puzzling, and messy: a real search challenge.

NOTES

1. Mary Ann Trail and Amy Hadley, "Faculty–Librarian Collaboration to Teach Information Literacy in an Online Environment," *Challenge as Opportunity: The Academy in the Best and Worst of Times*, Atlanta, GA, November 20–21, 2009, http://www.nyu.edu/frn/publications/challenge.as.opportunity/Trail.Hadley.html.

2. Amanda Duncan and Jennifer Varcoe, *Information Literacy Competency Standards for Students: A Measure of the Effectiveness of Information Literacy Initiatives in Higher Education* (Toronto: Higher Education Quality Council of Ontario, 2012).

3. Kristen Purcell, Joanna Brenner, and Lee Rainie, "Search Engine Use 2012," *Pew Internet*, last modified March 9, 2012, http://pewinternet.org/Reports/2012/Search-Engine-Use-2012/Main-findings/Search-engine-use-over-time.aspx, p. 3.

4. Kristen Purcell and Lee Rainie, *How Teens Do Research in the Digital World*, last modified November 1, 2012, http://www.pewinternet.org/~/media//Files/Reports/2012/PIP_TeacherSurveyReportWithMethodology110112.pdf.

5. James Shepperd, Wendi Malone, and Kate Sweeny, "Exploring Causes of the Self-Serving Bias," *Social and Personality Psychology Compass*, 2, no. 2 (2008): 895–908.

6. Dennis O'Connor's online course forum (unpublished).

7. Center for Talent Development, Northwestern University, online survey (unpublished).

8. "Action Zone Directory," *21st Century Information Fluency*, last modified February 17, 2013, https://21cif.com/rkit/actionzone/index.html.

9. Carl Heine, "Snowsport Challenge I," *21st Century Information Fluency*, last modified December 28, 2007, https://21cif.com/rkitp/challenge/nyms/snowsports/Nyms_snowsport1.swf.

10. Dave LeClair, "3 Video Games That Actually Made Me Laugh Out Loud [MUO Gaming]," *MakeUseOf*, last modified March 27, 2012, http://www.makeuseof.com/tag/3-video-games-laugh-loud-muo-gaming.

11. Carl Heine, "Pirates and Piranhas Users Guide," *21st Century Information Fluency*, last modified January 28, 2009, https://21cif.com/rkitp/curriculum/v1n7/use_flash_applications_v1n7.html.

12. "Do piranha's have fears?" *Answers*, accessed February 23, 2013, http://wiki.answers.com/Q/Do_piranha's_have_fears.

13. *The Homeless Guy*, accessed March 5, 2013, http://thehomelessguy.blogspot.com.

14. Carl Heine, "Information Researcher," *Searchwhys*, last modified August 6, 2012, http://searchwhys.com/pretest/practice-2.php.

15. Carl Heine, "Broadway Search Challenge," *21st Century Information Fluency*, last modified March 4, 2012, http://21cif.com/tutorials/challenge/SC001/SC_01.swf.

16. "What is the earliest Broadway show for which both the opening and closing dates were published?" *Answers*, accessed March 2, 2013, http://wiki.answers.com/Q/What_is_the_earliest_Broadway_show_for_which_both_the_opening_and_closing_dates_were_published.

17. Carl Heine, "Information Researcher," *21st Century Information Fluency*, last modified January 1, 2013, http://21cif.com/selfguided.html.

18. *Internet Broadway Database*, accessed March 3, 2013, http://www.ibdb.com.

19. See note 15.

20. Carl Heine, "Soccer Challenge," *21st Century Information Fluency*, last modified February 17, 2013, https://21cif.com/tutorials/challenge/SC001/SC_04.swf.

21. *DMOZ Open Directory Project*, accessed March 5, 2013, http://www.dmoz.org.

22. "Top: Sports: Soccer: Statistics," *DMOZ Open Directory Project*, accessed March 5, 2013, http://www.dmoz.org/Sports/Soccer/Statistics.

23. Carl Heine, "Citation Challenge," *Searchwhys*, last modified August 8, 2012, http://searchwhys.com/posttest/exam-10.html.

24. Robert Derstine, personal correspondence (e-mail), March 6, 2013.

25. Robert Derstine, "Top 10 Things to Know as You Begin Your Career," last modified June 4, 2012, http://web.archive.org/web/20120604165148/http://faculty.kutztown.edu/derstine/TopTenThingsToKnowToStartYourCareer.htm.

26. See note 25, last modified November 12, 2012, http://faculty.kutztown.edu/derstine/TopTenThingsToKnowToStartYourCareer.htm.

27. Carl Heine, "Thinking outside the Search Box (Confessions of a Search Challenge Designer)," *21st Century Information Fluency*, last modified January 20, 2010, https://21cif.com/rkitp/features/v1n9/outsidethebox.html.

28. Jakob Nielsen, "Search: Visible and Simple," *Nielsen Norman Group*, last modified May 13, 2001, http://www.nngroup.com/articles/search-visible-and-simple.

III

INVESTIGATIVE SEARCHING

5

Investigative Searching

The Internet makes no distinction between fact and fiction. The ability to post information without first passing it in front of editors and knowledgeable peers, traditional gatekeepers of quality assurance in print, puts every consumer of digital information face to face with a common dilemma: who and what to trust. In a modern parallel to the biblical wheat among the chaff, unknown authors and unfiltered content are caught up in the mix with trustworthy sources and content. It can't all be thrown into the fire. It can't all be believed.

Teachers know all too well on which side of the dilemma their students stand. Students are believers. They may insist not everything they read online is true, but in practice students readily mistake fiction for fact.[1] Obvious Web hoaxes and parodies, such as the endangered Northwest tree octopus, male pregnancy, dihydrogen monoxide, Stormfront's Martin Luther King Jr. site, the California Velcro crop, and the Institute of Delicious Whale Research cannot stop students from believing. Once anyone reaches the point of believing without considering the facts, a foolish choice may be only a click away.

Unqualified trust poses a serious problem not only for students and their academic pursuits but all digital consumers as well. Across the population the monetary toll alone is tremendous:

- *U.K. Guardian*: Consumers and businesses in the United Kingdom lost an estimated £27 billion in 2012 due to cybercrime.[2]
- Ponemon Institute: The average annualized cost of cybercrime for fifty-six benchmarked U.S. organizations is $8.9 million per year.[3]
- People's Public Security University of China: In 2012, economic losses from Internet crimes in China totaled an estimated $46.4 billion (RMB 289 billion).[4]

Losses to cybercrime, phishing, and scams are a growing, worldwide problem. The total cost of Internet-based identity theft, fraud, larceny, extortion, and corporate espionage does not solely rest on the gullibility of information consumers, but every time someone fails to resist an offer that sounds too good to be true or gives out personal information when solicited, there is bound to be a cost.

The ability to evaluate the credibility of offers, claims, and facts published online can be taught. Whether learners act on it is another matter. A discrete set of investigative techniques can help but may do little to deter consumers and students alike from the pitfalls of gullibility. Until a person has to pay for the judgment error of misplaced trust, knowing how to investigate digital information may not personally matter. Investigation, after all, takes time and effort. Until it's "my problem," it doesn't necessarily make sense to adopt a skeptical mindset and put an evaluation plan into action.

Taking human nature into consideration, along with the low probability that students can identify a significant "my problem" experience, an approach to teaching investigation is to allow students to fall for misinformation in an environment that will not cost them too dearly. This philosophy is similar to using Internet challenges to disclose inadequacies of self-taught search strategies. In this case, the challenge starts with information in hand. Whether students accurately determine the credibility of found information or not, the cost is immaterial. As they discover how quickly information can fall apart before their eyes, students become increasingly sensitized to red flags. Being told to "be more aware" has little impact compared to experiencing false information firsthand.

Evaluation challenges are centered on red flags—warnings—inherent in hoaxes and inaccurate, stale, and biased information. Red flags are useful for identifying problems affecting three facets of information: primary sources, content, and secondary references.

AUTHORSHIP RED FLAGS

The usual source of information is an author. Because authorship online has no governing standards, anything goes. Today everyone with access to a computer can become an author. Any author can be anonymous either by adopting a pseudonym or failing to supply a name at all.

Unknown authors and unqualified authors are red-flag warnings: Be cautious and investigate further. The symbolism of the red flag comes from its historic use as a warning sign. Instead of alerting passersby to the danger of flooding waters, wildfires, live fire exercises (military), or the need to stop immediately (traffic),[5] digital red flags warn readers to be attentive. Literal red flags are fairly rare, mainly limited to comments or warnings about message posts. For the most part, the red flags that invite attention are hidden. It is possible to plant a digital flag to warn others: Diigo members may compose a virtual sticky note and attach it to a page as a warning to other Diigo users.[6] But once again, trusting notes uncritically is just another opportunity to fall prey to information that needs to be personally evaluated.

Consequently, the vast majority of red flags on the Web have to be discovered as part of the searcher's ingrained process. Every searcher is obligated to watch for warning signs or pay a price for not doing so. In terms of authorship, warnings frequently appear relative to educational background, training, work and life experience, previous publications, bias, and opinions of others. The last two are discussed in subsequent sections on evaluation of content and secondary (i.e., external) references, respectively.

An author's education may or may not be relevant, depending on the nature of the publication. Academic and research-oriented work, if it is to be trusted, depends strongly—and only in part—on author credentials. Completion of coursework and a degree from a creditworthy institution are time-honored, standard fare for establishing expertise. These may not be enough, however, if an author chooses to write in an unrelated field or has too little relevant education; for example, writing about surgical procedures with only pre-med training. Normally, a knowledgeable audience dismisses an author who lacks experience or training.

What if the pre-med student somehow "gets it right," regardless of training? One factor is pitted against another: education vs. content. One bit of information can trigger a red flag, but that doesn't mean one warning is a deal breaker. Several factors may need to be taken into consideration. Minimal educational experience may satisfy the minimum credential threshold expected by some critics (or be forgiven if the content is good enough). Others will set the bar higher and, no matter how good the writing, expect the author to be a surgeon as opposed to a student who has yet to complete medical school.

The example is exaggerated but makes two points: that investigation of credibility 1) seldom depends on a single factor and 2) does not produce consensus. A single discrepancy may be a red flag to one person; to another person something else constitutes a warning. A third person may detect no red flag at all. An isolated factor about an author, unless it is egregious or establishes a pattern, is hardly sufficient for deciding if a person can be believed or not. The recommended practice is to consider three factors before making a determination of credibility. In addition to the author, the content and external references should be investigated.

A single red flag may be a tipping point if an author provides falsified personal information. This is the case for Lyle Zapato (surely a pseudonym), purportedly the author of the Pacific Northwest tree octopus site. Zapato claims to have a master's degree from Kelvinic University.[7] A fact check of that institution on the Web produces no corresponding names. Therefore, anything else this tree octopus advocate writes is suspect: not necessarily wrong, but the reader has been duly warned. In addition to questionable vitae, the site contains altered images and a really good keyword: the scientific name for a tree octopus (*Octopus paxarbolis*) that, oddly enough, is never referenced in any authoritative guide to marine or animal biology. External references consider the tree octopus a useful site for conducting Web evaluations.

There are enough red flags here for a small rally in Tiananmen Square. Nonetheless, discovering the flag related to academic falsification may be enough to discount the entire body of work and just leave it at that.

Novice researchers, like the middle-schoolers in the University of Connecticut study to whom similar evidence was given,[8] may still insist the tree octopus is real. Truth, like beauty, is in the eye of the beholder. Merely presenting students with evidence may not be sufficient to displace their perceptions. After all, they personally constructed their beliefs. It could take some effort to deconstruct them. Investigation is not something to be told, no more than speculative searching is something to be learned by just the teacher doing it. Querying, which takes practice, is not learned by proxy. Neither do students learn to investigate when a teacher does it for them. The argument here is that, when individuals investigate, it leads to discoveries that can dismantle and replace first impressions with more accurate knowledge. This won't happen if teachers do most of the searching.

Personal investigation can be framed as a detective game. It starts as a hunt for clues. What evidence is there on the site (or a specific page) that can be considered a clue? Because the author is the current suspect, the best place to start is the "Who is Lyle Zapato?" page: http://zapatopi.net/zapato, found by browsing the site. Investigative searches for authors often require first finding the name of the author, then stepping outside of the Web site to find the author using a search engine. The author of the tree octopus Web site is assumed here to be Lyle Zapato (it says so on the page). The following think-aloud is meant only as a guide to what students may find; it is not intended as a demonstration. The students need to find the clues and investigate them.

One of the prominent features on the page is a drawing of Mr. Zapato. This could be a clue. The image can be dragged and dropped into a Google Images search. The resulting match is a person with a different name: D. B. Cooper. Cooper was a passenger who hijacked a Boeing 727 over Washington State in 1971. After collecting $200,000 in ransom, he parachuted from the plane at 10,000 feet and was never seen again.[9] This connection to a fugitive from the law and finding a different name than Zapato are both red flags.

Other proper nouns located on the page include *Republic of Cascadia, M.A. in psychothermodynamics from Kelvinic University, Cascadese* (a language), and *Dr. Ernesto* (an arch nemesis). It's already been indicated that Kelvinic University does not exist. If it did, a search for degrees granted would be in order. A quick fact check for *psychothermodynamics, republic of cascadia, cascadese,* and *Dr. Ernesto* could turn up some interesting connections or none at all—telltale signs of a red flag. A query for *psychothermodynamics* retrieves pages that claim the tree octopus is a hoax, more red flags.

In addition to good keywords to fact check on the bio page, several terms occur repeatedly (black helicopters) that suggests paranoia. Zapato's mission statement is a marvel of incoherent thinking (or, perhaps, Cascadese) that might sound impressive to an eighth grader:

> End subjugation of humanity under Entropic yoke of clandestine and/or paraterrestrial
> agencies through technological, informational, and spiritual empowerment of individu-

als employing, but not exploiting, the synergistic leveraging of enterprise level subversion.[10]

Interpreting this page could easily be connected to Common Core language arts standards in reading.[11] What is he really saying in normal English? (One possibility: Some mysterious, otherworldly agencies are weakening humanity; people who use technology, information, and spiritual powers assertively can overthrow them.) What can be learned about the author through his writing? Is this an author who can be trusted? Why or why not? This could make an interesting discussion.

Finally, the obvious: search the Web for *Lyle Zapato*. Many articles about Lyle Zapato can be found. One article in Xconomy.com entitled "In Defense of the Endangered Tree Octopus, and Other Web Myths"[12] provides a good secondary source about the site. In it, Zapato is referred to as a Washington-based author and Web publisher, as well as a hoaxster who invented the tree octopus in 1998. Perhaps most intriguing are the comments left by readers at the bottom of the page: librarians who use the site to teach Web evaluation, students who recently discovered the octopus is a fake, and lots of other people making fun of them for believing it in the first place. Curiously, no one questions why the site exists. Why does someone spend the past fifteen years perpetuating an Internet hoax? Why hasn't the novelty worn off? Those are not questions with easy answers, but they are by far the best investigative questions—graduate-level challenges—to pose about Lyle Zapato, wherever he is hiding.

OWNERSHIP RED FLAGS

The plot thickens when ownership of the tree octopus site is investigated. If Zapato is the CEO of Zapato Productions Intradimensional, who is Kevin Fraites, and why does he apparently own the domain name zapatopi.net? The standard way to determine domain ownership is to search a database that indexes domain names. Whois.net is one of many search engines that can retrieve ownership records. Unlike a Google search, the only query that is effective in a Whois search box is the domain name, in this case, zapatopi.net. Google can find ownership information as well, but Whois is the ultimate authority and returns the only relevant result.

The registrant, administrative, technical, and billing contact is the same person: Kevin Fraites. Among other information are an e-mail address, street address, and telephone number. The address in Gig Harbor is located not very far from Hood Canal, home of the alleged, arboreal octopus. The pieces seem to fit. Mr. Fraites from Washington has not left much of a trail online. His house is hidden in the trees (Google Earth). That's as far as this casual search for information needs to go.

There's no need to be intrusive. If there is a pressing need to contact an owner, Whois often provides the connection. In some cases, a privacy service is used to mask the identity of an owner. An agency hired to represent an owner (who doesn't want to be contacted) can be considered a red flag.

Except when a privacy service is used, an author who cannot be positively identified may be traced through domain registration. Registered owners are often publishers. They may be an individual or an organization. A publisher could be the author, as is often the case with personal blogs and smaller Web sites. Larger organizations, such as *Education Week* or the *Guardian*, may have little to do with authors' content other than make it publicly available.

Finding the name of a publisher is also frequently achieved with browsing or truncation. Copyright information or "about us" information may indicate the name of a publisher. This requires some skimming, a method to use before conducting a Whois search. Another way to find the publisher is through the URL. Truncating back to the home directory often gives better information about the publisher than information on a specific article page. When one method doesn't work, try another.

To illustrate the persistence a fluent search must employ, consider this publisher challenge: find the publisher of the Harry Potter Sorting Hat Personality Test (http://www.personalitylab.org/tests/ccq_hogwarts.htm). The page claims to be a self-paced survey developed by professional psychologists that can determine into which Hogwarts house the famous Sorting Hat would place the respondent: Gryffindor, Hufflepuff, Ravenclaw, or Slytherin. The page contains no tell-tales signs of ownership, such as copyright or "about us." There is a link to read about the consent form, which is worth a click. No hint of a publisher is contained therein.

The next logical step is to truncate the URL back to personalitylab.org to see what that is. The home page describes and links to nine different personality tests, one of which is the Sorting Hat questionnaire. At the bottom of the page are a copyright (2004–2010) and a couple "about us" sentences that read like a disclaimer and give no indication about the publisher. Besides the nine links to different tests, there are two links to "e-mail us" and "our privacy policy." Both are worth checking because, based on the pronouns used, they might contain identity information. The e-mail page provides only a generic name: webmaster@personalitylab.org. The other link provides very general information as well and a further link: "e-mail us." Leaving no stone unturned, clicking that e-mail link produces the same "webmaster" e-mail address found on the home page: a dead end, unless one wants to take time to contact the Web master for more information.

At this point, there are two choices left, and both are queries. Search for personalitylab.org in Google or in Whois. Sorting through the results on the first page of Google, the best places to look are sites other than personalitylab.org. One of these, PsychCentral, claims psychologists at the University of California, Berkeley, developed the tests.[13] This is new information. But it would be nice to have a name or to confirm if the university is actually the publisher. If it is, the credibility of the site is definitely enhanced.

The same query in Whois.net produces one result.[14] A name for the owner of the domain finally appears: Christopher Soto, Department of Psychology, Colby College (Maine). Maine is a long ways from Berkeley, CA, so what is the connection? At this point, there is a name to fact check, which is what investigation is all about. It's not enough just to find information; the information has to be verified. Therefore, a logical query is to combine the new information with the old: *Christopher Soto Harry Potter*. Those are very specific keywords; it doesn't get much better than all proper nouns. The results are relevant: an article from 2004 about a student (Soto) who created the test, a Facebook page for Soto, Soto at Colby College, some blogs about Soto and the test, and even a short Prezi created by Soto dated 2013. By skimming several results, it starts to make sense: Soto was a grad student at Berkeley when he created the Sorting Hat test based on work by psychologists there. Now he is assistant professor of psychology at Colby College and still operates the site and the tests. To be absolutely certain, the query *Christopher Soto Colby College* leads to the Colby Personality Lab, where Soto tells his story, describes his research interests, and lists his publications.[15] The reader now has plenty of information upon which to decide the reputation of the publisher.

UNRELIABLE CONTENT AND RED FLAGS

Imagine for a moment, that no Christopher Soto could be found at UC Berkeley or Colby College, as claimed. That red flag would be a major blow, big enough to sour anyone on the reliability and reputation of personalitylab.org who checked into it. Soto's identity stands up to fact checking, so inaccuracy is not a problem. Plenty of other sites, however, do have trouble with reliability. Nonetheless, they are still in business. Just because a site has inaccuracies doesn't mean it can't thrive.

Fact checking is the digital consumer's main line of defense against ill-conceived sites and the information they contain. The fact-checking technique has been demonstrated numerous times in this book. It's the query after the query to make sure facts and claims are not just made up by an author or overlooked by a lax publisher. In addition to checking on an author's or publisher's identity, education, or reputation, fact checking is crucial when statements or outcomes need to be verified. Failure to fact check makes novice and seasoned Internet users vulnerable to spam, phishing attacks, and rotten deals.

Following is an actual e-mail with no known author. It is a familiar format that most readers would immediately suspect, but to a small percentage of people, it sounds plausible—it only takes a small percentage of unwitting consumers to keep spammers in business:

From: Mr. Ban Ki-moon
  Subject: ONLINE NOTICE!!!!

United Nations has deposited the sum of $10,500,000.00 USD to western union, which is to be shared among you and other 7 Email users. You are entitled to $1,500,000.00 USD in the on-going united nations poverty alleviation program. Please send your Name, Address; Phone Number, email ID:

  to union payment center via email (unionpayment768@sify.com) to apply for your payment. Or call Mr. David Young @ +60166561422 for more inquiries on the above message.

Regards,
Mr. Ban Ki-moon
Secretary-General (UNITED NATIONS) ©.http://www.un.org/sg/biography.shtml

This makes a good "find all the red flags" assignment and could prevent someone from disclosing name, address, phone, and e-mail as requested. The letter is goldmine for facts that don't add up. Here are all but two potential red flags[16:]

- Ban Ki-moon—Yes, he is secretary-general of the United Nations, but why is he writing personally?
- info@diaockhanglinh.com.vn—The sending e-mail address is a Vietnamese real estate Web site.
- ONLINE NOTICE!!!!—Not the message you'd expect if you actually won the money.
- $10,500,000 USD—Too much to be believable.
- "you and other 7"—The author needs some help with English.
- $1,500,000—A nice sum, and it is one seventh of $10,500,000, but remember, there are supposedly eight winners (seven others plus me), so this doesn't add up.
- Please send your Name, Address; Phone Number, email ID—Never share personal information online with strangers!
- union payment768@sify.com—sify.com has no believable connection to a payment center.
- +60166561422—What are the chances this is a real phone number? International code 6 is Argentina, 60 is Germany, and 601 is Mayotte Island (off the east coast of Africa).
- ©http://www.un.org/sg/biography.shtml—Not sure about the copyright symbol, but this is Ban Ki-moon's biographical page.

Just to make things interesting, two juicy "facts" that also turn out to be red flags have been left off this list. When incorporated in a learning activity, always let the students find the clues and red flags. Discuss the findings. Does everyone agree? Agreement isn't crucial, however a proponent of any red flag should be asked to explain the reason for labeling it so. The remaining answers are revealed at the end of this chapter.

STALE NEWS AND RED FLAGS

News on the Internet is rapid and relentless. Sites like Twitter are excellent sources for fast-breaking news coverage by eyewitnesses. Using subscriptions and search engines, almost anything that is newsworthy can be delivered almost instantly to one's digital doorstep. All this information has to go somewhere. Old news has a way of sticking around. Web pages grow old; links die. Fresh information fills in around it. With a basic search, stale information is just as likely to be retrieved as fresh. Advanced search interfaces, like the Internet Broadway Database discussed in the last chapter, can provide filters for specifying a range of publication dates. Otherwise it's not always clear how long the information has been hanging around.

Knowing the publication date of information is important in many cases. Historic research as well as current events depend on time-sensitive facts and figures. An analysis of the primary sources leading up to the popping of the dot-com bubble in 2000–2001 has little to gain by studying the housing bubble of 2006–2009. Moreover, a report on the current state of terrorism globally does not benefit much if the sources consulted were written before 9/11. The publication dates have to be relevant.

For most Web 2.0 information, establishing a publication date is not a problem. Blogs, tweets, and comments are date and time stamped. Journals and news articles are given a printed date by their publisher. However, finding the publication date on standard Web pages can be challenging. In addition to failing to include the name of the author, many pages are undated or not updated when modified. Therefore, when placing information historically as well as for citation, it is helpful to know how to track down a publication date.

An investigation starts at the scene of a crime by looking for clues. Information investigators adopt a similar procedure when evaluating content and looking for information about the source. When a publication date is not included at the top of an article, a fluent searcher first scans the page for date information. Possible locations include the end of an article, the URL, copyright, or other places, such as a sidebar or footer. A quick way to involve younger students in searching for date information is to provide hard copies of several Web pages where the date is found in a different part of the page and have them circle the date. To encourage kinesthetic learning, imagine the classroom is a giant flat Web page (aisles are margins, desks are type, etc.). Point to where the various parts of the page are in the room and have one or more students move to the corresponding area of the room when they find the date on their sample page. For example, if the date is in the URL, everyone moves to the front of the room—the footer would mean a move to the opposite end. To facilitate this page-mapping activity, the following pages from newmedz.com may be printed (by permission of the 21st Century Information Fluency Project).[17] Dates can be found at the:

- top of an article: http://newmedz.com/news/breakthroughs/epilepsy.html
- bottom of an article: http://newmedz.com/news/breakthroughs/cancer.html
- footer: http://newmedz.com/about/
- copyright: http://newmedz.com/
- URL: http://newmedz.com/news/breakthroughs/2011/July-11-bone-stretching.html
- sidebar: http://newmedz.com/news/breakthroughs/sensor.html

If the date does not appear in one of these locations, expand the investigation while staying on the site. This may mean truncating the URL to the directory index page. For the first example, this would mean trimming the URL to the breakthroughs folder (http://newmedz.com/news/breakthroughs) to see if any date information is given there. Another option is to browse pages one or two clicks from the article looking for publication clues.

The amount of effort to find the date depends on how important knowing the date is to one's research objectives. In some cases, time sensitivity is crucial; therefore establishing a date is necessary to validating information. A few years ago, one of the authors directed a program involving high school students in problem-based learning. The problem centered on the mining of conflict (blood) diamonds in Africa and what international policies should be enacted to stem the trafficking of these gems. This was an emerging discussion involving many nations, including the United States. A delegate from the U.S. State Department who was a participant in the Kimberley Process meetings mentored the students. After concluding their studies, eight student teams from across Illinois held their own summit and presented their findings and policy recommendations. The delegate was impressed with the depth of knowledge and relevance of the students' recommendations. She had one criticism. All the information the students were using as the basis of their decisions was more than six weeks old. The international situation had shifted since then; the students' recommendations were invalidated. A valuable lesson was learned: Pay closer attention to the freshness of information. Information can become stale quickly.

If the steps described previously do not help in determining freshness, there are several other methods to try. Many articles appear in multiple places on the Web, so another good idea is to query the name of the article or a unique string of words from the article using Google or a similar search engine. Other instances of the same work may be returned, one of which may have date information. Best not to put quotes around the string in case some small variation exists in the text (e.g., a paraphrased copy). If too many results are obtained, then try putting quotes around the string.

Descriptive metadata may offer further insights. This "data about data" may include time stamps when information was posted or last modified. One way to obtain date information is with a browser. As part of its tools menu, Firefox makes page info available (shortcut: right click on a Web page and select "Page Info"). Page info for http://newmedz.com lists "Modified" as August 22, 2011. Because many browsers do not offer last modified information, the Information Fluency Project created a search wizard that pulls this metadata from static (html) pages.[18]

The same date is returned using Javascript pasted in the omnibox of the page being investigated: *javascript:alert(document.lastModified)*. This code is an alternate to using Firefox and returns date metadata in all major browsers. For a site that purports to be about medical breakthroughs, the information on the page is no longer on the cutting edge, a potential red flag. The purpose of the site has a minimal connection to medicine or health. It is deliberately engineered to be an information-fluency playground: a place to practice and assess digital investigative skills.

"Page Info" often returns the time when the function is called, which has everything to do with the type of page and nothing to do with the original or modified publication. If *lastModified* seems too fresh, other processes are affecting the Javascript. More and more pages are dynamically created using server side script (e.g., PHP), therefore the Javascript alert function returns the current *server* time and date.

Archived information may be helpful in tracking down original information. The WayBack Machine described in chapter 4 ("Top Ten List" investigation) may be used to verify that information has or has not changed substantially, even if the modified date is recent.

Metadata is also available for documents. PDFs, DOCs, PPTs, and other file types shared online all have properties. Digital documents frequently omit dates. Nevertheless, last-modified information is captured automatically by the software and can be retrieved by clicking "Properties" for a document. How fresh is "The Myth of the Teen Brain" (drrobertepstein.com/pdf/Epstein-THE_MYTH_OF_THE_ TEEN_BRAIN-Scientific_American_Mind-4-07.pdf)?[19] The article doesn't really say. There is a clue in the URL: *4-07.* Using "Properties" in Acrobat Reader (File > Properties), the document was created February 27, 2007, and last modified April 9, 2007, which verifies the tenuous URL clue. The article could be useful in research on the teen brain, but more current findings need to be sought for college-level work.

Finally (or initially), the author may have to be contacted. Another assessment example, the "Top Ten Hikes in Southern Arizona" Challenge, provides a link to a page created by Dan Coombs: http://www.math.ubc.ca/~coombs/hikes.html. Conflicting date information is available for this page. The description at the top states this information was included in a talk delivered in 2000. The metadata for the page gives the last update as June 13, 2006. The page has not been crawled by the WayBack Machine. Therefore, the surest way to determine freshness is to contact the author, who in this case confirmed that the information is now "very out of date."[20] Better to consult a current trail guide than venture misinformed into the chaparral.

These means of locating the date may yield nothing, or they may produce multiple dates. In the former, assuming due diligence, a Web page may be cited without a publication date, using the "accessed on" option instead. With multiple dates to choose from, the question becomes, Which date is most accurate to cite: created on, published on, last update, or copyright? Citing an unreliable date can invalidate the content. Date inaccuracy can even be an ethical matter. Representing information as fresh when it is actually stale conceals a red flag. Hikers should be able to determine if trail directions are thirteen years old. The older a hiking guide becomes, the greater the risk in trusting it.

BIAS, THE FILTER BUBBLE, AND RED FLAGS

Bias is woven into the fabric of most authored works. Personal beliefs, perspectives, and opinions all contain a degree of bias: Some things are right, some things are wrong. A person who doesn't agree with a particular point of view might say the proponent is biased and vice versa. Sometimes the belief is benign ("It's cold out today"); in some cases a belief is malevolent ("Ethnic cleansing purifies society"). Acting on propaganda, hoaxes, and lies can precipitate harsh outcomes and severe reactions. Not to recognize them for what they are prior to taking action is a failure of bias detection.

In a democracy, no single opinion is necessarily right or wrong. What matters is the freedom to express it. This doesn't mean everyone is obligated to agree. The open exchange of ideas is valued in a developing society. Otherwise, once diversity starts to be suppressed, the free exchange of ideas starts to die and, along with it, growth in knowledge and new ways to understand the world and each other.

As much as some people dislike Stormfront's Martin Luther King Jr. site, it provides an opportunity for discussions about King, his ideas, as well as Stormfront's opinions. This type of diversity may cause uneasiness, but in general, perturbed thinking is considered good educationally if it causes one to examine previously unexamined beliefs and make reasoned decisions. An unproductive effect would be to visit Stormfront's site, accept what's stated as true, and not think twice about it. Of course, that's the present author's bias.

Martinlutherking.org is frequently cited as a Web evaluation resource by schools and colleges. It has been labeled as a hoax and misinformation[21;] it seems to be more about propaganda and persuasion than, as it states, the truth about Dr. King. The use of rap lyrics and a youthful appeal seem to be aimed at influencing young readers who know little about King. An examination of the language on just one page of the site, especially hyperbole and understatement connected with "The Beast as Saint,"[22] presents a strong portrayal of prejudice and mistrust:

- The speaker (this is a transcript of a radio program) claims that Communists have affected a revision of U.S. history as it applies to Martin Luther King Jr.
- The support of U.S. media for the annual Martin Luther King holiday is interpreted as a "spastic frenzy of adulation."
- The audience is admonished to "think for yourselves" while claiming, ironically, that the media is being controlled in order to promote King's values.
- The speaker calls King a "moral leper" and "Communist functionary" and criticizes any social indignation such words may elicit.

The hyperbole indicates an extreme perspective that leans far away from being rational. Based on word choices alone (*controlled media, spastic frenzy of adulation, moral leper*), the speaker's language is inflammatory and laced with paranoia. This is not normal elocution; people typically do not talk or write this way unless they are trying to provoke an audience. The use of language is a red flag. It is easy to tell where the author stands on the alleged truth about King.

Group discussions can be a healthy practice when it comes to talking about bias as a sign of an author's intentions and credibility. The lesson here is actually suggested by the speaker: "Think for yourself." A high school history class discussion could easily be wrapped around this story, exploring bias and touching on several Common Core standards all at the same time. Questions to launch a discussion could include "How does this information make you feel?" "Specifically, what does the author say that makes you feel that way?" "What was the author's purpose in sharing this information?" "Does the information have merit?" and "How do you know?" The last question depends on fact checking the allegations. The beauty of open discussion is that students get to voice their personal reactions to bias and hate, defend their ideas, weigh arguments, and ultimately make up their own minds. This is far better than being told what to believe, which Stormfront's publisher—who may be found using a Whois domain search—attempts to do by mounting a one-sided smear campaign.

Personal bias can also influence the information an individual retrieves online. Eli Pariser's book *The Filter Bubble*[23] and related TED talk[24] sparked public interest in how personalized searching creates selective content based on a person's search history. The downside is this: If two people with different points of view, one a conservative, the other a liberal, conduct an identical query, the results they see are different. The conservative is not likely to encounter liberal news and vice versa. Each person's information aligns with a self-selected persuasion but not necessarily by permission. The search engine makes the choices. Consequently, there is a world of disparate views that cannot be seen from within the bubble. Pariser's comments are aimed at Google.

Since the TED talk, Google altered its approach, permitting users to block personalization features.[25] The postmodern nightmare of a "World Wide Web of one" is always a possibility because the goal of using a search engine is to retrieve "relevant" information. What is relevant to one person may not be to another. The question is how a person would ever know results are being tailored to his or her views. What is hidden becomes important to know.

Ways to pop bias bubbles include using more than one search engine, turning off search-engine personalization, switching to private browsing, deleting Web history, dumping cookies, using online anonymity services such as Torproject.org,[26] and scanning information streams on open services, such as Twitter. Another way is simply to confuse the machine by venturing outside one's familiar interests and become informed about an ever-expanding range of topics and opinions.

SECONDARY SOURCE REFERENCES AND RED FLAGS

The last item on the investigative checklist involves discerning what other authorities think about published information. In brief, using specialized operators makes it possible to discover organizations and individuals who link to a site. The real challenge is how to understand what such a link means, if the linking source is an authority, and, if so, what kind of authority. Linking to a site creates a voluntary external reference that may boost credibility or reflect poorly on the site.

Several means are available to trace incoming links to a page: the *link:* operator, the *site:* operator, and backlink search engines. As mentioned earlier, the *link:* operator is less effective than it once was. Google has reigned in its powers so that fewer results are obtained. For a while, Yahoo!'s Site Explorer was the go-to source for link queries, but that was incorporated in the Bing Webmaster tool and now requires creating a Microsoft account. There is money to be made searching for backlinks, so most specialized engines provide lookup services for a fee. A good query to find such services is *backlink search*. Some current free alternatives include OpenSiteExplorer .com (up to three reports a day without a paid account), Blekko.com, and Ahrefs .com.

Using the *-site:* operator, it is also possible to locate pages with incoming hyper-links while filtering out all the same site pages. This is easier to demonstrate than explain. To find incoming links to the Martin Luther King site discussed earlier, this query should be used: *http://martinlutherking.org/ -site: http://martinlutherking.org/*. The *http://* prefix may be omitted to obtain similar results. Here is a representative sample of top Yahoo! results and snippets for the *-site:* query:

- Stormfront (Web site)—Wikipedia, the free encyclopedia
  "Stormfront is a white nationalist and supremacist neo-Nazi Internet forum that was the Internet's first major hate site. Stormfront began as an online bulletin board." en.wikipedia.org/wiki/Stormfront
- The Beast as Saint: The truth about Martin Luther King
  "The media fabricates history, turns a scoundrel into America's preeminent national 'hero.'" www.stormfront.org/history/martin_luther_king_adv.htm
- Evaluating Web Sites with Elvis, UCLA—YouTube
  "Hear what the ghost of Elvis Presley has to say about evaluating information found on the Internet." www.youtube.com/watch?v=VfLVAh6FA-o
- Evaluating Information on the Web: Oglethorpe University
  "http://martinlutherking.org: World Trade Organization: http://www.gatt .org/ http://www.wto.org: The Onion: http://www.onion.com/ Top; Recom-mended Tutorials:" library.oglethorpe.edu/libweb/resources/evaluating.aspx
- Home | Federation for American Immigration Reform
  "Seeking to improve border security, stop illegal immigration, and promote immigration levels consistent with traditional rates of about 300,000 a year." www.fairus.org

The Wikipedia reference makes a connection between martinlutherking.org and Stormfront, which is basically confirmed by the second result that comes from a Stormfront source. The third and fourth external references are about evaluating the credibility of Web information. The fifth is something of an anomaly, since no link to martinlutherking.org can be found on the page indexed. Taken together, external references suggest that martinlutherking.org is connected to a white nationalist and neo-Nazi organization and is the subject of Web-evaluation training. As for the authority of these sources, educators generally disregard Wikipedia as much of an authority, but here the volunteer Wikipedia authors are validated by Stormfront's own information. The YouTube video has a UCLA source, however it doesn't spe-cifically mention anything about Martin Luther King. Oglethorpe University does include the site in a list of Web content to evaluate. Having at least one authoritative university weigh in on the site as something to evaluate stamps a warning label on Stormfront's publication. A cursory reference search takes only a few minutes to locate sources of incoming links and determine whether they have authority and if it matters. A more thorough search using a backlink engine delivers more than 200 external sources that bring together proponents (white hate groups) and opponents (universities and libraries) around this flashpoint site. Providing students with a list of external references without saying more than "These are sites that link to martin lutherking.org; according to these references, what kind of a site is it?" creates a good opportunity for discovery and subsequent analytical thinking about secondary sources.

SUMMARY

The mixture of information and misinformation on the Web presents problems for unwary consumers. Failure to recognize inaccurate, stale, or biased information costs individuals, corporations, and countries dearly, approaching a trillion dollars each year. Students and adults alike can benefit from putting investigative searching into practice. Investigation, as opposed to speculation, involves using a finite set of tools and methods with very little guesswork. The challenge is to put them to use.

The source, the content, and secondary references to the source and content are the crucial components to investigate. Looking for red flags is a tangible activity that can motivate students to do Web detective work. Learning games and group analysis of evidence collected are potentially rich high-level-thinking experiences. Not only do investigative and subsequent deciphering activities promote information fluency, but they also directly address Common Core State Standards, ISTE NET-S, and ALA Standards for the 21st-Century Learner. Rather than summarize investigative procedures here, the following chapter illustrates how investigation is applied to a Web site that has been labeled a hoax but turns out to be something entirely different.

Answers to "Ban Ki-moon E-mail" Challenge: "united nations poverty alleviation program" and "(western) union payment center"—Neither entity exists when fact checked.

NOTES

1. Beth Krane, "Researchers Find Kids Need Better Online Academic Skills," *University of Connecticut*, last modified November 13, 2006, http://advance.uconn.edu/2006/061113/06111308.htm.

2. John Burn-Murdoch, "UK Was the World's Most Phished Country in 2012—Why Is It Being Targeted?" *The Guardian*, last modified February 27, 2013, http://www.guardian.co.uk/news/datablog/2013/feb/27/uk-most-phishing-attacks-worldwide.

3. "2012 Cost of Cyber Crime Study: United States," *Ponemon Institute*, October 2012, http://www.ponemon.org/local/upload/file/2012_US_Cost_of_Cyber_Crime_Study_FINAL6%20.pdf.

4. "Internet Crimes Cost China over $46 Billion in 2012, Report Claims," *The Next Web*, last modified January 29, 2013, http://thenextweb.com/asia/2013/01/29/china-suffered-46-4b-in-internet-crime-related-losses-in-2012-report.

5. "Red Flag," *Wikipedia*, accessed March 13, 2013, https://en.wikipedia.org/wiki/Red_flag_(signal).

6. "Collect and Highlight, Then Remember," *Diigo*, accessed March 23, 2013, https://www.diigo.com.

7. "Who Is Lyle Zapato?" *Zapato Productions Intradimensional*, last modified June 2, 2004, http://zapatopi.net/zapato.

8. See note 1.

9. "D. B. Cooper," *Wikipedia*, accessed March 14, 2013, https://en.wikipedia.org/wiki/D._B._Cooper.

10. See note 7.

11. "English Language Arts Standards," *Common Core State Standards Initiative*, accessed March 23, 2013, http://www.corestandards.org/ELA-Literacy/RI/7/8.

12. Wade Roush, "In Defense of the Endangered Tree Octopus, and Other Web Myths," *Xconomy*, last modified August 8, 2008, http://www.xconomy.com/national/2008/08/08/in-defense-of-the-endangered-tree-octopus-and-other-web-myths.

13. "Personalitylab.org," *PsychCentral*, accessed March 17, 2013, http://psychcentral.com/resources/detailed/4617.html.

14. "WHOIS Information for Personality.org," *Whois.net*, accessed March 17, 2013, http://www.whois.net/whois/personalitylab.org.

15. "Colby Personality Lab," *Colby*, accessed March 17, 2013, http://www.colby.edu/psychology/labs/personality/index.html.

16. Carl Heine, "Fact Checking Spam," *Internet Search Challenge*, last modified April 19, 2012, http://internetsearchchallenge.blogspot.com/2012/04/fact-checking-spam.html.

17. *NewMedz*, accessed March 19, 2013, http://newmedz.com.

18. Carl Heine, "Metadata Search Wizard," *21st Century Information Fluency*, last modified June 3, 2013, https://21cif.com/tools/evaluate/lastmodified.html.

19. Robert Epstein, "The Myth of the Teen Brain," *Scientific American Mind* (April/May 2007), last modified April 7, 2007, drrobertepstein.com/pdf/Epstein-THE_MYTH_OF_THE_TEEN_BRAIN-Scientific_American_Mind-4-07.pdf.

20. Dan Coombs, personal correspondence (e-mail), March 6, 2013.

21. Paul S. Piper, "Better Read That Again: Web Hoaxes and Misinformation," *Searcher*, 8, no. 8 (2000), last modified September 2000, http://www.infotoday.com/searcher/sep00/piper.htm.

22. "The Beast as Saint: The Truth about 'Martin Luther King, Jr.,'" *Stormfront*, last modified January 15, 2007, http://www.martinlutherking.org/thebeast.html.

23. Eli Pariser, *The Filter Bubble: How the New Personalized Web Is Changing What We Read and How We Think* (London/New York: The Penguin Press, 2011).

24. Eli Pariser, "TED Talk," *thefilterbubble.com*, accessed March 21, 2013, http://www.thefilterbubble.com/ted-talk.

25. Steven Levy, "Has Google Popped the Filter Bubble?" *Wired*, last modified January 10, 2012, http://www.wired.com/business/2012/01/google-filter-bubble.

26. "Tor: Overview." *Tor*, accessed March 21, 2013, https://www.torproject.org/about/overview.html.en.

6

Investigative Case Study

The *Los Angeles Times* calls it the "ultimate e-commerce site of the future." What is this next-generation moneymaker that vies for supremacy over Amazon, Facebook, or PayPal? The site is GenoChoice, and its appeal is the power to create genetically healthy children online.[1]

The premise isn't entirely far-fetched: Gene therapy and genetic engineering are increasingly in the news. But GenoChoice is a little ahead of its time. The site is more (science) fiction than fact. It's been called a hoax[2] and a fake.[3] There is a lot of evidence to challenge the credibility of the site—and its future as a powerhouse e-commerce site. But only on the surface is the site a hoax or a fake. Deeper down, it is something very different.

Unless there is a good reason to conduct a thorough investigation of a Web site, most evaluation efforts take only a few minutes. The average evaluation probes to see if any red flags appear, and if not, the information is put to use. It is rare to exhaust all the resources in an investigator's toolkit. Depending on the reliability of the source, little evaluation may be needed—enough to satisfy a skeptical mindset. The crucial dependency, however, is how important it is to make sure the information can be trusted. Most decisions are not life altering, but when something with momentous consequences comes along, it is good to know how to do thorough evaluation.

This chapter demonstrates what being thorough (fluent) looks like. The approach is to take a Web site that has been dubbed a hoax by secondary sources and to investigate its author and content. Part of the approach is strategic: In what ways does the information guide the selection of evaluative methods? In the process, many of the tools come out of the information-fluency toolkit, mainly to demonstrate their use. If this were a typical evaluation task, the work would be concluded in short order. In this case, few stones will be left unturned: not because the information warrants it but for the sake of modeling multiple ways to analyze a site.

GenoChoice allows for surprisingly deep study and has not been subjected to the same degree of popular scrutiny as the Pacific Northwest tree octopus, although it too could be considered to belong to a genre of tall Internet tales. Even though genetic science isn't advanced enough to achieve results online, for young learners, creating genetically healthy children online may be just as plausible as octopi that dwell in trees for part of their lives.

The home page is a good place to start by examining the titles, links, and images and by reading the content of the page (see figure 6.1). At first glance, this seems to be a hospital site that is aimed at singles or couples who want to plan a family. There is a welcome from a doctor whose name is Elizabeth Preatner, a prenatal geneticist and embryologist at GenoChoice. There are seven occurrences of the name *Geno-Choice* on the home page. In once instance, the name appears to be trademarked

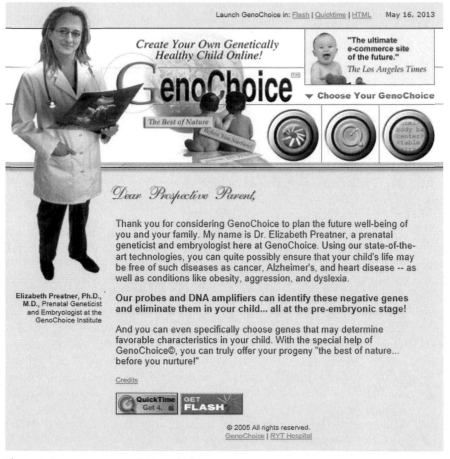

Figure 6.1.   Home Page of Genochoice.com

(™); in another it is copyrighted (©). A third usage pairs *GenoChoice* with the word *Institute*. There is a copyright date that may have been neglected; it reads *2005*.

The investigation begins by scanning for hyperlinks, each of which is a doorway to more information. There are eleven hyperlinks to investigate in the header alone. Some appear to point to a sponsoring agency (RYT Medical Center) and information regarding that organization ("About Us," "Patient Care," "Education," "Research," and "Contact Us"). A list of featured programs includes, in addition to GenoChoice, links to Nanodocs, male pregnancy, Clyven, and a Dr. Liu. By contrast, there are few links outside the header. A few of these launch different versions of the GenoChoice application, although the Flash Version is said to be coming soon. Farther down the page is a link to credits, and at the bottom of the page are links to GenoChoice (home page) and RYT Hospital, same as in the header.

The first phase of investigation gathers evidence available in plain sight. Students can easily be engaged in hunting for evidence on the home page. Rather than anyone forming premature conclusions, it's best to guide them to locate as many things as they can to be fact checked. Students need to be reminded to fact check because they often take Web pages at face value. In this case a long list can quickly be generated. The items should be prioritized, starting with the biggest objects and strongest keywords to query.

So far the evidence includes the name of a hospital, a medical center, two doctors, and the quote from the *Los Angeles Times* mentioned at the beginning of this chapter. GenoChoice appears to be a featured program or an institute under the jurisdiction of RYT Hospital–Dwayne Medical Center; it's hard to tell without browsing. But before browsing, it's best to consider what to fact check first and if any red flags have been uncovered. Because proper nouns make strong keywords, they are good to fact check. Additionally, the newspaper quote should be easy to verify. The highest priority is the biggest target: the hospital and the medical center. Institutions imply credibility. If the hospital lists GenoChoice as one of its programs, all is well and good. If not, that could be a serious red flag.

In addition to a primary strategy, a wary investigator has other options in case they are required. Other evidence on the page prompts secondary strategies. The old copyright date serves as a warning that this page has not been updated in a great while, despite the current month, day, and year showing near the top of the page (a check of page information might also return today's date and time). A 2005 copyright coupled with an announcement that a Flash version is coming soon makes for an uneasy combination. How long has the Flash update been on hold? If GenoChoice is the next big e-commerce site, why isn't the page being tended? Why hasn't the copyright been updated? What about the two buttons near the bottom of the page for downloads to QuickTime and Flash? Is the current release of QuickTime version 4 as it displays on the button? Is that icon the current version of Flash Player? This is a time for unbridled curiosity. Checking the publication or "last modified" date is a second investigative strategy. Freshness is an important consideration when dealing with medical breakthroughs.

Following good fact-checking procedure, the first investigative query is RYT Hospital: *ryt hospital.* The top link returned is *http://rythospital.com*. Unfortunately, the browser cannot find the server online; instead, an error is returned. This could be a temporary inconvenience or a life-and-death issue. It is definitely a red flag for something as prominent as a hospital to go missing online. A quick check of Whois to determine if the *rythospital.com* domain name has also expired reveals the name is currently good for another nine months. But the interesting finding is the registrant and administrative contact: Dr. Elizabeth Preatner. She is the doctor whose greeting appears on the homepage of GenoChoice. Since when does a doctor own the rights to the domain of a hospital? Unless she is the hospital administrator, this is a red flag.

Other records involving RYT Hospital from the fact-checking query point to the Museum of Hoaxes,[4] Snopes,[5] and similar secondary sources that come to the same conclusion: The hospital is fictitious. At this point the fluent investigator would discount what GenoChoice has to offer. Total elapsed time: a couple of minutes or less.

Individual students or small groups could fact check evidence from the page and report back. This is a valuable exercise in checking the accuracy of claims and can cover a lot of ground in a short amount of time. Using the fact-check query *"ultimate e-commerce site of the future,"* an interview with Virgil Wong, an artist and designer, is retrieved. In the interview he claims that the *Los Angeles Times* made this statement about GenoChoice. No match is found connecting the quote to the Los Angeles newspaper. Wong describes RYT Hospital as fictional.

As part of a whole-class investigation, another team could investigate the lead quotation. A search of the newspaper's archive is in order. The homepage of the *Los Angeles Times* has a search box. An "advanced search" option is available, which is always a good way to proceed when searching an unfamiliar site. That holds true here because one of the choices is a date range, and it is set to search only the last 30 days. This investigation needs to go back to 2005. It takes a lot of clicks to get the calendar back to 2005, but once there, the search is poised for a broad date range. The quote is pasted in the "this exact phrase" box. Zero matching records are retrieved. Moving the phrase to "all of these words" (in case the quote has been paraphrased) also returns nil. The *Los Angeles Times* quote is not recorded in the newspaper's database; the origin of the quote is unknown.

More red flags are raised by fact checking Elizabeth Preatner, QuickTime 4, and trademark records for GenoChoice. According to Whois, Elizabeth Preatner has an address in New York State. Doctors are registered to work in specific states, therefore it is possible to check the New York State Physician Profile site for Elizabeth Preatner.[6] Using "Advanced Search" on the New York doctor site, it is possible to enter not only the first and last name but to select a specialty as well. On the GenoChoice site, Preatner is listed as an embryologist and prenatal geneticist. Those are not specialties listed in the menu, so it is best to leave this field blank. Elizabeth Preatner is not registered as a physician in New York. It is possible she is registered in another state, so a national search could be attempted (still no matches).[7] On the "advanced search" page of the New York State Physician Profile site is list of hospitals. There is neither an RYT Hospital nor a Dwayne Medical Center in the state of New York even though Whois lists a P.O. box for them in New York City. Both missing records are red flags. At this point there are enough red flags to supply a May Day parade. But there is more to investigate.

QuickTime 4 was released in 2001. Version 7 was available in 2012. Dragging and dropping the image of "Get Flash" into a Google Images search retrieves matching images as early as 2000. The current Flash-Player icon has a very different look, another confirmation that some very stale information has been left on GenoChoice's home page.

Not to be overlooked are the trademark and copyright signs appended to Geno-Choice. A skeptic might wonder: If a name is trademarked, why copyright it? Can a name even be copyrighted? The clue that GenoChoice is trademarked invites an excursion into a government database, the United States Patent and Trademark Office.[8] TESS (Trademark and Electronic Search System) is the government's tool to locate pending and registered trademarks. For new users the basic search is recommended. All that is needed is a very simple query: *genochoice.* No matching records are retrieved. GenoChoice is still available for trademarking.

So far, every fact check of content has either come up empty or led to a hoax/evaluation site. The site is covered with red flags. Based on any one of them, it is hard to trust anything on the Web site. There is, however, one thing that does check out.

Back on the home page is a link to credits. The "Credits" page takes the investigation in a new direction.[9] For a medical site, the content is incongruous. It would be beneficial to see if students realize this. One way to help them make this discovery is to split a class into two groups. Assign one group the home page and the other the credits page. The task is to describe in keywords what kind of a site it is based on the content. The home page is medical in orientation. The credits page is artistic. How do these two pages fit together on the same site? That is a deeper investigative question. Now the hunt is diverted from chasing the accuracy of medical details to the reason for the very existence of the site.

The credits page contains numerous names, all of which could be fact checked and could lead to answers. Five names stand out: Virgil Wong, Nicholas Mount, Miranda Hope, and Jennifer and John Ruffing. A Google Images search for Miranda Hope matches photos of a singer/songwriter who bears an uncanny resemblance to Elizabeth Preatner.[10] Of all the names credited, however, Virgil Wong's is paramount. The page provides a great amount of detail about him as well as a link to *http://virgilwong.com.*

Unlike just about everything else on GenoChoice, Virgil Wong is real. This is an important finding because he is also the author of GenoChoice. Virgil Wong is listed as the registrant for the domain name *genochoice.com.* Whois doesn't provide this information, but a GoDaddy domain search does—a good reason to know more than one way to search for Whois information. External confirmation of ownership is established. The bio page available on http://virgilwong.com[11] is recently updated and profiles the author:

- cofounder, Medical Avatar LLC
- artist and researcher, Columbia University
- vice president of Interactive Media, Element 115
- adjunct assistant professor, Media Studies, The New School

Each of these positions can be independently verified by searching *Medical Avatar LLC, Columbia University, Interactive Media,* and *The New School.* For example, the query *virgil wong site:columbia.edu* provides links to an announcement of a lecture by Virgil at the Faculty Club of University Medical Center:

> Artist and filmmaker Wong's work grapples with bioethically vexed medical technologies—including nanorobots, a smart-as-human genetically engineered mouse, and a male pregnancy program. His fictional "RYT–Dwayne Medical Center" (www.ryt hospital.com) had been called "disarmingly authentic" by the *New York Times.*[12]

Here, a credible educational source removes any remaining doubt about the fictive nature of RYT Hospital and provides strong clues to the reason GenoChoice was first created. At the same it confirms that Wong is both an artist/filmmaker and someone with sufficient credibility to speak about novel medical technologies to an audience at a university medical center.

On the New School site, Wong is credited as a part-time assistant professor.[13] In addition to teaching film, photography, and interactive media since 2000, he served as cochair of the Clinical Translational Research Science Center (CTSC) Cross-Institutional Web Portal Working Group, "whose primary mission is to leverage new technologies in rapidly moving advanced biomedical research from the laboratory bench to the patient's bedside."[14]

As an investigative activity, students could be assigned the task of collecting and fact checking evidence about Wong in order to compile a comprehensive profile (see lesson 1, following). In addition to the findings already mentioned, he appears in a TED talk, a video format dedicated to "ideas worth spreading."[15] As head of Web services for two prestigious medical institutions, Wong developed 120 Web sites, won awards for eHealthcare leadership, produced experimental medical-themed films, served as a conference keynote speaker,[16] and is currently a Ph.D. candidate in the field of cognitive science.

Forming this profile leads to a nagging question and provides a terrific discussion starter for older students: "Why would Wong be associated with a hoax Web site?" "Does being the author of GenoChoice hurt his credibility as an authority on the future of human health?" Students can be encouraged to develop hypotheses to explain the paradox. Knowing more about the author really challenges the ubiquitous *hoax* hypothesis. If GenoChoice, male pregnancy,[17] and Wong's other fictitious Web creations are hoaxes, why are they still online? Other theories are more believable. They could be part of an elaborate joke. Maybe the sites are part of an artist's Web design portfolio. Maybe they are intended to trigger thinking about medical ethics and where medical technologies could go in the future. Students may brainstorm other possibilities. What matters most is how they present the evidence to support their hypotheses.

The activity described here starts with an information fluency task—research to build and present knowledge—and comes full circle to a level of critical thinking aligned with Common Core standards (e.g., Grades 9–10):

> CCSS.ELA-Literacy.W.9-10.8: "Gather relevant information from multiple authoritative print and digital sources, using advanced searches effectively; assess the usefulness of each source in answering the research question. . . ."[18]

> CCSS.ELA-Literacy.RI.9-10.8: "Delineate and evaluate the argument and specific claims in a text, assessing whether the reasoning is valid and the evidence is relevant and sufficient; identify false statements and fallacious reasoning."[19]

In developing and defending hypotheses, students are not limited to the specific claims of one text but information gathered from many. Integrating lessons in information fluency with critical thinking as defined by the Common Core is accomplished seamlessly. Investigative searching is the catalyst for deep critical thinking.

It is well known that students neglect evaluation as part of digital research. They assume that if it's on the Internet, it must be true. Taking time to blend evaluation into instruction helps to instill healthy skepticism; strengthens skills that depend on questioning, integration, argument, and synthesis; and most importantly, transforms classrooms into places of hypothesizing and learning, not just rote learning.

GenoChoice is a single example that can be used this way. The Pacific Northwest tree octopus site is another. Why is that site—as opposed to GenoChoice—continually tended and updated? If it were just a hoax, wouldn't the novelty be wearing thin for the author/owner? According to archived versions in the WayBack Machine, the tree octopus site was already active in the summer of 2000.[20] That's a long time to tend a hoax. What other theories make more sense and explain the motives of the site creator?

FOUR MINI-LESSONS

As part of the International Society for Technology in Education's annual conference model lesson series, the authors created four mini-lessons on GenoChoice that demonstrate how students may be engaged in learning through the use of a Web-site challenge.[21] The ready-to-go lesson plans are reproduced here to facilitate embedding them in a lesson or unit on evaluation.

Lesson 1: "Think-Aloud"[22]

Objectives

- Learners evaluate the quality of a search result to determine the reliability of its content (Information Fluency 2.A)

- Learners evaluate the quality of a search result to determine the reliability of its source (Information Fluency 2.B)
- Gather relevant information from multiple print and digital sources, using search terms effectively; assess the credibility and accuracy of each source (CCSS-ELA Literacy 6-12.WST.8)
- Analyze the author's purpose in providing an explanation, describing a procedure, or discussing an experiment in a text (CCSS-ELA Literacy 6-12.RST.6)

Time

30 minutes as follows:

- 5 minutes think-aloud
- 5 minutes individual searching
- 5 minutes share findings, draw conclusions
- 15 minutes explore GeneScan2000, discuss credibility

Materials

- http://www.genochoice.com
- Computers, one with a projector
- Whiteboard or red-flag chart

Create a red-flag chart with three columns: Accused | Suspicious | Acquitted (or similar terms). The findings in this mini-lesson will all likely go in the "Suspicious" column. However, red flags may travel from one category to another as a result of investigative activity. Furthermore, students may not agree on where to place a red flag, which makes for a good discussion starter.

This lesson could take place in the context of a science course where DNA, genetics, and "designer babies" are the topic. It is used here for demonstration purposes—imagine that among the results for *designer babies, genochoice.com* is discovered. Use GenoChoice to demonstrate how an investigative searcher might approach the material. Students need to see an example of good searching in practice. Focus on authorship in this instance. Open the page and browse to find information about who wrote this or is responsible for its content. As part of the search, note the "Credits" link on the page.

Click "Credits" and point out information about Virgil Wong. Also note that this is not what you expected to find: a medical site written or designed by an artist and performance credits for several other people. Point out that now you have some good keywords to fact check. Proper nouns make good fact-checking terms because they are so specific, so unique.

Start a list of things discovered about Virgil Wong. The first red flag is that he's an artist, not apparently a medical expert. Assign the students to fact check Virgil

Wong: "Discover as much as you can about this person." Everyone is permitted freely to search for information about Virgil—the more eyes looking for information the better.

After five minutes, have everyone freeze. "What are you looking at now?" Have students report their findings. The results may be summarized on a whiteboard, sticky notes, or any online app that is made for group collaboration. Or merely have the students call out what they found, trying to build as complete a picture of Virgil Wong as possible. Among the findings possible, he is:

- a Web designer
- featured in a TED video
- a Ph.D. candidate in cognitive science
- an artist
- a keynote speaker at conferences
- A.K.A., Dr. Liu

Follow this profiling activity with discussion. Ask: "Is this really the type of person you think would be the author of a credible site on designer babies? Why or Why not?" Answers to "Why Nots" are red flags. Invite students to update the red-flag chart. "How do these red flags affect how much this information can be trusted? Do you trust it?" Allow students time to conclude it would be wise to be skeptical. If they don't reach this conclusion, encourage them to think about the consequences of what might happen to them if they trusted (consumed) the information on GenoChoice.

If time is available, a hands-on activity is built into GenoChoice. The Flash version has never been published, but a QuickTime version has. Click the QuickTime link. Play the three videos. The first depicts Sally and Steve Meyers, prospective parents who endorse the GenoChoice procedure. The second video features Dr. Elizabeth Preatner, whose calm demeanor instills confidence in state-of-the-art genetic technology that "can ensure that your child's life can be free from such diseases as cancer, Alzheimer's, and heart disease." The last video is an introduction of how to use one of four methods to create a genetically healthy child online.

Preatner continues: "Just keep your left thumb on the oval button and be sure to keep it there until we are done scanning." The GeneScan 2000 analyzes a subject's DNA (*sic*) and produces a report. A screen prompts the subject to enter a name and a password to keep the information confidential. The fields are not required. Ask the students: "How many of you are still comfortable with the process?" The results really are worth seeing. Leave the name/password fields blank or insert any name you like—nothing is being saved here. In one sample, these "personal" disease susceptibilities were observed:

- 89 percent, Premature Baldness/Alopecia, $6,989
- 76 percent, Arthritis, $10,425

- 42 percent, Sickle-Cell/Anemia, $8,878
- 33 percent, Diabetes, $9,875
- 22 percent, Tay-Sachs Disease, $3,542
- 18 percent, Neurofibromatosis, $4,251
- 13 percent, Retinitis Pigmentosa, $4,253
- 12 percent, Duchenne Muscular Dystrophy, $3,251
- 8 percent, Lesch-Nyhan Syndrome, $3,121
- 3 percent, Polycystic Kidney Disease, $2,397

The dollar amounts are the costs to upgrade, that is, to eradicate the likely defect from the future child. For example, an 89-percent chance of premature baldness can be genetically zapped for under $7,000. After examining the "shopping list," ask the students, "Who here is willing to be a consumer, to spend money to ensure that a future child is protected from such disorders or diseases?" Click a box by any upgrade to add it to an invoice. No financial information is solicited; no one is asked for a credit card. This isn't really a hoax or a money grab attempt (a good point to make in the discussion), but it brings the reality home: Who is willing to risk money to take advantage of something that sounds too good to be true? Sadly, if this were a real scam, some small percent of the population *would* risk the money. Better to discover this type of lesson in class and save students from an uninformed, impulsive purchase down the road.

Lesson 2: "Teamwork or Jigsaw" Method[23]

Objectives

See Lesson 1

Time

10–15 minutes as follows:

- 2–3 minutes instructions
- 4–6 minutes group searching
- 4-6 minutes to share findings

Materials

- http://www.genochoice.com
- Computers, one with a projector

This is a follow-up session to lesson 1 but could be used without the previous lesson. Divide the class into groups of two to four learners each. Instruct each group to choose one fact or claim from the GenoChoice site to fact check as a small group.

Display the site and have students suggest facts or claims that could be investigated. Among possible suggestions are:

- Who is Elizabeth Preatner, MD?
- What is RYT Hospital?
- Can DNA amplifiers identify negative genes and eliminate them in your child?
- Is there such a device as GeneScan 2000®? (Found by browsing http://www.genochoice.com/clone.shtml)
- Did the *Los Angeles Times* really state: "The ultimate e-commerce site of the future"?
- If Virgil Wong wasn't investigated previously, include him now.

Give each group several minutes to verify (triangulate with three external sources) their selected fact or claim. To improve the diversity of findings, members of a team do not need to consult same sources. Teams may use a red-flag chart (see lesson 1) to categorize their findings. Call time and give teams one to two minutes to share what each member found. The jigsaw method comes into play by forming new groups, with a member of each team placed in a new group. Each person serves as the expert for his or her investigation of a fact or claim. Findings are shared with the new team members. Then each team prioritizes red flags that cause them to doubt the facts or claims being made. Combine all the red flags into one chart. Call for group or individual conclusions: "Does the information on the Web site warrant a thumbs up (approval) or thumbs down (rejection)?"

Lesson 3: "Flipped Discussion" Method[24]

Objectives

- Learners evaluate the quality of a search result to determine the reliability of its source (Information Fluency 2.C)
- Gather relevant information from multiple print and digital sources, using search terms effectively; assess the credibility and accuracy of each source (CCSS-ELA Literacy 6-8.WHST.8)
- Support claim(s) with logical reasoning and relevant, accurate data and evidence that demonstrate an understanding of the topic or text, using credible sources (CCSS-ELA Literacy 6-8.WHST.1.b)

Time

15 minutes as follows:

- 3–4 minutes demo
- Homework: backlinks investigation
- 11–12 minutes discussion

Materials

- http://www.genochoice.com
- Computers, one with a projector
- Red-flag chart (see following discussion)

The search method being applied is "finding backlinks" (incoming links to a page from another site). Demonstrate using a think-aloud the three ways to find backlinks (following). Explain how backlinks serve as external or secondary source references for a site and why it is important to gather opinions of writers other than the author of the site being investigated. Gathering several other opinions is called triangulation. Provide a link to step-by-step instructions for a backlink query (e.g., *http://newmedz.com/first-aid/linkcheck-1.html*).

- Method 1: *link:http://www.genochoice.com*
- Method 2: *http://www.genochoice.com -site:www.genochoice.com* (finds examples of the hyperlink on sites other than genochoice.com)
- Method 3: (Deep Web) Use Google to find backlink search engines. One of these is opensiteexplorer.org. This returns many more results for an external search of genochoice.com than methods 1 or 2. However, there is a daily limit to how many backlink searches may be done for free (three); multiple searches from the school IP address exhaust the free searches quickly.

Allow each student fifteen minutes in class (or homework outside) to do one or more backlink searches. Driving questions are: "Why does this site link to genochoice.com? By linking, does this external link support or discredit the information on genochoice.com?" When students return, follow up the backlink search activity with a discussion of findings and their implications.

It may be helpful to create a red-flag chart (see lesson 1). Place the findings in the appropriate column. Red flags may move from one category to another as a result of investigative activity (e.g., from "Suspicious" to "Acquitted"). Furthermore, students may not agree on where to place a red flag, which makes for a good discussion starter.

As a result of investigating backlinks, ask the learners, "Should the information on GenoChoice be trusted?" To probe deeper, ask, "Did the external sites get it right? Why would an artist–medical keynote speaker–Ph.D. candidate–Web master create such a hoax site? Wouldn't that hurt his reputation? Why do you think genochoice .com was created? Did any new red flags appear? Did any red flags disappear?" Discussion may lead to a number of interesting hypotheses, which may be further investigated in another session or assigned as homework. GenoChoice looks less and less like a hoax the more it is studied.

Lesson 4: "Search Challenge Method"[25]

Objectives

- Learners evaluate the quality of a search result to determine the reliability of its content (Information Fluency 2.A)

- Gather relevant information from multiple print and digital sources, using search terms effectively; assess the credibility and accuracy of each source (CCSS-ELA Literacy 6-12.WST.8)

Time

15–20 minutes as follows:

- 5–8 minutes working on a search challenge
- 5–7 minutes consulting the "Quick Reference Guide"
- 5–5 minutes applying the methods to investigate genochoice.com

Materials

- Quick Reference Guide: http://searchwhys.com/CTD12/QR/freshness-1.html
- http://www.genochoice.com
- Computers, one with a projector
- Red-flag chart (see lesson 1)

The search method applied here is "determining freshness": When was the site created or last updated? Have students try the following search challenge. If students get stuck (no progress after eight minutes), stop the challenge and review the steps in determining freshness[26:]

- Scan the page for publication date
- Browse the site for publication date
- Use "Page Info" to look "inside" the Web page for metadata
- Search Archive.org to locate archived copies of the information
- Browse "Preferences" if the information is from a PDF, DOC, PPT, or similar file

It won't be necessary to use all of these. Start with the first one. If that doesn't work, work down the list.

Challenge

Is the material on genochoice.com fresh or stale? When was it last updated?

Choose three pages on the site. Use appropriate search technique to find the date each page was last updated (this may not be the same as the copyright date). Without previous instruction, students will likely not know how to find the date. Be sure they use the "Quick Reference Guide" (following) rather than become frustrated.

The "Quick Reference Guide" was created to help students enrolled in 21CIF online courses that teach research skills. It is a free resource that provides methods to locate and interpret missing dates for articles and Web pages (plus a lot more). The complete guide may be accessed from http://newmedz.com/first-aid/index.html. For date-tracking information, refer to the "Page Information" link.

Once students grasp several techniques, have them research genochoice.com to locate missing date information. Add or move red flags on the red-flag chart as a result of investigation (see lesson 1 for an explanation).

GenoChoice is tricky but not unusual in regard to finding a publication date. The site has no files that can be downloaded to check freshness. The JavaScript on each page updates any page opened to the current server time. Archive.org can be useful in this case to compare saved versions of the site going back a number of years. Students can also find sufficient date evidence on the Web site from visual clues, such as the old versions of QuickTime and Flash download buttons described earlier in the chapter.

Help students talk about what the date information means for the credibility of the content. The findings point to a site that has not been updated lately. Ten-year-old medical procedures can hardly be called "state of the art," to quote Elizabeth Preatner, M.D.[27]

SUMMARY: MODEL LESSON TEMPLATE

One case study doesn't make a curriculum; it provides a model. Using GenoChoice as a means to teach investigative searching and attain English language arts literacy is not a solution for every school. However, the model could be if used with some imagination. The four mini-lessons offer a framework for lesson planning that can be integrated in the majority of language arts, social studies, and science courses—wherever research skills are needed.

Generalizing the design elements from the four model lessons results in this investigative template for teaching and learning both information fluency and critical thinking:

- The topic is a wild card and can involve anything from literature to term papers to lab experiments—anything that requires looking up information online. A hoax site need not be used.
- Objectives are essential to guide the learning. Focus on one or two investigation techniques. In so doing, one or more of the three information fluency competencies should be addressed. One or more Common Core standards are associated with each competency. For a collated list of competencies and standards, the reader is referred back to chapter 2.
- Time-frame guidelines are used to keep up momentum. Investigative techniques don't take long to teach, though they may take time to master. Don't plan to master the skills in one session. Repeated exposure and practice is best. In general, move activities along. Even when the majority of students are still searching, call time to avoid boredom or frustration. One-minute searches can be productive. Leave time for interaction and discussion.
- Materials need not be elaborate. Even one computer with a display is adequate for an entire class as long as students take turns "driving" it.

- Start with an investigative challenge. This should be derived directly from the local topic of study (Mark Twain, the Civil War, climate change, etc.) and involve either the source or the content (or both) of digital information on the topic. Any secondary source on any subject can be subjected to investigation.
    - What is known about the author? What makes the author an authority? In what way does the author show signs of bias?
    - What claims should be fact checked? Is the information accurate? When was this material written? Is it still relevant today? Be skeptical about facts online: Misreported facts are not hard to find.
    - What do other sources say about this author or the content? Triangulate information; don't take one author's word for granted.
- If necessary, demonstrate a technique using a think-aloud.
- Permit hands-on investigation. Break up large tasks into small chunks assigned to small groups or individuals.
- Encourage dialogue. Students need opportunities to process their findings. Have them talk about 1) what they discovered, 2) what this means, and 3) if there's another way to think about it. When students are challenged to think about the meaning of investigative findings, they engage in hypothesis making. The best discussions are not aimed at getting everyone to agree to a "right answer" but to contribute new perspectives and possible meanings. Investigative discussions are not likely to fail because students haven't done their homework.[28] Here, the discussion immediately follows the preparation. The subject is not something remote from the students' experience. It is an authentic, personal question: What do your findings mean?

NOTES

1. *GenoChoice*, accessed March 25, 2013, http://www.genochoice.com.

2. "Gallery of Hoax Websites A–J," *Museum of Hoaxes*, accessed March 30, 2013, http://www.museumofhoaxes.com/hoaxsites.html.

3. "Avoiding Fake Web Sites," *Township High School District 214*, accessed March 30, 2013, http://www.d214.org/district_library/Fake_sites.aspx.

4. See note 2.

5. "Topic: RYT Hospital," *Snopes.com*, accessed March 30, 2103, http://msgboard.snopes.com/message/ultimatebb.php?/ubb/get_topic/f/81/t/001144.html.

6. *New York State Physician Profile*, accessed March 30, 2013, http://www.nydoctorprofile.com.

7. "DoctorFinder," *American Medical Association*, accessed March 30, 2103, https://extapps.ama-assn.org/doctorfinder/recaptcha.jsp.

8. "Trademarks Home," *The United States Patent and Trademark Office*, accessed March 30, 2013, http://www.uspto.gov/trademarks.

9. "Credits," *GenoChoice*, accessed March 30, 2013, http://www.genochoice.com/credits.shtml.

10. "Miranda Hope: Home," *Leaving Eden*, accessed March 30, 2013, http://miranda hopemusic.com.

11. "About | Biography," *VirgilWong*, accessed March 30, 2013, http://virgilwong.com/bio.

12. "Narrative Medicine Rounds: Virgil Wong," *Columbia University School of Continuing Education*, accessed on March 30, 2013, http://ce.columbia.edu/narrative-medicine/events/narrative-medicine-rounds-virgil-wong.

13. "Faculty: Virgil Wong," *The New School for Public Engagement*, accessed March 30, 2013, http://www.newschool.edu/public-engagement/faculty-list/?id=87942.

14. See note 13.

15. "Virgil's TED Talk: The Medical Avatar," *YouTube*, last modified March 28, 2012, http://www.youtube.com/watch?feature=player_embedded&v=ePlB2W66zWc.

16. "12th Annual Healthcare Internet Conference," Orlando, Florida. Sponsored by Greystone.net, Staywell Communications, in cooperation with the Forum for Healthcare Strategists.

17. *Pop! The First Male Pregnancy*, accessed March 30, 2013, http://www.malepregnancy.com.

18. "English Language Arts Standards: Grade 9–10: 8," *Common Core State Standards Initiative*, accessed March 31, 2013, http://www.corestandards.org/ELA-Literacy/W/9-10/8.

19. See note 18, http://www.corestandards.org/ELA-Literacy/RI/9-10/8.

20. "The Pacific Northwest Tree Octopus," *Archive.org*, last modified August 18, 2000, http://web.archive.org/web/20000818130120/http://zapatopi.net/treeoctopus.html.

21. Carl Heine and Dennis O'Connor, "Information Fluency in the Classroom: Evaluation and Critical Thinking" (workshop presented at the annual conference of the International Society for Technology in Education, Philadelphia, Pennsylvania, June 26–29, 2011, and San Diego, California, June 24–27, 2012).

22. "ISTE Model Lesson: Lesson 1: 'Think Aloud' Demonstration," *21st Century Information Fluency*, last modified January 1, 2013, http://21cif.com/iste-lesson-1.html.

23. "ISTE Model Lesson: Lesson 2: 'Teamwork or Jigsaw' Method," *21st Century Information Fluency*, last modified January 1, 2013, http://21cif.com/iste-lesson-2.html.

24. "ISTE Model Lesson: Lesson 3: 'Flipped Discussion' Method," *21st Century Information Fluency*, last modified January 1, 2013, http://21cif.com/iste-lesson-3.html.

25. "ISTE Model Lesson: Lesson 4: 'Search Challenge' Method," *21st Century Information Fluency*, last modified January 1, 2013, http://21cif.com/iste-lesson-4.html.

26. Carl Heine, "Quick Reference Guide: Freshness," *21st Century Information Fluency*, last modified June 30, 2012, http://searchwhys.com/CTD12/QR/freshness-1.html.

27. Elizabeth Preatner, "home.mov," *GenoChoice*, accessed April 5, 2013, http://www.genochoice.com/quicktime/home.shtml.

28. Diana Hess, "Discussion in Social Studies: Is It Worth the Trouble?" *Social Education*, 68, no. 2 (2004): 151–155.

IV

ETHICAL AND FAIR USE

7

Ethical Consumption

At the conclusion of the search process stands an essential question: How may the information found be used ethically? This is a question of information consumption and one that must be answered continually. It's simple to say just, "Yes! I'll review the work of others with care." If the object of a search is just food for thought, ethical use isn't a big concern. However, if searchers plan to write about the ideas acquired, they must develop a system to organize resources and remember the origins of materials that spark insight. When it comes time to write or develop new media, the researcher becomes an author. Authorship demands a detailed understanding of copyright law, standards of fair use, plagiarism avoidance, and citation.

Authorship has many responsibilities and challenges. It takes determination and courage to make sense of ideas, write original insights, and then creatively share the writing with an audience. The days of a paper being read by just the teacher are over. The opportunities to reach a wide audience with digital content abound. Authorship now includes creating original works; critiquing the work of others; and collecting, sharing, and developing derivative work. It is in the ambiguous arena of online publishing that ethical use is important. A fear of copyright violations can hamper thinking and research. This fear leads to rigid restrictive approaches with strict formulas that limit the creative process.[1] Many educators are so fearful of violating hard-to-understand copyright laws that they avoid the use of any media in their classrooms.[2] An unfettered approach can lead to piracy and plagiarism. An overly cautious approach can lead to paralysis and stagnation. As becomes evident later in this chapter, there are specific provisions allowing teachers to use and publish copyrighted materials without seeking permission.[3] Answering the question "How do I ethically use information I've found" depends on the information environment, an understanding of copyright law, personal courage, and commitment to communicating ideas in the twenty-first century.

Ethical use of digital information requires numerous skills and competencies. The information-fluent searcher has a well-grounded understanding of copyright law, fair use standards and best practices, how to cite online materials, and how to avoid plagiarism. This requires a commitment to focus on goals, adjust strategies, and adapt and revise thinking when faced with ambiguous circumstances.

COPYRIGHT

This discussion starts by considering the kind of content copyright law does not cover. The question to keep in mind is "Who is the author?" Copyright exists to protect the following authorship rights[4]:

- Unfixed works: These include conversations with people or a tune or rhythm created spontaneously. Once something is written on paper or published online, it becomes fixed.[5]
- Lists of ingredients or recipes cannot be copyrighted. However, original explanations or directions that accompany ingredients are covered by copyright.
- Work in the public domain includes blank forms. Whenever copyright coverage expires, the author's work transfers to the public domain. This means it can be used, transformed, remixed, or repurposed without the permission of the author.
- Titles, names, short phrases and slogans, common symbols, and numbers cannot be copyrighted. Company names like *Google*, *Apple*, and *General Motors* cannot be copyrighted. However, names may be trademarked; branding issues fall under U.S. patent and trademark law. The reader will recall this was a red flag when *GenoChoice* was paired with both a copyright symbol and a trademark.
- Ideas, systems, or methods of operation fall outside copyright law. It may be argued that very few ideas are new. When a new idea comes along, the idea itself cannot be copyrighted. On the other hand, original works that spring from that idea can be copyrighted. An original written description of an idea may be copyrighted, not the idea itself.
- Facts and basic information that can be verified by observation or experimentation cannot be protected by copyright. This speaks to the underlying intent of copyright law that society and mankind benefit from the creative work done by individuals. Again, written descriptions or interpretations of facts can be copyrighted.
- Federal government publications are not copyrighted. Government documents written for the people of the United States become the property of all.

TIME LIMITATIONS OF COPYRIGHT

Copyright exists to protect the intellectual property rights of "original works of authorship."[6] Copyright laws attempt to balance the commercial interests of content creators against the cultural benefits derived from the free flow of information. For that reason, copyright protection is granted for limited times. The length of term or duration of copyright varies. In general, copyright lasts the life of the author plus seventy years. Work for hire or anonymous work has a 95-year protection from date of first publication or 120 years from the year of creation, whichever is less.[7] The intent of an expiration date on a copyright is that eventually the material will pass into the public domain. In the broadest sense of the concept, copyright ensures that the creator of the content derives the economic benefit. Others who benefit financially and deny the author profit by using the copyrighted materials without permission are in violation of the law.

A copyright is granted automatically to the author of new materials once the content is fixed in print or online. The copyright holder has exclusive rights to the original work. These rights include the ability to reproduce copies; create derivative works; and distribute the work for sale, display, and performance.[8] Copyright is implied and inherent. No specific applications must be filled out. No copyright symbols need be present. The assumption is, unless otherwise stated, the material is copyrighted. An application does need to be filed, however, if copyright infringement has occurred and the injured party wishes to file suit.

Copyright law was written to give authors of printed materials, such as pamphlets, books, and maps, protection for a limited period of time. This promotes creation and discovery by protecting an author's exclusive right to make money from created works. Copyright law is also a national issue. Each country has unique copyright laws, although there has been some international standardization. If online publication is interpreted as if it were ink on paper, it would seem that most digital sharing and all remixing of copyrighted material violates law.

CREATIVE COMMONS

One way to sidestep copyright concerns for teaching and research is to use only Creative Commons–licensed content. However choosing to use nothing but Creative Commons content would severely limit access to new ideas. Use of Creative Commons–licensed content is a good choice in some circumstances, but knowledge of how to work with copyrighted materials will open the door to a richer writing and learning experience. It's important to understand that all Creative Commons content is copyrighted. The difference lies in the layers of nuance and permission that this voluntary program brings to the copyright agreement. Creative Commons works along with traditional copyright to spell out an author's wishes about use and distribution. Licenses are managed by Creative Commons, a nonprofit group; authors are given tools to modify the traditional reach of copyright law. The stated vision of Creative Commons is "nothing less than realizing the full potential of the Internet—universal access to research and education, full participation in culture—to drive a new era of development, growth, and productivity."[9] In many ways, Creative Commons helps overcome the problems of restricted markets and fear of copyright infringement that can be the unintended side effects of traditional copyright protection. A writer or musician who locks down his or her work with a copyright may miss the potential audience and be doomed to labor on in obscurity. In the twenty-first century, viral buzz and Internet sharing are the way to find an audience. By using a Creative Commons license, the artist not only opens the door to wide distribution via search engines but also promotes the possibility of collaboration and future creative projects with others in the open resource community.

Authors are reassured that they will be able to "easily change . . . copyright terms from the default of 'all rights reserved' to 'some rights reserved.'"[10] The system operates on the premise that authors of original work will benefit from the free distribution of their works. For many, free mass distribution, as long as it involves attribution of authorship, is like casting bread upon the waters. The work is seen by potentially a vast audience and may indeed open doors to new opportunities. Creative Commons promotes online collaboration, sharing, and evolving use of content while still retaining for the original author some rights. Licenses may be easily modified based on the author's needs. Every license includes attribution, meaning some form of citation must be employed when using Creative Commons–licensed content.

Creative Commons licenses have three layers: legal terms written for lawyers, the Commons Deed written for the public, and a machine-readable element that makes Creative Commons license material easier to find with search engines. Indeed, much of the power of Creative Commons licensing comes from its ready availability via search engines. The basic license is "Attribution" only. This grants international free use with the only requirement being attribution to the original author. A much more restrictive license is "Attribution–Noncommercial–No Derivative Works." At first glance, forbidding commercial use may seem like a logical choice. However this does limit the potential audience significantly. If the intention is to get ideas to as many as possible, why forbid commercial use? Between these two extremes is a particularly potent kind of licensing that should appeal to anyone interested in open-source education. The international "Attribution Share Alike" license allows anyone to "alter, transform, or build upon" the original work.[11] Added to this is the requirement that any work derived must be published under the same license. This means that the original author has the right to use both commercial and noncommercial content derived from his or her content. On the playground this would be called "share and share alike." Creative Commons goes on to instruct authors to display the appropriate Creative Commons logos. These logos include a code that leads the reader back to the license page where copyright permissions are spelled out. This approach is a best practice for open-source publishing.

However, in a digital age, the vast majority of information is not released under a Creative Commons license. Standard copyright applies, and the application of the law, especially in the digital world, is far from black and white. Indeed, copyright is all about shades of gray. The vague nature of copyright law means that many kinds of uses are open to interpretation. Some argue that remixing copyrighted material should be exempt from all copyright restrictions, reasoning that the original constitutional intent of the copyright laws was to promote progress.[12] Given the freely available tools and almost instantaneous publishing capability of the Internet, remixing words, songs, images, and video is claimed as a new art form protected under freedom of expression. The original works are transformed by the interpretation of the remixer. Lawyer and author Lawrence Lessig, in his book *Remix: Making Art and Commerce Thrive in the Hybrid Economy*, compares remix artistry to cooking: Each uses original ingredients to create something new. Lessig explains that the "remix artist does the same thing with bits of culture found in his digital cupboard."[13] Here the argument is that remixing is a form of authorship that creates new content, even if the original ingredients are copyrighted. The societal benefit, Lessig argues, is the extension of multiple aspects of culture to a community around the world. Lessig also points out that remixing is a way to "excite interest-based learning"[14] and that engaging students in remixing is one new way to learn with media.[15]

The music industry is a hot spot for copyright controversy. Mixing songs, downloading music, and swapping music are all activities common today. Many claim the digital age has destroyed the music industry. Headline cases of copyright prosecutions by the Recording Industry Association of America (RIAA) produce a wave of fear and intimidation as a way to enforce copyright protections. The case of Sara Ward, a retired schoolteacher charged with pirating millions in hard-core rap music, has been widely reported. As it turned out, Mrs. Ward didn't even own the technology needed to download a single song. Eventually the charges were dropped by the RIAA, which showed no remorse for pillaring an innocent schoolteacher saying, "When you go fishing with a driftnet, sometimes you catch a dolphin."[16] However, music and song writing were not always covered by copyright protection. Indeed, music piracy and copying are nothing new.[17]

The social nature of music makes sharing a natural impulse. Additionally, music is more than words and notes on paper; it is also performance. For music to be copyrighted, it must be thought of as property, however it is much more. Alex Cummings, in his book *Democracy of Sound: Music Piracy and the Remaking of American Copyright in the Twentieth Century*, documents the long history of music piracy while exploring the inadequacies of copyright law. Of particular interest is Cummings's insight into the current distribution of digital music on the Internet: "If the music industry is the thesis and piracy is the antithesis, social media and online streaming sites offer a kind of synthesis—driven by user choices, and based on a model that does not necessarily involve the sale of a good, but instead the provision of a service that makes music readily and widely accessible."[18]

All teachers understand that music is a passionate interest of their students. Any discussion of fair use will inevitably collide with the common attitude that sharing music is a community activity and not an abuse of copyright. This outlook is rooted in more than blind self-interest. Cummings sums up the problem succinctly: "the idea of preventing any item from ever being shared is unrealistic in the context of a culture and an economy that thrive on the unencumbered communication of ideas and expression."[19] If a teacher takes a stand that demands students choose between sharing music and deeply engaging in the practice of ethical use, the conclusion is foregone; students do not see music sharing as theft or piracy. No one is making money; everyone is enjoying the music. Cummings argues that attacking music sharing as piracy is a mistaken interpretation of the marketplace: "In the case of recorded sound, anti-piracy efforts attempted to curtail the web of social relations through which so much of the meaning and value of music emerges—the desire for it, the sharing of it, and the surprises piped through illicit and unofficial channels of sound. Fight piracy, home taping, and file sharing means fight demand rather than satisfying it."[20]

So what is a teacher to do? The sharing issue must be addressed. However a repressive, narrow reading of copyright law leads only to a do-it-my-way experience. This approach destroys a true chance for engaged learning. As shown next, there are ways to share and use commercial music and other copyrighted materials in student projects and performances that are sanctioned under fair use standards. As with most things concerning copyright law, understanding the context for use is everything.

FAIR USE

Ultimately fair use is determined in a court of law on a case-by-case basis. The goal is to determine if the use was fair according to the equitable rule of reason. The task is to determine if the social good generated by unlicensed fair use is greater than any damages suffered by the copyright owner. Indeed, a powerful way to interpret fair use is to take an honest look at how the use might impact the bottom-line finances of the original author. If use promotes sharing and adds publicity that might ultimately lead to a sale, a strong argument for fair use has a common-sense foundation. If someone posts a copyrighted song on YouTube that goes viral, leading to a recording or song-writing contract for the original author, no one will be claiming copyright abuse. On the other hand, if a new CD is burned to MP3 format and distributed via BitTorrent,[21] a claim might be made.

Fair use provisions are part of copyright law. It is of utmost importance to know that fair use factors are based on section 107 of the copyright law.[22] This clearly states, "the fair use of a copyrighted work, including such use by reproduction in copies or phonorecords or by any other means specified by that section, for purposes such as criticism, comment, news reporting, teaching (including multiple copies for classroom use), scholarship, or research, is not an infringement of copyright."[23] Clearly much of the use of copyrighted content is covered under the broad description: "criticism, comment, news reporting, teaching." However this use is modified by what is often called the four factors:

> 107. Limitations on exclusive rights: Fair use. . . . In determining whether the use made of a work in any particular case is a fair use the factors to be considered shall include—
>
> 1. the purpose and character of the use, including whether such use is of a commercial nature or is for nonprofit educational purposes;
> 2. the nature of the copyrighted work;

3. the amount and substantiality of the portion used in relation to the copyrighted work as a whole; and
4. the effect of the use upon the potential market for or value of the copyrighted work.

The fact that a work is unpublished shall not itself bar a finding of fair use if such finding is made upon consideration of all the above factors.[24]

Teachers and writers should feel some sense of freedom when reading these conditions. However, applying the four factors is a matter of interpretation of the law. When push comes to shove, legal decisions about fair use are made in a courtroom.

In addition to the fair-use section of the copyright law, the U.S. Congress enacted the Technology, Education, and Copyright Harmonization Act of 2001,[25] more commonly known as the TEACH Act. This bill was passed in part to deal with the increasingly complicated landscape evolving from the use of copyrighted materials in distance education. The TEACH Act trims some of the liberal fair use practices available in the physical classroom. The four-factors test establishes that, in face-to-face settings, teachers are free to use copyrighted work related to their curriculum. This freedom includes the right to use photos, movies, books, and music as seen fit by the teacher without formal permission. The TEACH Act restricts distance-education classroom use to "reasonable and limited portions" of copyrighted content. The law does permit instructors to copy digital works and digitize analog works as long as these copies remain under the control of the educational institution and associated with specific curriculum. Compliance is usually met by keeping this kind of media in a password-protected environment and not on the open Web. The law also covers performances supervised by an instructor and limited to the members of a class. These provisions apply only to nonprofit educational institutions. The complexities of the TEACH Act have led most educators to fall back on the criteria detailed in the fair-use section of the copyright law.

THE FOUR FACTORS

Briefly stated, the four-factor fair-use test is a method of judging ethical use by balancing four different elements of fair use. These elements or factors can be summed up in these questions:

1. Has something been added that transforms or enhances the value of the original work? Is it just a copy or something different from the original work?
2. Was the original work creative or primarily factual? (Use of factual work is easier to justify under fair use.)
3. How much of the original work was used, and was that amount necessary? (Limited sampling of materials makes it easier to establish fair use.)
4. Does the use of the work damage the bottom-line finances of the author? Did the use harm the market for the original work? For example, would people buy this work instead of the original?

UNDERSTANDING TRANSFORMATION

The first factor is considered to be the most important of the four. Transforming copyrighted material for artistic, critical, dramatic, or educational audiences speaks directly to the concerns of any educator. Transformation of a copyrighted work means that the work has been altered or added to in some way. Transformation may mean the work is repurposed for a new context or to interest a new audience. Consider the use of a popular cartoon strip to illustrate a teaching technique. The entire cartoon strip can be used to help make the point because the original purpose of the cartoon (entertainment) is transformed to that of illustrating a concept. On the other hand, photocopying an entire textbook and using it in place of legitimately printed copies does not transform the content; it simply violates copyright by making a copy. The latter would not be fair use. Transformation is at the heart of online creations, such as remixes and mash-ups. If the intent is to comment or critique a cultural issue, use of copyrighted music or videos is considered fair. The essential question is, "Was value added to the original by creating new information, new aesthetics, new insights, and understandings?"[26]

CASE STUDIES

The application of the four-factor test to several case studies helps clarify an understanding of fair use as it occurs in the real world. In each case it involves an educator using ethical practices and in situations that many teachers would find intimidating if they did not have a strong understanding of fair use.

Case 1

Mr. Huckaby teaches tenth-grade English. He scans a published poem by Gary Snyder from a printed anthology with a standard copyright. Mr. Huckaby also adds a full citation to the lower right-hand part of the page. Additionally the teacher adds space for the student's name and a set of directions asking the students to color code the poem for the following literary devices:

- Internal Rhyme
- Consonance
- Imagery
- Rhyme
- Simile

Mr. Huckaby also posts the assignment in a PDF format with a Creative Commons "Attribution Only" license on his class blog. Students are able to complete the form online or download and print the form and complete it by hand. Has Mr. Huckaby violated the copyright of the poet or the publisher?

Mr. Huckaby has transformed a poem into a teaching tool. His changes add value (for students and English teachers) to the poem by providing a guide for critical analysis. Although the poem is not a factual work, the transformation is considered fair use for educational purposes. The poem relates to the curriculum. A single poem is a small sample from the larger anthology. Clearly, the heart of the entire original content has not been used. Because the online worksheet includes a citation that credits the publisher, the added publicity for the original book neutralizes any possible negative economic impact on the publisher. It may even lead to a few sales for the anthology publisher or the poet Gary Snyder. Mr. Huckaby has the right to copyright his original literary analysis directions. His choice of an "Attribution Only" license indicates Huckaby is a supporter of open-educational resources.

Case 2

Ms. Anderson is teaching a unit about media, politics, and persuasion. She directs her students to search for online videos that display the classic characteristics of propaganda: lying by omission, loaded emotional messages, transfer, name calling, glittering generalities, bandwagon approach, celebrity testimonials, and plain-folks appeal. Working in teams, groups are each assigned a specific form of propaganda. Students then download Internet videos and remix several longer videos into one-minute segments to illustrate each method of propaganda. Each video has a themed music track playing behind the original audio found on the video clips. The class then publishes a Web site with hot links to each of the video segments, as well as their own expository and persuasive essays discussing propaganda techniques and media. A comment thread eliciting viewers' opinions about the videos accompanies each video. Social media sharing buttons are included. The remixed student videos are published with a Creative Commons "Attribution–Share Alike" license. Have Ms. Anderson and her students violated the copyright of the original video producers?

Ms. Anderson is actively engaged in teaching her students how to remix video as a form of critical thinking and social commentary. Her students are actively transforming nonfiction and fictionalized video into new, original works. They meet most of the elements of factor 1 and factor 2. The use of nondocumentary footage, such as television shows or commercials, are confined to a few short segments. The limited use of the video clips conforms to TEACH Act requirements regarding media. Students contribute insights and original composition speaking to propaganda techniques, which strengthens the case for transformational use and falls under the critique and commentary intent of the law. A strict interpretation of copyright law would emphasize that the authors of the video hold the exclusive rights for any derivative product. However, in addition to the strong four-factor alignment of the assignment, Ms. Anderson is also supported by the code of best practices developed by the documentary filmmakers community[27] and the "Code of Best Practices in Fair Use for Media Literacy Education."[28] She can justifiably argue that her students are engaged in a form of documentary filmmaking and social commentary. The student-generated one-minute videos are made up of a number of shorter clips, so the size of the individual copyrighted samples is small. Even the use of a single sixty-second clip from a copyrighted song is mitigated by the fair use for criticism and commentary rights reserved for students and educators. As far as economic impact goes, no financial loss to any of the copyright holders is likely. Once again, by sharing snippets of video online, the likelihood is that the number of viewers of the original materials will go up, conceivably bringing some financial gain to the copyright holders. Ms. Anderson might consider adding a filmography, citing all original videos remixed by her class. By including a back link to the originals, the argument that more viewers may reach the original copyright holders is strengthened.

Case 3

Mr. McNeal's senior AP science classes are conducting a research project on alternative energy. Lacking an up-to-date text, McNeal turns to the Internet as a primary source for research. Students are tasked with locating the most reliable and credible information about alternative energy. Breaking into groups assigned to solar, wind, geothermal, tidal, biomass, and hydrogen energy, students are tasked with developing an online, curated magazine dedicated to energy research. To sharpen students' critical-thinking abilities, he also instructs them to find dubious or hoax-driven examples in their field of study. All articles are published using a curation system that provides a page for researcher's annotations. Each annotation page includes the student-author's name, a synopsis of the article, and a link to the original article. Students assemble, annotate, and publish introductions to more than one hundred articles on alternative energy sources. The curation-publishing platform prompts readers both to "like" and comment on articles. Students are to click "Like" for credible articles while rooting out hoax articles. They must debunk specious sources in the comments area. However, Mr. McNeal forgets to require formal annotations as part of the synopsis, so it's left up to readers to figure out who the authors of the original articles really are. Have Mr. McNeal and his students violated the copyright of the authors of the original stories?

Although Mr. McNeal will probably include a more formal citation in his next version of the alternative energy unit, there is no fair-use requirement to provide formal citations. However, if formal citations were provided, the research aspects of the project would be greatly enhanced. When students use the curated site for writing, they will appreciate having citations waiting for them. The transformation factor is at work here as well. While none of the original authors' content is changed, extra value is added to the entire publication by collecting and annotating articles on this timely topic. The original authors could sustain no commercial loss argument because readers can click through to the original articles. Once again, financial gain is more likely as readership goes up. One possible problem that might cause a copyright holder of an article some financial harm arises with the inclusion of hoax articles in the curated contents. If students incorrectly identify a legitimate article as a hoax, the author could claim damages. It would also be possible for the author of a hoax article to claim damages. (However, authors of hoaxes usually prefer to fly below the radar.)

CODES OF FAIR USE

An important step in clarifying the gray areas of fair use is to codify best practices. Codes are created as guidelines for specific communities. They are powerful arguments in case a suit is brought against a member of the community. Documentary filmmakers, historians, K–12 teachers, college and university instructors, open-education resource advocates, and librarians belong to communities with established codes of fair use. These codes influence legal decisions by detailing a shared common approach to fair use. However, community codes are not laws or even agreements with specific copyright holders. Instead, they are statements of principles and guidelines for ethical behavior. The codes are not meant to constrain use but expand ethical use; best practices codes help illuminate the gray areas of copyright law.

This is just what the Association of Research Libraries (ARL) did when they issued a "Code of Best Practices in Fair Use." Note the audience for this document: librarians in generally traditional settings. Fair use for this population is the "right to use copyrighted material without permission or payment under some circumstances, especially when the cultural or social benefits of the use are predominant."[29] The best practices codified by the ALR are summarized here. The code identifies the relevance of fair use in eight recurrent situations for librarians:

1. Supporting teaching and learning with access to library materials via digital technologies;
2. Using selections from collection materials to publicize a library's activities or to create physical and virtual exhibitions;
3. Digitizing to preserve at-risk items;
4. Creating digital collections of archival and special collections materials;
5. Reproducing material for use by disabled students, faculty, staff, and other appropriate users;
6. Maintaining the integrity of works deposited in institutional repositories;
7. Creating databases to facilitate nonconsumptive research uses (including search); and
8. Collecting material posted on the Web and making it available.

Recognizing the quality of this code, the Consortium of College and University Media Centers (CCUMC) recently endorsed this code and retired its own set of guidelines. This banding together of stakeholders produces a strong united front should members of this community have to go to court to assert their fair-use rights.[30]

CODE OF BEST PRACTICES IN FAIR USE FOR MEDIA LITERACY EDUCATION

Understanding fair use will help teachers calm their fears about using online materials. Many feel confined by the tyrannical reliance on rigid sets of rules. The very nature of fair use precludes rigid interpretation. Better teachers push the boundaries in their attempts to educate students rather than knuckle under to unjustified fear. The simple intention to educate is a very strong argument for fair use. The fair-use guidelines set down in the "Code of Best Practices in Fair Use for Media Literacy Education"[31] provide a wide umbrella for all teachers working online or in blended classrooms. This code is widely endorsed by the Action Coalition for Media Education, the Media Education Foundation, the National Association for Media Literacy Education, the National Council of Teachers of English, and the Visual Communication Studies Division of the International Communication Association. The John D. and Catherine T. MacArthur Foundation funded the creation of the code. The express intent of the code is to help educators everywhere become leaders in the use of media and free themselves from the "Tyranny of Guidelines and Experts."[32]

The code goes into great detail, describing current conditions, principles of use, and limitations of use. The main principles of the code affirm that educators are allowed to:

- Use copyrighted materials in media literacy lessons and
- Create curriculum content with embedded media.

Additionally, the code supports student rights to:

- Create their own original material using copyrighted materials and
- Distribute their creations digitally as long as it represents a significant transformation of the copyrighted material.

Limitations are crafted to acknowledge and promote an understanding of the fair-use factors stated in the copyright law. These limitations include:

- Providing attribution;
- Modeling formal citation;
- Limiting amount of media sampling;
- Following professional standards for curriculum creation;
- Seeking permission when using copyrighted materials for promotional purposes; and
- When appropriate, focusing access to copyrighted materials to students within the institution.

The code provides sage advice about digital distribution of student works: "Educators should take the opportunity to model the real-world permissions process, with explicit emphasis not only on how that process works, but also on how it affects media making."[33] In this way, understanding fair use becomes one of the objectives in any curricula that encourage digital publication: "In particular, educators should explore with students the distinction between materials that should be licensed, materials that are in the public domain, or otherwise openly available, and copyrighted material that is subject to fair use. The ethical obligation to provide proper attribution also should be examined."[34] This kind of instruction provides a strong foundation for reading, research, and content production in the digital age. It can also be seen as a foundation for a meaningful understanding of plagiarism.

AVOIDING PLAGIARISM

Ethics meets information consumption and real-world consequences in cases of plagiarism. Most educators know that a student's first response when confronted with a charge of plagiarism is to claim, "I didn't know . . ." Most educators also assume that the student has a working knowledge of the subject. It seems simple enough: Don't copy another's work and claim it as your own. However, like most aspects of information fluency, plagiarism is a complex issue with many shades of gray. Where is the line drawn between paraphrasing and plagiarism? What if portions of a resource are mixed in with mostly original writing? What if personal work is reused? Does that require a citation? Is it unethical to create a false citation just to meet the demands of an instructor? Teaching the subtleties of this topic takes precise understanding and significant specific effort.

Just about any teacher will admit there just isn't time or space in the curriculum to teach plagiarism. This reality creates a serious problem when confronted with the "I didn't know I was doing anything wrong" defense. In an effort to solve this issue, the 21st Century Information Fluency Project designed a self-paced training module called the "Plagiarism Dropbox"[35] that assesses the students' understanding as they interact with many types of plagiarism. The Information Fluency Project believes "if you can detect plagiarism, you can avoid it." The most common types of plagiarism are described in this training as:

- Photocopy Plagiarism: copying an original source word for word.
- Patchwork Plagiarism: copying or paraphrasing without citing multiple sources.
- Paraphrasing: poorly disguising the content of an original by rewriting it and not citing the original. Whether a little or a lot, paraphrasing without citing is plagiarism.
- Misinformation: intentionally providing a bogus citation so the original source is difficult or impossible to find.
- Missing Quotes: word-for-word copying without using quotation marks, even though a citation is included.
- Self-Borrowing: copying your own work without citing it.

Notice the repeated references to citation? Attribution by formal citation is the best defense against plagiarism.

The first part of the training steps a student through each type of plagiarism, presenting the learner with both the source material and a sample excerpt written by an unknown student. The learner is put in the position of being a teacher who must accurately detect the presence or absence of plagiarism.

After comparing the original source with the student paper, the learner makes a choice: plagiarized or not plagiarized. The system keeps track of an individual's score. Feedback is provided immediately following the learner's choice, helping to reinforce a proper understanding of each type of plagiarism. The training starts with easy-to-distinguish cases of patchwork and photocopying-style plagiarism. The second part of the training directs the student to repair an excerpt of plagiarized text. Once again, the student is given the opportunity to compare the original to a plagiarized paper. The challenge is to repair the paper by choosing from a list of suggested edits. Full points are awarded when a student selects only the necessary repairs. The list of editorial suggestions includes:

- Put quotation marks around copied sections,
- Paraphrase the existing content,
- Add some new content,
- Cite the quoted sections in the text,
- Cite the paraphrased sections in the text,
- Correct the citation, and
- Do nothing.

Successful completion of the entire training earns the student a competency badge that can be used to verify their accomplishment in online social venues. This training takes maybe an hour to complete and may be done at the students' desired pace. It's unlikely that a student who has earned an "Avoiding Plagiarism" badge based on this training will ever again claim, "I didn't know it was wrong." Best of all, this on-demand, self-paced training can be done out of class as a homework assignment.

In these scenarios, the user compares the original source and the plagiarized excerpt so a determination of plagiarism is easy to make. Students must understand that copying others' work isn't acceptable, even if it is easy to do. In the real world of online research and writing, it's said that plagiarism flourishes because it is so easy to copy. What's not always understood is that it is also easy to discover plagiarism using a few common techniques that leverage the power of the Internet.

Technique 1

Search for sentences that don't sound like the writer's usual voice. Teachers can develop an ear for copying. If the sentence fluency and word choice of a writer suddenly change gears, place quotation marks around the suspect sentence, and use a search engine to check for the original source. This simple search will provide proof for an accusation of plagiarism.

Technique 2

Use a specialized plagiarism database to analyze the paper under question. Turnitin[36] is the best known of these systems. A paper submitted to Turnitin is compared to millions of other texts in the database. A percentage score comparing works already analyzed by Turnitin to the new student submission is calculated. The Turnitin system can be used as a sophisticated writing tutor if the student is allowed to send in drafts and get automated editorial advice. Using Turnitin for automated feedback is one way to teach students how to avoid plagiarism. Ultimately, this use of the system could be highly beneficial to all involved. However, most of the time, Turnitin is used when instructors suspect plagiarism. One of the strengths of the system is that it assembles strong evidence of plagiarism for the instructor. Accusing a student of plagiarism is always a tense and high-stakes action. Legal consequences may follow. The time and energy spent pursing plagiarism cases can be immense. Having well-organized, solid proof of plagiarism is essential if a teacher must go forward with an adversarial case.

CITATION

The best way to avoid plagiarism is accurately to quote and cite all references used when writing expository or research pieces. Unlike many elements of information fluency, quotation and citation is currently taught in school. However, too often with citation, form trumps function. Citation is often taught in isolation from the research process and divorced from the concept of ethical use. Students are asked to produce citations following one of the required forms, such as MLA, APA, or Chicago. The intricacies of matching the form to the source (print journal article, book, online article, e-book) often overshadow the fundamental purpose of a citation. Students, with a checklist mentality, see the number of citations required and the specific format required but may not understand that citations actually help a reader check resources. Without seeing the bigger picture, citation is a rote ritual with little meaning.

Why cite a source?

- To provide a complete and systematic back trail to the sources used,
- To avoid plagiarism,
- To improve the credibility of one's writing,
- To drive the need to actually research information from expert and primary sources,
- To showcase the ideas of other writers in an ethical manner,
- To engage ethically in the process of understanding others' ideas to support one's point of view, and
- To provide the reader with additional quality resources about the topic at hand.

Rather than focus on the minutia of constructing a proper citation, educators are encouraged to consider and teach the kind of investigative skills necessary to render a proper citation, thereby giving context to the citation process. Citations were originally designed to document the use of print materials and help researchers delve more deeply into texts. Working with print materials, it's highly likely that all of the required information is relatively easy to find. However, most contemporary research materials, especially in the science and social science fields, are digital. With digital content, the information required (and dictated form) may be more difficult to discover.

Citation of digital materials is a form of investigative searching. Being able to find the author of a blog post or determine the date of publication requires technical abilities described in detail in chapter 6. One way to unpack the requirements of a citation is to approach the process as a search challenge.

ONLINE CITATION GENERATORS

Creating a citation used to require a reference book like the *Chicago Manual of Style* or the *Modern Language Association Handbook*. The writer would page through the table of contents, identify the type of source, and then turn to the appropriate chapter looking for models to mimic in order to create the citation. Online citation generators now present a series of empty fields for each element required. Fill in the fields, and the software processes the citation. Depending on audience expectations, an automatically generated citation may be all that's needed. However, it's the writer's responsibility to understand the demands of the audience. A misplaced comma or incorrectly rendered author's name in a Ph.D. thesis biography is likely to be more closely scrutinized and penalized than a similar error in a high-school term paper. However, all require a citation complete enough to direct a curious reader back to the source material. In most cases, title, publication date, publisher, author, and page numbers are sufficient for a citation. The additional format and spacing requirements are specific to the field of study.

CASE STUDY

For this study, a citation is deconstructed better to illustrate the investigative skills needed to provide an accurate and ethical citation. The launch page for the 21st Century Information Project's "Online Citation Wizards"[37] is the information to be cited. The page is located at http://21cif.com/tools/cite and contains orientation information and hyperlinks to citation templates for APA, CSE (a.k.a., CBE), MLA, Chicago, and Harvard style citations. The templates are specifically designed to cite Web pages, online journals, electronic books, and databases. Additionally, annotated links to other MLA and APA citation wizards are provided.

One unique feature of the 21CIF tools is that many templates have links to short on-demand tutorials that explain citation options and formatting specifics. In some cases mini-tutorials link to online training games, for example, "What Is the Date?"[38] and "Who Is the Author?"[39] The intent is to provide more than just a citation template. This system is also a self-paced teaching tool.

Using American Psychological Association (APA) format, the citation looks like this:

Online Citation Wizards. (2012). Retrieved April 5, 2012, from http://21cif.com/tools/cite

The APA citation for this particular site is fairly easy to create (see figure 7.1). Most of the required information is clearly visible on the page. The only investigation necessary is to track down the author. Because the citation wizards are Flash-based tools, there is no way to dig into the code looking for the author. Browsing the Web site leads to clicking "About Us" in the navigation panel, then selecting "Our Team." This Web site is maintained by two people: Dr. Carl Heine and Dennis O'Connor. In this citation, it should not be assumed that the Web site owners are the authors of this content. In this case, APA allows for the citation not to include an author's name. When authorship can't be established using investigative search tactics, the most reliable method of discovery is to write the authors of the Web site. (If this were done it would be revealed that the author of the content is Carl Heine.) If this activity is used as a lesson, have the students find the information and fill in the citation template.

Council of Science Editors Format

Online Citation Wizards [Internet]. Warrenville (IL): Information Fluency; [2012 Feb 12, cited 2012 Apr 5]. Available from: http://21cif.com/tools/cite

Compared to APA, the CSE citation is significantly more detailed. This provides multiple opportunities for investigative searching. In this case, assume there isn't time to write the Web-site authors. This means that authorship cannot be determined and

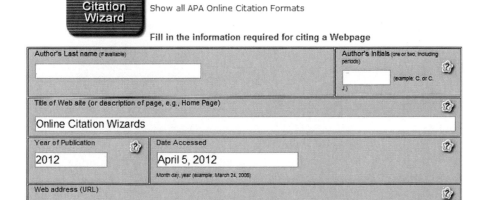

Figure 7.1.   Template for an APA Web Page Citation

that part of the citation form is left blank. The copyright notice on the page indicates the publisher. Clicking the "About Us" button and selecting the "Contact Us" link reveals the city and state. The publisher information is also verified on the "Contact Us" page. The original publication date presents a true search challenge. Unlike the APA citation that is satisfied by a last-updated notation, CSE wants the original publication date. In this case, the information needed is found outside of the 21cif.com domain using the Internet Archive WayBack Machine.[40] When the URL for "Online Citation Wizards" is searched, a first archive dated April 26, 2009, is found. This is the date when the Internet archive crawled and copied the site. Because there's no way to know exactly when the page went online, only a best guess can be ventured: the original publication date is sometime before April 26, 2009. Based on the archiving history, first publication sometime in 2009 is highly likely.

Each citation format is different. Each presents unique challenges and opportunities for investigative search. The audience for the writing often determines the type of citation. Different organizations have stated preferences. However, when there is no firm citation style requirement, perhaps it is wise to use a citation that provides the user with the most information. In the case of the "Online Citation Wizards" page, CSE provides the most information for the reading audience. To maintain consistency, use only one style per paper.

NOTE TAKING AND CITATION

Bookmarks, notecards, and page highlighting are old standbys when doing research with printed resources. This is a cumbersome but accepted method of work. The information-fluent researcher is more inclined to use digital tools to pursue search and evaluation tasks. When using traditional library resources, relevant quotations are often written on notecards or typed into a word processor. This means recording, at a minimum, the title and publication date of the book, the publisher's and author's name, the chapter title and subtitle, and the exact page numbers of quotations planned for use. Books are then returned to the library.

This tedious mechanical process can be automated when using online resources. With tools like Diigo,[41] the researcher bookmarks and tags a resource. It's also easy to highlight the passages that might make good quotations and to place virtual sticky notes capturing fresh ideas right on the Web page. Social bookmarking systems are covered in greater depth in chapter 9, "Curation." This form of markup isn't allowed with traditional library resources. When it's time to write the paper (including quotations, footnotes, and bibliographic citations), the bookmarks and annotations are saved, along with copy and paste techniques, insuring correctness and accurate citation with less tedium than traditional methods.

Properly citing resources requires the disposition fully to engage in the information fluency process by using digital resources and investigative search techniques to locate, evaluate, and cite online materials in a manner that meets the needs of the audience. In an ideal world, every time one searches for important information, accurate citation and annotations would be captured on a cloud-based server ready for instant recall. In the real world, the process of searching and the ethical use of information are rather sloppy. The key is to practice the more formal approach often enough to have an internalized and systematic approach to research. Such an approach requires ethical use of information, complete with citation and a healthy respect for copyright, tempered by a solid confidence in how to practice fair use. All of these qualities develop as the disposition to be an information-fluent searcher evolves.

NOTES

1. Ad Hoc Committee on Fair Use and Academic Freedom, International Communication Association, "Clipping Our Own Wings Copyright and Creativity in Communication Research," *Center for Social Media*, last modified 2013, http://www.centerforsocialmedia .org/fair-use/related-materials/documents/clipping-our-own-wings-copyright-and-creativity -communication-r.

2. James G. Lengel, "Teaching with Technology: Copy, Right?" *PowerToLearn: CSC Holdings, LLC*, last modified January 22, 2008, http://www.powertolearn.com/articles/teach ing_with_technology/article.shtml?ID=67.

3. "S.487—Technology, Education, and Copyright Harmonization Act of 2001," *Library of Congress*, last modified September 25, 2002, http://www.gpo.gov/fdsys/pkg/BILLS -107s487es/pdf/BILLS-107s487es.pdf.

4. "What Does Copyright Protect?" *U.S. Copyright Office*, last modified June 4, 2012, http://www.copyright.gov/help/faq/faq-protect.html.

5. "Copyright and Fair Use in the UMUC Online or Face-to-Face Classroom," *University of Maryland University College*, last modified June 4, 2012, http://www.umuc.edu/library/ libhow/copyright.cfm#copyright_notincluded.

6. See note 4.

7. "How Long Does Copyright Protection Last?," *U.S. Copyright Office*, last modified March 10, 2010, http://www.copyright.gov/help/faq/faq-duration.html.

8. "Copyright Law of the United States of America and Related Laws Contained in Title 17 of the *United States Code*: Circular 92," *U.S. Copyright Office*, accessed April 21, 2013, http://www.copyright.gov/title17/92chap1.html#106.

9. "About," *Creative Commons*, accessed April 26, 2013, http://creativecommons.org/ about.

10. See note 9.

11. "About the Licenses," *Creative Commons*, last modified month day, year, http://cre ativecommons.org/licenses.

12. "Recast Copyright Law for the Digital Era: It's Time to Regain Public Respect with Laws That Make Sense," *We the People*, last modified April 14, 2013,http://gslis.dom.edu/ newsevents/news/call-action-recast-copyright-law-digital-era.

13. Lawrence Lessig, *Remix: Making Art and Commerce Thrive in the Hybrid Economy* (New York: Penguin, 2008). p. 71

14. See note 13. p. 71

15. See note 13. p. 80

16. "RIAA v. The People: Five Years Later," *Electronic Frontier Foundation*, last modified September 30, 2008, https://www.eff.org/wp/riaa-v-people-five-years-later.

17. Noah Berlatsky, "The Long, Fruitful History of Music Piracy: Music and Intellectual Property Law," *Reason.com*, last modified April 9, 2013, http://reason.com/archives/2013/04/09/the-long-fruitful-history-of-music-pirac.

18. Alex Sayf Cummings, *Democracy of Sound: Music Piracy and the Remaking of American Copyright in the Twentieth Century* (New York: Oxford University Press, 2013), p.272.

19. See note 18, p. 140

20. See note 18, p. 272.

21. "Home Page," *BitTorrent*, accessed April 26, 2013, http://www.bittorrent.com.

22. "§ 107 . Limitations on Exclusive Rights: Fair Use," *U.S. Copyright Office*, August 16, 2012 http://www.copyright.gov/title17/92chap1.html.

23. "Copyright Law of the United States of America and Related Laws Contained in Title 17 of the United States Code," *U.S. Copyright Office*, accessed April 26, 2013, http://www.copyright.gov/title17/92chap1.html#107.

24. See note 23.

25. See note 3.

26. "Copyright and Fair Use: Measuring Fair Use: The Four Factors," *Stanford University Libraries*, last modified 2010, http://fairuse.stanford.edu/Copyright_and_Fair_Use_Overview/chapter9/9-b.html.

27. "Documentary Filmmakers' Statement of Best Practices in Fair Use," *Center for Social Media*, accessed April 26, 2013, http://www.centerforsocialmedia.org/fair-use/best-practices/documentary/documentary-filmmakers-statement-best-practices-fair-use.

28. "The Code of Best Practices in Fair Use for Media Literacy Education," *Center for Social Media*, accessed April 26, 2013, http://www.centerforsocialmedia.org/fair-use/related-materials/codes/code-best-practices-fair-use-media-literacy-education.

29. "Code of Best Practices in Fair Use," *Association of Research Libraries*, http://www.arl.org/focus-areas/copyright-ip/fair-use/code-of-best-practices.

30. Patricia Aufderheide, "CCUMC Adopts Librarians' Code, Retires Previous Fair Use Guidelines," *Center for Social Media*, last modified January 29, 2013, http://www.centerforsocialmedia.org/blog/fair-use/ccumc-adopts-librarians%E2%80%99-code-retires-previous-fair-use-guidelines.

31. See note 28.

32. See note 28.

33. See note 28.

34. See note 28.

35. Carl Heine, "Plagiarism Dropbox," *Information Fluency: Avoiding Plagiarism*, accessed April 23, 2013, http://searchwhys.com/plagiarism-dropbox-2.swf.

36. "Home Page," *Turnitin*, accessed April 23, 2013, http://turnitin.com.

37. Carl Heine, "Online Citation Wizards," *21st Century Information Fluency*, last modified February 12, 2013, http://21cif.com/tools/cite.

38. Carl Heine, "What Is the Date?" *21st Century Information Fluency*, accessed April 23, 2013, http://21cif.com/rkitp/challenge/evaluation/date.swf.

39. Carl Heine, "Who Is the Author?" *21st Century Information Fluency*, accessed April 23, 2013, http://21cif.com/rkitp/challenge/evaluation/author.swf.

40. *WayBack Machine*, accessed April 26, 2013, http://archive.org/web/web.php.

41. *Diigo*, accessed April 26, 2013, http://diigo.com.

V

INSTRUCTIONAL
APPLICATIONS

8

Embedding Information Fluency

Information fluency instruction does not require a dedicated class period. It fits well into other instruction if done right. The marriage of information fluency and language arts, social studies, and science starts with competencies. Multiple competencies can be met by embedding simulations or live searches in classes. Two or three Common Core standards can be addressed by a single lesson. In many cases, experiences that support digital information fluency can augment other language arts standards.

Not every lesson plan will benefit from an infusion of information fluency, so what makes a good pairing? Knowing how the competencies align is key. Direct correlations between Common Core and digital information fluency are the most obvious opportunities for integration. If a lesson is designed to address the standards for reading information text—key ideas and details, for example—there is a natural intersection with keyword-selection activities. These opportunities for addressing multiple standards are the easiest to identify. Other correlations may be more indirect, a stated objective might be beyond the usual proximity of information fluency, but working on the objective in the information fluency environment enhances the process of instruction. A third type of pairing involves more of a disruptive force-fit, where information fluency transforms the original lesson into something entirely new. All three ways of embedding information fluency into existing curriculum are demonstrated in the following course activities excerpted from the Library of Congress lesson plan database:

- Language Arts—"Explorations in American Environmental History"[1] (example of direct correlation)
- Social Studies—"Out of the Dust: Visions of Dust Bowl History"[2] (example of a lesson enhancement)
- Science—"Thomas Edison, Electricity, and America"[3] (example of transformation)

COMMON CORE STANDARDS ARE
INTENDED FOR STUDENTS, NOT TEACHERS

"Explorations in American Environmental History" is an English language arts lesson developed for grades 6–8 and 9–12. The lesson places emphasis on the Common Core Reading Standards for Writing:

- Text types and purposes (W.8.2, W.8.2f)
- Production and distribution of writing (W.8.4)
- Research to build and present knowledge (W.8.7, W.8.8)
- Range of writing (W.8.10)

Research to build and present knowledge is directly correlated with information fluencies in terms of gathering information from digital sources, evaluating the accuracy and credibility of the sources, and avoiding plagiarism. It should be relatively easy to embed digital information fluency into the research activities of this lesson.

As it turns out, this is a lengthy lesson, consisting of two units and spanning up to twelve weeks. For the purpose of demonstration, only unit 1 is examined here: "The Photographer, the Artist, and Yellowstone Park." The photographer is William Henry Jackson, and the artist is Thomas Moran. For more background on the lesson and these individuals, the reader is referred to the published online lesson plan. An objective that provides a point of contact with information fluency involves selecting digital images from the Library of Congress's online collections. Here is an excellent opportunity to use a search engine other than Google and to learn how an unfamiliar search engine works and how to optimize its use.

The lesson plan for unit 1 consists of three main sections: preparation, procedure, and evaluation. The first section provides the teacher with links to Library of Congress resources on the topic, including background information on the environmental movement, specific regions of Yellowstone National Park, photographs from the World's Transportation Commission, and a teacher's guide to analyzing photographs and prints. Each link takes the teacher to a section of the "American Memory" collections, "a digital record of American history and creativity."[4] The home page of the "American Memory" collections (http://memory.loc.gov/ammem/index.html) is a search interface that provides both a search box and a subject directory. This page is referenced again in the second section of the unit, procedure, where learning activities for students are found.

The teacher briefly explains the origins of Yellowstone National Park (step 3), and proceeds to step 4:

> Invite students to participate in a "voyage of discovery" as they work within the American Memory collections to discover the impact of William Henry Jackson and Thomas Moran.

- Ask students to consider why an artist and a photographer were members of this geological survey team.
- What contribution did these men make as a result of that journey?
- What is the relationship between the advent of photography and the creation of a National Parks system?[5]

Step 5 provides information about how to go about answering these questions by giving students links to preselected pages, such as the timeline of William Henry Jackson (http://memory.loc.gov/ammem/wtc/wtcjack.html). This could be a search task, but from an information fluency perspective, this task is an exercise in reading that includes clicking hyperlinks. It is a fine lesson, but there is a missed opportunity to learn something about gathering "relevant information from multiple print and digital sources, using search terms effectively," to quote Common Core standard W.8.8. Presumably, the lesson authors gathered the source material (demonstrating their proficiency) and provided the teacher with the search results, who in turn are instructed to pass them along to the students.

Not having to gather the information saves time, but the cost is not learning how to use the Library of Congress search engine. An alternate approach would be for the teacher, who has been told what is available, to direct learners to find relevant resources about Jackson and Moran. Instead of giving students the link to Jackson's timeline, show the students the "American Memory" search page (see figure 8.1).

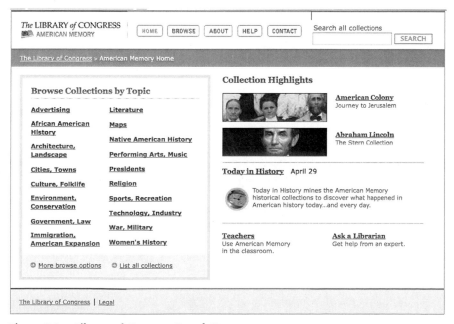

Figure 8.1. Library of Congress Search Page

For younger students, the embedded objective could be to use the search box to find information about the two characters in the lesson. William Henry Jackson and Thomas Moran are both combinations of keywords. There's a fair chance that no one else has these names. This could be an opportunity for the teacher to demonstrate how to use the names, with or without quotes, to find information about the men. Beyond that, it could involve a group effort to look at the search results and determine which ones are most relevant—based solely on the abstracts—for answering the questions presented in the lesson.

A trial query, *William Henry Jackson*, returns 5,000 results; the query *"William Henry Jackson"* does the same. From this it can be determined that the quotes operator makes no difference, a first step in learning how the Library of Congress search engine works. Clicking the "Help" button and reading the extensive guide to search engine use results in the same conclusion: Don't use quotes. That being the case, one can conclude this is a well-maintained engine. Note that there is no "Advanced Search" interface, just a simple search box, yet the results claim to come from an advanced search. The best advice for learning how to use an unfamiliar search engine is to go to the "Advanced Search" features. There is no longer such an interface for this engine. It makes one wonder why.

The large number of records also indicates that other keywords are necessary to home in on information pertaining to the question. This need directly addresses the competency "use search terms effectively." The learners should suggest what words would be good to add to the photographer's name. Including the word *Yellowstone* with Jackson's full name produces 86 results, a marked difference. *National park* and Jackson's full name yields more: 358. Students could be asked to explain why: What's going on here? *Yellowstone* is a more specific term than *national park* and therefore is likely to occur fewer times. Which term is more effective? Is it better to have more results or fewer results? Or does it depend on what the results are? This is a natural segue into evaluating abstracts.

Answering the question about the contributions of a photographer and an artist on a geological survey is a really good critical-thinking task. There isn't a right answer. Some answers are bound to be better than others, but the challenge demands diving into primary and secondary source material for inspiration. Without a doubt this process takes longer than giving students a link to the "right" information, which arguably doesn't exist. On the other hand, it will be time well spent if students make a discovery using information they find.

What students find using these queries are lists of resources and the collections where they are kept. If these are clicked open, it becomes obvious they are photographs and notes about them, such as the photographer's name and date of publication. If a picture were worth a thousand words, what effect would pictures like these have on Americans seeing them for the first time? Here is the heart of the lesson, and students should be the ones to discover and articulate it.

On the second page of search results is something that is conspicuously not a photograph: "U.S. Statutes at Large, Vol. 17, Chap. 24, pp. 32–33": "An Act to set apart a certain Tract of Land lying near the Head-waters of the Yellowstone River as a public Park." It is not an obviously relevant find but worth a look because it is the first record that is something other than a photograph. Here's an excerpt of the statute where Jackson's name is mentioned: "The photographs of William Henry Jackson and the paintings of Thomas Moran, both from the Hayden Expedition of 1871, provided Congress with powerfully persuasive images of the region as a place of uniquely American wonders."[6] This resource is not mentioned in the lesson but certainly sums it up. It's a gem waiting to be found by a student. Aside from being a powerful source to help answer the question and possibly support what students were thinking, there is a search lesson here as well. It is worth looking past the first page of results. Relevant information can be found on page 2 and thereafter. Furthermore, it's hard to tell relevant information by a title; here is a case where it pays to click open something that stands out because it is different to see how the search terms are used.

Returning to the search page, another potential mini-lesson is waiting. The same information can be accessed using the search box and the directory (see the "Browse" button). It makes an interesting word and concept exercise to use only the words provided in the directory to find a path to information. Which link will lead to information about Jackson? "Environment and Conservation" seems promising, given the topic of the lesson. This leads to five choices, one of which is mentioned in the lesson plan (mapping the national parks). Without knowing what was in the lesson, it would be difficult to see that Jackson could be found by clicking on the "Maps" link. But, in terms of word usage, here is a good clue that the path is relevant. The lesson is about Yellowstone, a national park. This is a close term, so the search is getting warmer. Is it more efficient to use the search box or the directory? Almost everyone finds it a frustrating task to find specified information by browsing a directory. It can be done but not without a lot of mistakes. A live-browsing challenge in chapter 5 helps to drive home this point. For the sake of this adapted lesson, it's probably enough just to make students aware that there are two different ways to find the information on the search page.

The first lesson provides ample opportunities for embedding information-fluency training. Older students could be expected to search and report their discoveries, sharing interesting finds with the group so everyone benefits from a broader gathering of primary and secondary sources. Of course, one mini-lesson like this is not enough to make a lasting difference in how students search, but it's one step in the right direction.

PICTURES WORTH A THOUSAND KEYWORDS

The second curricular example takes a different approach. Instead of starting with a lesson aligned with information fluency, "Out of the Dust: Visions of Dust Bowl History"[7] is a unit consisting of several sessions with no significant search activity (one of the later sessions does). Nevertheless, speculative search skills can be addressed without significantly altering the objectives. In fact, it could be argued that the lesson benefits from the complementary addition.

"Out of the Dust" addresses two main areas of Common Core Standards for Reading History for grades 3 through 8:

- Reading standards for literacy in history/social studies (RH.6-8)
- Writing standards for history/social studies/technology (WHST.6-8).

The first of these strands has no direct connection to information fluency but provides an interesting opportunity regardless. As part of the first lesson, students are shown several photographs from the Library of Congress's "Dust Bowl" collection and directed to answer four questions.[8] The first of these questions, "Speculate as to when and where these photographs may have been taken," could be combined with an information-fluency task. The speculation seems to function as a lesson hook, a way to get students interested in the topic. Instead of having students look at the pictures to guess where the photos might have been taken, there is another way to speculate using a search engine. Google's image search box[9] enables searchers to drag and drop photos and find matching photos online. This takes the guesswork out of figuring out where the photo *might* have been shot. At the same time, this activity serves as a lesson hook. It's engaging to drag and drop and get immediate results.

With Google Images open in a different browser, the first photograph, "dust piled up around farmhouse," can be dragged into the Google search box—it's not just for keywords. The search results show several different locations where the identical photo may be found online, including the Library of Congress. Some of these provide information about the photo, including the state and when it was taken (Oklahoma, April 1936). The other photographs reveal county information. Another way to get this information is by clicking on the links provided with the pictures in the lesson. Simply by browsing, the name of the photographer can be discovered. There is no reason to guess; besides, guessing isn't really an objective of the lesson but just a way to create interest. The embedded search-related activity takes no time away from the rest of the lesson but shows students that guessing isn't necessary when search skills are applied.

To make using a search tool more interesting, a teacher could divide the class in half. The "offline team" could pool their knowledge of history and clues they see in the three photos to answer the "when and where" question. The "online team" could search for information using either of the aforementioned techniques. After a minute or two, the groups could report their conclusions, although the online team has the researched answer. If students can find the information from the photos, the teacher does not need to tell anyone the answers.

Questions 2 and 3 of the lesson retain their value, getting students to think about their reactions to the images and the stories they tell—for which there are no right or wrong answers. The fourth question could be augmented from "What questions do these images evoke" to "What questions does the information about these photos evoke," driving students back to the primary source material. For example, the same photographer took each photo in April 1936. Who was Arthur Rothstein? Did he live in Oklahoma? If not, why was he there? Did the Dust Bowl reach its apex in April 1936? If it looked this bad in the spring, what about the following summer when it was hot? What does Cimarron County, Oklahoma, look like today? The last question is entirely within reach using Google Images and other search strategies. An image search for *Cimarron County Oklahoma* retrieves additional stunning photos from the same period that are missing from the lesson, along with more recent views that make an excellent study in contrasts. Other effective ways to find present-day photos of Cimarron County may be discovered by answering this investigative question: "Who might take pictures of Cimarron County today, and why?" Answers include residents, tourists, real estate agents, and Google Earth. Anyone interested in buying land in that part of Oklahoma will find an abundance of photos online.

The embedded lesson in this second example is useful for introducing ways to conduct image searches in Google, encouraging browsing to discover hidden information, and engaging in detective work to determine the source of additional information and, more importantly, where to find it.

SECONDARY SOURCE SUSPICION

The third lesson example, "Thomas Edison, Electricity, and America," is appropriate for middle-school or high-school classes in history or science. Embedding information fluency in the material transforms the lesson, turning it into something different without losing sight of Edison and electricity. The second lesson of the Edison unit examines Edison's role in the electrification of America. Written for middle-school and high-school grades and covering topics in science, technology, and business, the following Common Core standards are targeted:

- Reading standards for information text (RI.9-10.9)
- Writing standards (W.9-10.10—information fluency is included here)
- Speaking and listening standards (SL.9-10.2)

One of the Web resources provided is biographical: "The Life of Thomas A. Edison."[10] The first paragraph contains an impressive fact: Edison obtained 1,093 patents. The rest of this secondary source describes only a fraction of Edison's output: improvements to the telegraph, electric lights, and a motion picture camera as well as a viewer. To the curious-minded, some questions arise: With so many patents, what else did Edison patent? Did he invent everything he patented? Did he patent everything he invented? The first question could be turned into a scavenger hunt for Edison inventions and their relation to patents.

Students may not know much about patents or why they are necessary. The biography suggests that patents have a commercial and legal use, as they can be sold and patent infringement can ignite heated battles in court. A patent is a legal document that establishes the ownership of an invention. By acquiring more than 1,000 patents, Edison owned a huge inventory of inventions. For students drawn to innovation, information about patent protection and filing for a patent can be valuable information. This need not become an objective of the lesson, but investigating Edison's patents does fit in with getting acquainted with the man because so much of his life involved the patenting of inventions.

The following embedded activity addresses the first two stated objectives of the unit:

- Students analyze the role of Thomas Edison in the electrification of America and
- Students demonstrate an understanding of electrification as both a technological and social process.

A good place to start this departure from the lesson—it need not be a long one—is to consider "Where can information about all of Edison's patents be found?" With computers handy, give students two to three minutes to search for what they think is a good source. After sufficient time has elapsed, ask everyone to freeze—hands off the computer. Call on individuals to report what page they are on now and why. Compare the answers and reasons for the choices. Students who search for *Thomas Edison patent list* will discover complete lists on About.com and Wikipedia. If students go to the U.S. Patent and Trademark Office[11] and search there, they won't find the complete list. Students who go to Google's patent search will obtain about 28,000 results.[12] Research that someone has already compiled is more readily available than having to start from scratch. If students have not discovered the U.S. Patent and Trademark Office search or Google patent search, suggest they try to answer the question with those search engines. Frustration may ensue after a couple minutes. Simple keyword searches do not yield the neatly arranged information found on the compiled patent lists. This raises the question "Why?" which could prompt a discussion of whether this search engine is intended for the average person.

The search for Edison's patents from original sources is time consuming and not recommended. This leaves secondary sources, such as Wikipedia, a more efficient alternative. Here is an excellent opportunity for students to distinguish between primary and secondary sources. Primary sources, like many artifacts in the Library of Congress, consist of original information, like photographs, statutes, and patent applications. Secondary sources, for example, the biographical page on Edison or the lists of his inventions, are developed from original information with an author's intervention. Consequently, secondary sources are susceptible to human error and cannot always be trusted. For this reason, many educational institutions advise students not to rely on popularly curated sources, such as About.com and Wikipedia. In this particular case, the lists of patents—at least the total number of them—agree. About.

com and Wikipedia are exonerated this time as a result of triangulation. Investigating at least three sources supports the claim that Edison patented 1,093 inventions, designs, and processes. Triangulation is the process for answering the question from several sources "Did Edison really receive so many patents?" Thus concludes a mini-lesson in investigative searching. By devoting some time to patent searching and the various sources of information to search, students start to differentiate primary and secondary sources and understand why investigation is important in the latter. Depending on time, students could search for evidence that Edison or someone else invented the things he patented. In this regard, Edison was not always the one to make the breakthrough discovery. Sometimes he made improvements on an existing practice; other times workers in his West Orange, New Jersey, laboratory came up with the ideas that Edison adopted and patented in his name.[13]

Skimming the long list of patents is a powerful way to grasp the extent of Edison's accomplishments. The list of patented inventions tells stories of successive improvements (note how many references there are just to the phonograph), the breadth of Edison's interests, and, paramount for this lesson, American life at the time. Inventions, both then and now, are solutions to problems people face. Entrepreneurs call them pain points.[14] Through his inventions, Edison was responding to the pain points of his day; otherwise his output would not have had such widespread public appeal. An extension of this lesson could be to describe the pain points or needs of the American public through the eyes of Edison's inventions. At this juncture, the diverted lesson could rejoin the published lesson with a discussion of Edison's contributions to entertainment. Or it could move into a richer conversation about the electrification of America in terms of devices he and his team invented that are predecessors of equipment still in use today: perforating pens (tattoos), voice recorders, gummed paper tape, electrical railways, wireless telegraphy, alkaline storage batteries, and much more—a task that calls forth higher-order thinking skills. Adding search emphasis to the lesson doesn't detract from the topic or divert from the competencies targeted. Instead, depending on whether the next step is writing or speaking, students are equipped to:

- Develop the topic with well-chosen, relevant, and sufficient facts; extended definitions; concrete details; quotations; or other information and examples appropriate to the audience's knowledge of the topic (W.10.2b) and
- Come to discussions prepared, having read and researched material under study; explicitly draw on that preparation by referring to evidence from texts and other research on the topic or issue to stimulate a thoughtful, well-reasoned exchange of ideas. (SL.10.1a).

The three lesson excerpts represent ways to embed information fluency in standards based mainstream curriculum. Absent from this trio is any overall integration or plan for addressing information fluency across the curriculum and grade levels. There simply isn't space in this book to compile a comprehensive guide that serves as a blueprint for integrating digital research education in schools. The point is that there are instructional models for achieving this one lesson at a time. Ample opportunities exist in schools for teachers and librarians to create lessons of their own from models like these.

NOTES

1. Marta Brooks and Jodi Allison-Bunnell, "Explorations in American Environmental History," *Library of Congress*, accessed February 26, 2013, http://www.loc.gov/teachers/class roommaterials/lessons/explorations.

2. Jan King and Rena Nisbet, "Out of the Dust: Visions of Dust Bowl History," *Library of Congress*, accessed February 27, 2013, http://www.loc.gov/teachers/classroommaterials/lessons/dust.

3. Robert Gabrick and Barbara Markham, "Thomas Edison, Electricity, and America," *Library of Congress*, accessed March 1, 2013, http://www.loc.gov/teachers/classroommaterials/lessons/edison.

4. "Mission and History," *Library of Congress American Memory*, accessed February 26, 2013, http://memory.loc.gov/ammem/about/index.html.

5. See note 1, http://www.loc.gov/teachers/classroommaterials/lessons/explorations/pro cedureone.html.

6. "The Evolution of the Conservation Movement, 1850-1920," *Library of Congress*, accessed July 17, 2013, http://memory.loc.gov/cgi-bin/query/r?ammem/AMALL:@ field%28NUMBER+@band%28amrvl+vl002%29%29

7. See note 2.

8. See note 2, http://www.loc.gov/teachers/classroommaterials/lessons/dust/photo.html.

9. *Google Images*, https://www.google.com/imghp.

10. See note 3; "The Life of Thomas A. Edison," *Library of Congress American Memory*, accessed June 30, 2013, http://memory.loc.gov/ammem/edhtml/edbio.html.

11. "Search for Patents," *United States Patent and Trademark Office*, last modified October 3, 2012, http://www.uspto.gov/patents/process/search/index.jsp.

12. "Patent Search," *Google*, accessed March 1, 2013, https://www.google.com/?tbm=pts.

13. A. Axelrod, *Edison on Innovation: 102 Lessons in Creativity for Business and Beyond* (San Francisco: Jossey-Bass, 2008), p. 61 (cf., "Edison never publicly gave credit to any of his small army of employees, experimenters, scientists, and craftsmen.").

14. Jeffrey Carter, "What's a Pain Point?" *Points and Figures*, last modified April 27, 2012, http://pointsandfigures.com/2012/04/27/whats-a-pain-point.

9

Curation: Applied Information Fluency

Curation is not a new idea. *Curation* comes from the Latin verb *curare* which means "taking care of someone." It's a short leap to thinking of a curator as one who takes care of things or ideas. Museum curators, for example, are often experts in multiple disciplines. They specialize in arranging artifacts to tell stories and represent concepts. The museum curator may be the first to identify and categorize a new item. Curators do not work alone but are part of a community of experts that consult with each other and discuss trends in the field. If libraries are considered to be museums of printed knowledge, it is easy to accept librarians as curators of processed information. They specialize in careful selection, categorization, and organization to aid patrons as they do their research, casual or formal, in the library. Anyone who has ever asked a librarian for a recommendation or browsed a display of new books has benefited from special curation expertise.

DIGITAL CURATION

A fundamental change has occurred that expands the role of curation from a science performed by specialists to a process within the reach of any skilled researcher. Curators are able to locate, select, contextualize, and interpret information and then share their insights with an audience of like mind. Digital curators practice information fluency as they pursue their interests and discover pearls of quality information in the ocean of content accessible via the Internet. Curated selections are based on an appreciation for what an audience will enjoy or appreciate. Curation develops skills for focusing attention. Creative hunger drives curators to turn over new rocks and keep looking long after they've saved dozens of articles on the same topic. It's not just what's new but what remains to be discovered that fuels the search. Creative insight and deep understanding of complex interactions between subjects inform this search.

First efforts at organized curation grew with the advent of the Web browser. Projects sprang up to create subject directories curated by subject-matter experts. These early efforts were assembled by vetted but generally anonymous editors who developed commercial directories like the Yahoo! Directory,[1] academic creations like INFOMINE,[2] and crowd-sourced encyclopedias like Wikipedia.[3] Professional librarians and information specialists built directories that gained reputations for reliable and credible resources. Wikipedia led the way in community-driven editing to create an encyclopedia with remarkable breadth and depth. With the advent of high-powered social media–driven sharing, curation efforts today are diverging. Groups of curators now build communities around specialized platforms that allow an individual curator to develop a personal brand. This brand can then be leveraged into a more powerful media profile. Unlike the aforementioned subject directories, there is no editorial board overseeing curation communities. Some would argue the lack of oversight makes the curated resources less credible. This has to be balanced against the extraordinary vigor and creativity promoted by open access to curation tools. Active curation has become a way of both learning and social sharing that powerfully promotes information fluency skills.

The complexity of ideas being actively discussed on the Internet provides a rich field for curators who follow multiple subjects with an eye toward spotting relationships. Take for example the TED Talks[4] series of lectures found online. Typically a TED talk will bring new perspectives and an appreciation for interrelationships to the viewer. The TED topic lists[5] offer a fascinating archive of insights from thought leaders in all fields. TED Talks are one lens on the modern topics that curators favor. Each of the following topics has 30 or more talks in the archives: alternative energy, architecture, astronomy, biology, biotechnology, brain activity, collaboration, communications, creativity, critical thinking, economics, education, freedom, gender equality, genetics, global awareness, global governance, God, human behavior, humanity, information, innovation, inspiration, knowledge, life, peace, quantum physics, renewable energy, social networks, society, sustainability, and technology. Any curator looking at this list of tagged resources will soon disappear in the archives of multidisciplinary ideas only to return with new thinking to share. The practice of following current thought on complex topics by selective curation of content is a way to learn and teach as part of a process of the continuous refinement of information fluency.

Compare the in-depth reading, thinking, and sharing implied by the TED archive with the simple social sharing of a Facebook "like" or retweeting of untagged comments on Twitter. This kind of simple information broadcasting is not content curation. The ephemeral unorganized churning of information on social systems can be tagged and transformed by a curator's discerning eye. Indeed the focus and categorization in hash-tag–driven[6] messaging on Twitter is a prime example of freelance curation that makes accurately tagged 140-character Tweets keys to Internet riches.

All of this is part of building a collective brain on a specific topic. Curation involves finely calibrated, technically enhanced curiosity that focuses a collaborative expert lens on a particular "niche" of information. Instead of broadcasting to the world what one "likes," a content curator serves a particular audience within a self-defined niche interest. Indeed, relying solely on casual sharing limits a person's source of ideas to an unfocused stream of random content that can soon feel like information overload. Limiting one's information input to friends on Twitter and Facebook creates a kind of "filter bubble," which Eli Pariser describes as a self-fulfilling prophecy.[7] Pariser speaks to the idea that relying too heavily on "personalized information" delivered by social media systems or the predictive algorithms of search engines invisibly limits access to information. These prescribed filters prevent diverse ideas from passing through, fostering a biased worldview.

The first step in becoming a curator of information is to find great curators to follow. The authors' beginning efforts at social curation (tagging photos, sharing links, creating blog posts, etc.), when combined with skimming the work of experts, helps mitigate the unorganized filter bubble. Information-fluency skills are invaluable for evaluating and sharing information. According to Steven Rosenbaum, author of *Curation Nation,*[8] the curation movement strives to answer the question "Whom do you trust?" Rosenbaum contrasts the traditional editor who labors in obscurity to improve prose and fine-tune punctuation with the curator who develops a personal and trusted brand. Curators endorse content with their reputations. They have skin in the game. They read widely and select carefully, convinced that people will embrace clarity.[9] The game is to help others find valuable, quality information in an age of exponential information growth.

Google CEO Eric Schmidt asserted that there were five exabytes of information created since the dawn of civilization through 2003, but that much information is now created every two days, and the pace is increasing.[10] While the exact amount of information being generated is hard to pin down, all experts agree that the pace of generating data is rapidly increasing. Digital information is growing exponentially.

To grasp the concept of exponential growth, consider the fable about a great sage who sat down to a game of chess with the king. A wager was made. The king promised the sage any gift he could name if he won the game. The sage asked that he only be given grains of rice that would be calculated using the chessboard. On the first square was placed a single grain. The second square doubled that on the first and so on through the remaining squares of the chessboard. The geometric progression is simple at first to comprehend: 1, 2, 4, 8, 16, 32, 64, and 128 completing the first row of the chessboard. The first row represents the accumulated knowledge of mankind prior to the printing press and provides a baseline for future growth. The next row of 8 squares is the output of knowledge to the industrial revolution: 256, 512, 1,024, 2,048, 4,096, 8,192, 16,384, and 32,768. By now, only a quarter of the way across, the chessboard is overflowing with rice. The rice continues to double. The end of the third row approximates Eric Schmidt's description of digital data in 2003. The 24th square now represents 8,388,608 grains of rice. Think of today as the 32nd square: 2.14×10^9 rice grains at the halfway point. The exponential growth of the sage's demands cost him his head in some versions of this tale. In the real world, there is no emperor to terminate the explosive growth of information.

Today's counterparts, information consumers, are left with a seemingly insurmountable problem: how to organize and understand digital information without being buried by it. The answer, to borrow a page from Douglas Adams's *Hitchhiker's Guide to the Galaxy*, is: Don't panic![11] Those who complain about information overload and bemoan the constant flow of random information that only serves to confuse and muddy their thinking usually do not understand how to manage information. Indeed, current research suggests that most Americans enjoy the variety and immediacy of information available on the Internet.[12] Perhaps a better answer to the question of how to live in the information age is to create information filters. Clay Shirky coined the phrase "It's not information overload; it's filter failure" at the Web 2.0 Expo in 2008.[13] He then drove home the point that information overload is nothing new.

It's been many centuries since anyone could claim to have read all the books in existence. Who first cried info-glut? Did having more books than one could read in a lifetime cause a retreat from the enormity of human knowledge? Is it right to claim a migraine and condemn smart phones? No, people educated themselves. Lifelong learners selected realms of knowledge and immersed their minds in traditional studies. Some who went on to earn doctorates might claim that, for a brief moment, they read everything of note on the subject of their fascination. They may even have added something new (and hopefully worthy) to their field of study. Nowadays, the traditional role of academic gatekeeper that worked so well before the Internet is wearing thin. New ways to filter information are needed. Seeking out the work of curators is one way to build new filters while avoiding a filter bubble. Partially relying on the recommendations of expert curators is a way to organize the information sought based on the credibility and commentary of informed others.

A curator locates and shares meaningful information by searching diligently with a variety of tools. The process begins with finely constructed queries to answer specific questions. Over time, curators develop a set of keywords that lead to the information they seek. Because most curators are experts in their fields of interest, they are familiar with the essential tags or keywords that describe their subjects. Not that one needs to be an expert to begin curating information. It is the process of curating using the applied principles of information fluency that will widen and deepen an individual's expertise.

TAXONOMIES AND TAGS

Taxonomies are formally organized descriptors within a field of study that describe and help classify information into named groups. Biology, in particular, is a science organized by the taxonomy of nature. The taxonomy of information is less neatly categorized than biology. The nature of information is so broad and interconnected that there is an almost infinite range of names and descriptors for the fast-growing universe of digital information. Consequently, curators categorize the information using keywords they feel best describe the content. The large-scale public process of tagging information and sharing information with personally generated descriptors results in a folksonomy. Creating commonly understood tags is a collaborative process shared by researchers and curators in an attempt to organize content. This is sometimes referred to as social classification or collaborative tagging.

Tags are powerful keyword search terms. Using tags both to organize and search for information leverages the power of social collaboration. This is a particularly important tactic when searching for fresh information on topics related to modern communications. Flipping through the traditional card catalogs of just a few years ago would produce little or nothing about blogs, wikis, Web 2.0, crowd sourcing, online discussion, social media, or digital footprints. Today, each of these terms is a powerful tag that, combined with professional vocabulary, become highly effective and efficient search queries. Tags are also an essential aspect of dynamic curation systems.

Curators, like librarians or museum specialists, seek to locate, organize, and share information via the Internet. They create automated queries that help them acquire an initial search field. As they select articles, they evaluate the quality of the information they recommend. Information that stands up under evaluation is tagged and displayed in a curation system so that anyone who shares a curator's interests can benefit from the curiosity and hard work of an expert searcher and consumer of information. Curators use keywords/tags as they practice fluent searching. They add tags as they select and organize resources. Tags allow users to sort a collection of articles by specific interests. In some curation systems, tags can then be used to create newspaper- or magazine-like displays of content on demand.

It should be understood that curators do more than locate and organize information. They share their information as well as provide commentary (annotations) to introduce their finds. A synopsis of the content along with personal insight provides context for the source material.

Before curators can share information, they must find credible resources worth sharing. Curators become experts in the evaluation of content as they build digital collections. They know where the information is to be found. They seek Web collections that have credibility (which is established using the evaluation techniques discussed in depth earlier in this text). Blogs, university portals, social networks, open-educational resource archives, subject-matter indexes, and the published work of other curators are all examples of organized digital collections. Many of these collections are found using professional language and tags in queries. At other times, the desired information is contained within databases housed on various servers. Typically, the contents of databases are not crawled and indexed by Web robots. This means the information housed in most databases is invisible to direct search via engines like Google and Bing. This information is often referred to as the "Deep Web" or "Invisible Web."[14] Curators understand that search is a multistep procedure: First, find credible Web sites, and then dig down into the databases looking for additional "hidden" information.

As curators participate in a long-term and ongoing search for information, their skills become finely honed. Typically this means the use of a variety of digital tools to amplify and automate the search process.

SEARCHING WITH MORE THAN ONE SEARCH ENGINE

Information-fluent curators understand that searching with more than one search engine will produce more wide-ranging results. Searching Google and Bing with the same keywords produces similar but not exactly the same results. Valuable information can be found in the differences produced by querying multiple engines. Web services like Bing vs. Google[15] or Twingine,[16] which compares Yahoo! and Bing, make it convenient to compare results.

Table 9.1 illustrates a case in point: a sample search using the query *information fluency* (without quotations). Note that some results are the same in all three search engines. A quick glance reveals that curators who depend on a single search engine will miss important results. Driven by curiosity and employing information-fluency tactics, curators also consider results well beyond the first page of search results. Knowing that different search tools yield different results drives them to integrate multiple sources and pages of information.

Table 9.1. Results of the Query *Information Fluency* Found on the First Pages of Yahoo!, Bing, and Google

	Yahoo!	Bing	Google
21st Century Information Fluency (21cif.com; the authors' home page)	X	X	X
Information Fluency, University of Central Florida (if.ucf.edu)	X	X	X
Information Age Inquiry: Information Fluency (http://virtualinquiry.com/inquiry/inquiry5.htm)	X	X	X
Digital Information Fluency Model (http://21cif.com/resources/difcore/index.html)	X	X	
Information Fluency, Indiana University, Bloomington, Libraries (http://www.libraries. iub.edu/index.php?pageId=8544)	X	X	
Information Fluency Project, Teacher Librarian (http://teacherlibrarian.ning.com/group/informationfluency)	X		

AUTOMATED SEARCHING

Directly searching with Google, Bing, or any other search engine is just part of the curation process. Tag searching Twitter and developing RSS feeds from blogs and other news sources are also involved. Armed with a powerful set of keywords, curators can create automated searches that scour the information flow and deliver an ongoing stream of digital information about the topic of interest. A number of tools are available to automate searching:

- Google Alerts[17]: This system searches Google for any customized search string a user sets. The results are delivered via e-mail.
- Prismatic[18]: This clever site displays feeds from blogs, Twitter, Facebook, and other social media sites matching self-described subject interests. Stories are graphically displayed, giving Prismatic a visual appeal superior to most RSS aggregators.
- RSS Feed Aggregators (Really Simple Syndication): This is a feature that streams the information being constantly published by social media. A feed reader captures that information in one place for easy reading. By subscribing to the feeds of different news sources, a curator has a constant flow of articles at hand. Google Reader (shut down in early 2013) was the best known of the RSS feed readers. Strong options remain with popular choices Feedly,[19] Feed-Demon,[20] and FeedReader.[21]
- Curation Tools with Onboard Search: Most curation platforms include self-search and keyword search of social networks. These results might be delivered on demand or compiled as suggestions available to the curator, as needed.

Effective curation requires remaining open to new ways to find credible information. One of the most valuable sources for credible information is found by following the work of other curators. Because curation is essentially a public act of sharing, following other curators becomes a way to access the information organized by knowledgeable guides. Social bookmarking is an example of this. The power of social bookmarking comes from the community of searchers willing to share their interests publicly. Typical social bookmarking sites use a browser-based widget that captures the URL of the site or page to be bookmarked. The user is prompted for an annotation and keywords (tags) to classify the content. Curators go the extra mile to annotate, tag, and organize their work. Otherwise, social bookmark files quickly become a kitchen junk drawer of odds and ends that obscure useful information. Another important aspect of social bookmarking is the personal profile of the user. This helps information consumers evaluate the background and credentials of the individual saving the sites. By finding solid thinkers, others who share similar interests can peek over their shoulders to profit from their efforts. Their bookmarks may easily be added to one's own lists. Often this means changing tags and adding new annotations. Users are able to browse the selections of curators they decide to trust and selectively republish their finds.

Consider a new system, Scrible,[22] and two of the most popular social bookmark-ing sites, Diigo[23] and Delicious.[24] All of these systems allow users to store and orga-nize Internet bookmarks "in the cloud." Social-bookmarking systems allow users to assemble their own search fields of treasured resources for access from any computer, tablet, or smart phone. These libraries of curated content can then be shared with other users of the system. These systems also suggest tags based on previous choices, enhancing consistency while improving organization. Tagging also helps others in the system to find and use the work of the community. Searching in the rich, human-selected content of social-bookmark systems is one of the many places a curious curator can find valuable information.

Diigo provides a rich set of tools empowering users to treat virtual pages much like they do traditional text. With Diigo, members can highlight text and attach notes. Other Diigo members can read the highlights and notes and leave comments of their own. In this way the social-sharing power of the Internet radically expands on simple underlining and note taking. Additionally, RSS feeds and automatic blog publishing enhance the Diigo bookmark system, helping curators repurpose and publish con-tent they discover. Diigo provides user-initiated interest groups for sharing around specific topics. Bookmarks and annotations shared within a group are then offered as an e-mail newsletter on a subscriber-defined basis.

Delicious is one of the earliest and most popular social systems. To this day, the enormous number of Delicious members provides an extensive search field as an alternate to using search engines. Like Diigo, Delicious offers a way to organize and share bookmarks using tags, automated blog publishing, interest groups, tag lists, and systemwide promotion of the most popular bookmarks. Those who want the rich Diigo toolset but don't want to abandon their Delicious accounts can import and export their work to Diigo, automatically synchronizing bookmarks across both platforms, maintaining the best of both worlds. Many curators maintain both systems as a way to combine the huge resource collection on Delicious with the sophisticated toolset of Diigo.

Scrible is a new online research tool now in public beta. It is supported by a grant from the National Science Foundation. Like Diigo and Delicious, Scrible is a browser-based social-bookmarking tool that collects and organizes resources in the cloud. It offers an exceptional rich editor with text markup, tags, sticky notes, library sharing, and more. Like Diigo, Scrible creates an archive page that will remain online even if the original page disappears. Scrible features a rich highlighting and annotation system. Thirty-two different colors and fonts can be used when marking up Web-page text. Virtual sticky notes (multiple colors) can be attached to any saved page. A clever addition to the system is Legends, a way to organize the highlighting and notes with a self-generated table of contents. Legends enables deep categoriza-tion and sorting. Scrible also keyword indexes the full text of each page saved. This is particularly important because it permits searching beyond the title and annotations of a bookmark. Of particular interest are the citation and bibliography generators that extract available information from a Web page to populate a citation. Available formats are MLA, APA, and Chicago. These citations are saved along with the Web page in research libraries. Citations remain available for bibliographic generation when the need arises. Scrible is a new feature-rich, cloud-based research tool worth exploring.

MAGAZINE-STYLE CURATION TOOLS

A new type of dynamic curation tool combines automated search and magazine-style publication with a rich social-sharing community that promotes cross-pollination of ideas and resources. These tools use a browser-based widget and make it easy to select and save articles of interest. Moreover, they encourage the use of article snippets to capture the reader's attention. The graphic display created by these systems is an attractive and easy-to-browse online magazine. The curator chooses an image and a selection of text to be displayed from the source article. Depending on the system, a curator is prompted to add personal annotations and comments on the quality of the information. This makes the curator's endorsement of the content explicit and helps a curator build a trusted brand. A hyperlink is automatically included, pointing to the source of the content. The reader is a single click from the source, driving them to the source, providing a boost in traffic for the content creator. These kinds of sites also allow active displays of video content; most will display a live window of YouTube or Vimeo streams.

Curation tools are relatively new but are catching on quickly as the power of curated content is recognized as a quality alternative to traditional search engine results. Among quickly growing curation systems are Pinterest,[25] Storify,[26] and Scoop.it.[27] Pinterest has exploded in popularity over the last year. It's been called a social media award winner, growing 1,047 percent during 2012.[28] Initially, Pinterest facilitated sharing of images, which may be tagged, noted, and pinned by the member/curator. Today, Pinterest encourages users to collect and share their favorite Internet-based images and videos using a browser-based widget. At present, PDF or word-processed content cannot be displayed. Like the other systems, clicking on the pinned image guides the user back to the original source. Pinterest populates a text box with information scraped from the original site. The curator may replace this text. Individual selections can be commented upon or repinned by other members. Pinterest members can follow Pinboards that are displayed on the user's home page. This encourages sharing and exploring. Like all curation systems, consumers of information, not search engine algorithms, make the selections. Pinterest, in an effort to build community norms, suggests specific etiquette: Be respectful, be yourself, give credit, be alert, and let us know. These guidelines are designed to encourage personal curiosity and authenticity and honor creators of content while self-policing a family-friendly community.[29] It is important to note that the system does little to prompt attribution other than state users should honor content creators. Issues of fair use and copyright are left up to the user.

Storify is a favorite of journalists. A newspaper metaphor is built in. Upon logging into Storify, the "best stories" on any topic are displayed on the front page. These stories are gathered from Storify users and from major television and print publications. Users are encouraged to like, comment upon, and reuse the front-page stories. Each page has a search box to encourage users to search Storify for the latest content posted by users of the system. Social networks are also easy to curate. Users are prompted to collect content via Twitter, Facebook, YouTube, Flickr, Instagram, Tumblr, RSS, and other social media sources. The system uses a drag-and-drop editor to assemble social media images into subject-themed pages. However, content layout is limited to a standard, centered-down-the-middle display. A browser-based widget is used to add Web content to one's Storify workspace. When a story is selected with the widget, the user has an opportunity to comment. However, once the article is posted, these comments cannot be edited. On the Storify page itself, the user can edit the header, but there is no way directly to add original text. Storify also generates an embed code, making it easy to add work to other Web sites. A noticeable weakness in this system is the absence of tags. Content is fully searchable but lacks the deeper organizational power of tagging.

Scoop.it is distinguished by its exceptional graphic appeal and powerful social media–broadcasting features (see figure 9.1). A Scoop.it page is made vivid by the

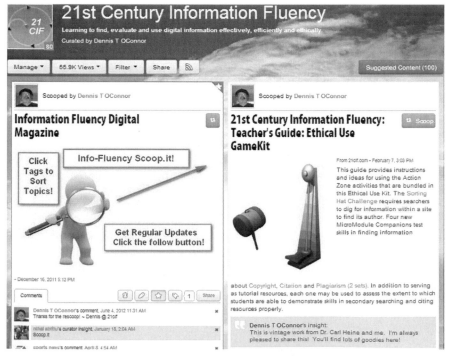

Figure 9.1.   21st Century Information Fluency Scoop.it Page

variable sizing of graphics and page layout choices for each article selected by the curator. Initially, any graphics available in the article being curated are captured and can be resized and arranged on the page. There is an option to upload other graphics as well. The curator is prompted to provide a snippet of text from the original source to intrigue the reader. A second text box is preformatted to separate the curator's comments from the original publication. These text boxes have rich editing tools with a variety of fonts and hyperlink capabilities. Tags can be added to each post. The system will suggest tags based on previous use to improve consistency. By filtering the content with tags, it is possible to assemble a tag-driven publication on demand. This means readers can assemble magazines to match their interests. Scoop.it also acts as a social media dashboard. New curated posts can be forwarded to Twitter, Facebook, Linked In, WordPress and Tumblr Blogs, Google+, Pinterest, and StumbleUpon. This makes a curator's selections instant social media. Comments and thumbs-up support are available. Similar to Pinterest, Scoop.it users are encouraged to "rescoop" the content of other curators. They also have a built-in recommendation system that will send resources to other curators being followed within the system. By following the work of other curators, a rich search field is generated that becomes one of the first places a skilled curator scans when looking for new information. In addition to the other social media push features of Scoop.it, there is a newsletter-generation feature that leverages the power of e-mail lists. Tag-driven newsletters can be easily assembled and then exported to the MailChimp newsletter system. This provides yet another way to share content with followers.

CASE STUDY: 21CIF SCOOP.IT MAGAZINE

Using Scoop.it, the authors have curated information-fluency content for several years. A quick look at the most popular tags describes the search universe and interest area of the *21st Century Information Fluency* publication.[30] These tags can be used to assemble an on-demand information fluency–oriented magazine dedicated to the tagged topic. Content tagged "21cif" indicates materials from the 21st Century Information Fluency Web site. Other tags will call up content from across the Web (including the original work of the authors).

Here are the most used tags, a digital snapshot of the universe of information fluency:

- 21cif
- bias
- citation
- collaboration
- common-core
- copyright
- creative commons
- critical-thinking

- curation
- digital-citizenship
- digital forensics
- evaluation
- fact-checking
- fair use
- games
- Google+
- information-fluency
- information-literacy
- knowledge-management
- library2.0
- plagiarism
- research
- search
- Web2.0

Scoop.it provides a powerful way to rebroadcast the resources found on the 21st Century Information Fluency Website.[31] At the same time, Scoop.it opens a door to the many new resources found online. The process of curation using Scoop.it is straightforward:

- Open the Web page to be curated.
- Select and copy a representative passage from the Web page.
- Look for an explanation of concept or purpose that will quickly orient the reader.
- Click the Scoop.it widget embedded in the browser toolbar, launching the curation window. Scoop.it then opens a quarter-page-sized window on top of the resource being curated. The system scans the page and fills in the initial values. A title is suggested based on the <title> html field of the page. The curator is free to edit this title for clarity. An image from the page—if one exists—is visible. This image can be changed at the curator's discretion. The idea is to use an image that communicates the big idea of the article or page being curated. Awareness of the visual design of the publication will help the reader have a more satisfying experience. Image size and placement can be manipulated by the curator to maximize impact on the page.
- A text field is available where the curator pastes the descriptive text copied earlier from the page.
- Another text space is available for the curator's comments.
- The curator is prompted to add tags.
- The curator can share the content with other social media outlets.

As the curator begins to key the tagged words, the system suggests tags that have already been used. This helps maintain consistency. The curator tags with the intent of being able to assemble a page of tag results. This allows any user to assemble a magazine of articles that share a common tag.

Additionally, to leverage the social-media power of the Internet, a curator can forward a new post to a customized list of WordPress blogs, Twitter, Facebook, LinkedIn, Pinterest, Google+, and StumbleUpon accounts. This kind of social sharing is semiautomated by Scoop.it. Each post broadcast to social media includes a backlink that returns the viewer to the curator's page. The article is highlighted on the curator's home page. From there the user can scan the article snippet and curator's comments and then click through to the source of the article or close the article and browse the curator's entire collection of resources.

Another feature encourages Scoop.it curators to follow and share articles with each other (see figure 9.2). With a few clicks, it is possible to rescoop any article from any curator in the system. By following other curators interested in information fluency and literacy, one can build a rich field of suggested articles from trusted curators. It's no surprise that Internet-oriented librarians like Joyce Valenza[32] and Buffy Hamilton[33] are active Scoop.it curators. Scoop.it serves up a display of the most current articles from curators being followed. This delivers pages of articles selected by trusted curators. This is information delivered by other thoughtful minds rather than a search engine algorithm. It is also possible to search the Scoop.it database using keywords or tags, thereby discovering new curators and new content. With time, a Scoop.it member can build a community of curators on a variety of topics that deliver a steady stream of high-quality articles.

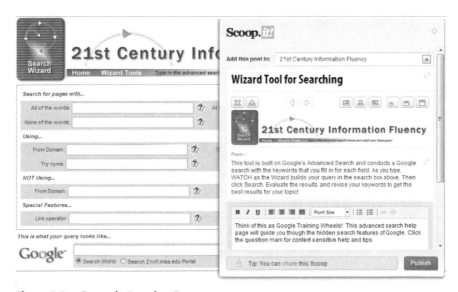

Figure 9.2. Scoop.it Curation Frame

EVALUATING A CURATOR'S CREDENTIALS

Thus far in this recapitulation of the information fluency model, curation has been viewed through the lens of "What information do I need?" and "Where will I find it?" Following "How will I get there?" comes "How good is the information?" Evaluation leads directly to questions of trust. As consumers of information, curators are acutely interested in a broad range of informed opinion as well as solid facts on their topics of interest. To verify the abilities of fellow curators, they employ the same techniques used to determine the credibility of an author. Look at the quality of the articles a curator chooses to share. Are they lightweight popular pieces, press releases, or links to ad-dominated pages? Do they promote a specific product? These issues could be red flags. On the other hand, if the selections and comments made by a curator show quality judgment, their work may be followed with a critical eye. The intent is not to rescoop everything they post. Instead, curators selectively browse the posts of others to rescoop work valuable enough to endorse.

Evaluation is driven by the quality of the search results shared by the curator. Do the article choices speak to an area of shared interest? If so, proceed. Some curiosity about the curator is wise. Search out the curator on other social media. A good choice is LinkedIn because it tends to profile members' fields of expertise. One might also check Twitter, Facebook, or Google+. Furthermore, many curators are active on social-bookmarking systems, making it possible to see their work in a different venue. Due diligence of this sort is required only one time. The most important measure is clear evidence-informed judgment as demonstrated by the selections and annotations provided with each selection. Another evaluative measure is the freshness and volume of the information shared. Inactive curators fade from view. Current information is publicly valued. Curators with multiple pages of current content are most likely to provide information of interest. Additionally, the number of followers and community engagement metrics provided by Scoop .it is an indicator of quality. Ultimately, whom to follow and whom to ignore is a decision based on a reader's educated judgment of the quality of the article and the credibility of the curator.

EVALUATING THE QUALITY OF THE ARTICLES TO CURATE

Answering the essential evaluation question "How good is the information?" the process of evaluation can move very quickly. The following description examines a curator's evaluation activities step by step.

First, evaluate the quality of a search result. Does the article under consideration answer the natural-language question? If one is interested in the old Washington Senators baseball team, reading articles about old-time politicians doesn't answer the basic question. In that case the query should be revised until the search retrieves relevant answers.

Next, it must be determined if the article is reliable. Investigate the author using a search engine. It's best not to rely solely on the "About Us" link or profile information supplied by the writer. What is the author's experience in the subject area? What does the author do for a living? Does the author have a good reputation with other experts? Is contact information provided?

The online publisher should also be considered. Is the publisher a mass provider of blog space? Is the publisher an established organization with a mission statement? Does the publisher broadcast work by only one author, or are other writers at work? Is it easy to find the publisher and related contact information?

Is the article itself accurate? Do the facts need to be checked? If so, triangulate fact checking using three reliable sources. Specific data, like statistics and dates, are easy to check. Do other topic-area specialists accept the evidence provided by the author? Does the information contain typos or grammatical errors?

The voice of the writer is also important. Can bias be detected? Is the author presenting a full range of facts, or is the focus so narrow that relevant information is ignored? Is there evidence of exaggerated or extreme language? Is a commercial intent hidden in the message? If "the voice" is trying to sell something, the material invites a deeper look.

This isn't necessarily a process to be employed for every article curated. However, it is helpful to have what Howard Rheingold calls a good "crap detector."[34] If something seems amiss, information-fluency investigative techniques should be applied to verify the information before it is consumed and shared. After all, one's reputation as a curator is on the line with every article endorsed.

CURATION AND ETHICAL USE

As discussed in chapter 7, the heart of ethical use is citation. A reader must understand that a curator is recommending and commenting on someone else's work. When curating content, hyperlinks act as an informal citation, taking the reader directly to the source material. Special attention should be paid when copying snippets of text from the original material into a curation post. Copied text should be enclosed in quotation marks and credited to an author whenever possible. An apt quote, the author's name, and a hyperlink to the original source create a useful online citation.

The conscientious content curator always digs down to the source material. When curating a blog article about the American Library Association, there is an opportunity to also curate the main page of the ALA and any subpages in discussion. This does require a judgment call. If a blog piece on the ALA contains a link to a specific ALA page, the source is covered. The curator must make a decision: Which is more vital: an article discussion on an ALA resource or original material itself? If the blog writer has provided value-added insights, curate the article. If the source is rich and deserves more than a passing comment, curate the original content.

FOUR-FACTOR TEST FOR FAIR USE

One might also raise the question of fair use in the curation process. Is the curator, by republishing links to another's intellectual property, violating the principles of fair use? "The Four Factor Fair Use Test"[35] is a guide to best practices of fair use for curators when selecting articles.

Factor 1: Does the purpose and character of the use add new meaning or added value to the original?

- Curators choose a short representative sample of the original to orient the reader.
- Curators use an illustration from the article or provide an image that captures the concept of the article.
- Curators add an annotation that provides background, context, or additional information supporting the article.

Factor 2: What is the nature of the copyrighted work?

- Curators select from published work, usually work that is published on the Internet.
- Curators generally work with factual materials.

Factor 3: What is the amount and substance of the portion taken?

- Curators use only a brief snippet (less than 10 percent) of the original work.
- Curators leave the "heart of the work" to be discovered when reading the original source.

Factor 4: What is the effect of the use upon potential market?

- The copyright owner's income is likely to be helped by increased readership.
- Curation expands the market for the copyrighted work.

CURATION AS EDUCATION

Noam Chomsky wrote, "The purpose of education is to help people determine how to learn on their own."[36] The mission of 21st Century Information Fluency Project (and this book) is to unpack the skills and explain the digital tools that make self-determined learning possible. Curating information on a topic demands fluency with information. Fluency arms the curator, who is also following the work of other curators, to engage in self-determined education. Teachers who use curation purposely have a way to engage students in the active practice of information-fluent thinking. As students participate in a dynamic world of research, fanning their curiosity and exploring new interests, they gain lifelong skills for knowledge discovery.

Modern educators understand that simply memorizing and regurgitating facts does not work in an information age. New ideas and new discoveries are the norm. Information moves faster than the printing press. Most new knowledge is digital. The old literacies are giving way to the new. This shifting landscape of information is real for both teachers and students. When change is constant, the ability to locate and select reliable and relevant digital information is essential.

Practicing curation helps students develop the advanced skills needed to evaluate and select content to meet complex goals and solve real-world problems. Simply collecting facts won't help students make sense of complex issues. College-ready thinking can only be accomplished by practicing the higher levels of Bloom's taxonomy: acquisition, interpretation, categorization, creation, evaluation, and synthesis. Throughout the curation process, searchers begin to comprehend complex relationships between different subjects that may have been obscured by the silo-driven approach of traditional education. Teaching the information-fluency research process—as a way to explore personal interests—fosters a better understanding of complex relationships. That process can be put into action by helping students learn to use dynamic curation tools. This may be achieved as part of interdisciplinary units and lessons that explicitly teach the research process infused with information fluency.

As students become curators, the research phase of specific discipline writing is transformed from copying encyclopedia facts to notecards to curating content from credible sources. Students who find fresh articles or information graphics that explain real-word issues gain clarity and insight as they assemble their sources. They become engaged with real-world problems and a range of solutions. The act of curation provides authentic practice in the skills of locating, evaluating, and ethically using information.

Instead of handing students canned information with preprocessed questions and answers, learners are encouraged to practice critical thinking as they grapple with the slippery mess of online information. The process of curation can start simply and evolve into increasingly demanding formal comparison, analysis, and synthesis of ideas. Curation front-loads the idea-generating activities of the writing process in an organized and public way that can be the basis for important lessons about the mechanics of search, the interpretation of information, and the composition of research papers.

MODEL LESSON: CURATION AND THE RESEARCH PROCESS

Subject Area: (Open)
    Students: Grades 9–12

Established Goals:

- Create an online magazine of curated articles by engaging deeply in the information-fluency process
- Demonstrate an understanding of how to locate, evaluate, and ethically use digital information
- Share results of collaborative research via social media (Facebook, Twitter, Google+, Project Blog)
- Write an expository or persuasive paper, including direct quotations from curated content, citations, and a bibliography

Common Core Standards[37]:

- W-7, WHST-7. Conduct short as well as more sustained research projects to answer a question (including a self-generated question) or solve a problem; narrow or broaden the inquiry when appropriate; synthesize multiple sources on the subject, demonstrating understanding of the subject under investigation
- W-8, WHST-8. Gather relevant information from multiple authoritative print and digital sources, using advanced searches effectively; assess the usefulness of each source in answering the research question; integrate information into the text selectively to maintain the flow of ideas, avoiding plagiarism and following a standard format for citation
- RH-7. Integrate and evaluate multiple sources of information presented in diverse formats and media (e.g., visually, quantitatively, as well as in words) in order to address a question or solve a problem
- RH-8. Evaluate an author's premises, claims, and evidence by corroborating or challenging them with other information

Understandings:

- Students will understand the online research process.
- Students will understand investigative searching when evaluating digital content.
- Students will understand that curation involves mindfully searching, evaluating, and ethically republishing digital resources.

Essential Questions:

- What information are you looking for?
- What is the optimal search strategy?
- Where will you find the information?
- How will you get there?
- How good is the information?
- How will I ethically use the information?

Students will be able to:

- Locate and evaluate digital information for creditability and bias
- Contribute to a collaboratively generated Scoop.it magazine
- Tag curated content with accurately descriptive keywords
- Write an expository or persuasive composition with proper use of quotations
- Assemble Chicago-style (or other assigned style) citations into a bibliography for curated Web content

Performance Tasks:

- Assemble keywords into queries used on multiple search engines
- Search for relevant content in Scoop.it archives and Open Educational Resources (OER) archives
- Evaluate Web pages for credibility
- Investigate the author of an article or Web site
- Investigate the publisher of a Web site
- Recognize multiple types of plagiarism
- Create accurate Chicago-style citations

Self-Assessments:

- Complete self-paced learning modules for:
  - Identifying author[38]
  - Identifying publisher[39]
  - Recognizing plagiarism[40]
- Use 21CIF Evaluation Wizard to investigate one Web site in depth[41]
- Use 21CIF Citation wizard to complete citations[42]

Alternate Assessment:

- Complete 21CIF "Information Investigator 5.0" self-paced class.[43]

Learning Activities:

1. Working as a group, students brainstorm a list of subject-appropriate topics. (This plan can be used to combine information-fluency skills with any curriculum.)
2. Students complete self-paced 21CIF training modules. (Authenticate performance with screen-capture of final results and save as image files.)
3. Individual or group topics assigned.
4. Generate keywords (proper nouns, professional language) to describe search topic.

5. Revise keywords based on initial search results.
6. Each student finds X number of articles on the research topic.
7. Students check essential facts by triangulation.
8. Search OER archives.
9. Search Scoop.it archives.
10. Search topics with Google/Yahoo!/Bing.
11. Revise keywords based on initial search results.
12. Document search results by curating articles to a Scoop.it magazine.
13. Each curator selects a brief snippet of text from the curated article that best represents the big idea presented in that article.
14. Using the curator's insight text field, each curator writes an annotation explaining the significance of the curated article.
15. Using the curator's insight text field, each curator provides a Chicago-style formatted citation for the curated article.
16. Curators carefully tag articles to indicate their topic and annotation authorship.
17. Keep in mind that a specialized magazine dedicated to individual topics will be generated using tags. Teachers may want to develop a strong tag strategy ahead of time to maximize the tag-generated magazine features of Scoop.it.
18. Curators review each other's articles, leaving comments and thumbs-up feedback.
19. Curators broadcast curated posts to social media outlets (class WordPress blog recommended).
20. Curators review the articles of their peers, looking for interconnections between articles.
21. Curators write a reflective-process journal describing the steps they took to complete their research tasks.
22. Curators write and (blog) publish an expository or persuasive essay detailing the topic they researched. The essay includes properly quoted content from articles curated during the research phase of project.
23. Curators generate a bibliography of resources published on Scoop.it to be included in an essay.
24. Curators enable hyperlinking of resources in a bibliography to curated articles in a Scoop.it magazine.

THE ADVANTAGES OF INFORMATION FLUENCY

The ability to locate, evaluate, and ethically use content provides a learner with the tools to use the rapidly multiplying OER portals offered by major universities like Stanford,[44] Harvard,[45] MIT,[46] and Berkeley.[47] OER portals are typically published with a Creative Commons license encouraging consumption and free redistribution. Subject-matter experts contribute indexed works as a way to provide quality information to the world. The open courses now available on the Web represent another major development in self-directed learning. These courses present original sources for student research.

Teaching students to curate quality content from a rich field of sources takes them beyond the search box and the automated results of Google, Yahoo!, or Bing. Curation teaches students to appreciate the human qualities of reliability and reputation. Instead of blindly accepting information provided by algorithms promoting advertizing interests, a student turns to quality information selected by a reputable curator or assembled by knowledgeable editors.

Information-fluency curation skills do more than foster a self-directed approach to learning. They prepare students for a rapidly changing job market. The Apollo Research Group suggests in their report "The Future of Work"[48] the following essential work skills for the year 2020. These skills also describe the abilities of an advanced curator:

- Trans-disciplinarity
- Sense-making
- Novel and adaptive thinking
- Social intelligence
- New media literacy
- Design mindset
- Cognitive load management
- Virtual collaboration
- Cross-cultural competency
- Computational thinking

Surely, anyone adept at using higher-level thinking skills to discover the interconnectedness of information can become an editor, a teacher, a publisher, or an expert coach in their areas of passionate interest. Students taught these skills will be better prepared for college studies and emerging worlds of work. Information fluency practiced via content curation helps lay a foundation for future success.

UNIVERSAL DISPOSITIONS

Curation is a holistic approach that promotes creative and critical thinking. To curate a topic requires certain universal dispositions that promote information fluency.[49] Curators must be confident in their abilities to locate appropriate information. Curators are also persistent as they practice the craft of locating, evaluating, and sharing digital information. This persistence is demonstrated by a focused pursuit of timely and accurate information retrieval. Good curators are seldom distracted by off-topic content. At the same time, they remain open to new concepts relating to their chosen topics. This includes new methods of acquiring information about their interests.

Discovering new archives of primary sources, utilizing advanced search tools and specialized search engines, applying social search tools, innovatively using tags, and collecting visualizations of data all help curators better to understand, interpret, and share information. This process is fueled by an unending curiosity about the world of information and questions that will yield answers. Info-glut isn't worrisome. Curators don't drown in information; they revel in it.

Careful searching and reading expressed as curation is a combination of intuition, art, and science. Curation documents a path to new ideas, new tools, and new techniques for finding and sharing answers about everything. This pursuit fosters the resiliency and persistence needed to overcome frustration and work around or go through roadblocks to collect the best thinking on any given topic. These dispositions are developed through the active pursuit of curation; they are useful in every walk of life.

Truly, to be a curator is to navigate the world of digital information with a growing sense that one can find or create answers for any question posited. The dispositions described here cannot be taught and tested in a few lessons. Dispositions are not quickly developed or mastered. Information-fluency dispositions are built over time by the repeated application and enthusiastic exploration of the research process. Curation is one way to acquire and strengthen information-fluency dispositions that evolve over a lifetime and act as a foundation for an open, curious, confident mindset.

NOTES

1. "Yahoo! Directory," *Yahoo!*, accessed April 30, 2013, http://dir.yahoo.com.
2. "INFOMINE: Scholarly Internet Resource Collections," *The Regents of the University of California*, accessed April 30, 2013, http://infomine.ucr.edu.
3. *Wikipedia*, accessed April 30, 2013, http://www.wikipedia.org.
4. *TED*, accessed April 14, 2013, http://www.ted.com/talks.
5. "TED Conversations: Topics," *TED*, accessed April 14, 2013, http://www.ted.com/conversations/topics/communication.
6. "Using Hashtags on Twitter," *Twitter*, accessed April 30, 2013, https://support.twitter.com/articles/49309-what-are-hashtags-symbols.
7. Eli Pariser, *The Filter Bubble: What the Internet Is Hiding from You* (New York: Penguin, 2011).
8. Steven Rosenbaum, *Curation Nation: How to Win in a World Where Consumers Are Creators* (New York: McGraw Hill, 2011).
9. Steven Rosenbaum, "TED[x] Grand Rapids: Innovate: Curation!" *YouTube*, last modified June 6, 2011, http://www.youtube.com/watch?v=iASluLoKQbo.
10. M. G. Siegler, "Eric Schmidt: Every 2 Days We Create as Much Information as We Did up to 2003," *Techcrunch*, last modified August 4, 2010, http://techcrunch.com/2010/08/04/schmidt-data.
11. Douglas Adams, *The Hitchhiker's Guide to the Galaxy, 25th Anniversary Edition* (New York: Del Rey Books, 2009).

12. Eszter Hargittai, W. Russell Neuman, and Olivia Curry, "Taming the Information Tide: Perceptions of Information Overload in the American Home," *The Information Society*, 28, no. 3 (2012): 161–73, accessed April 14, 2013, http://www.indiana.edu/~tisj/28/3/hargittai.html.

13. Clay Shirky, "Web 2.0 Expo NY: It's Not Information Overload. It's Filter Failure," *YouTube*, last modified September 19, 2008, http://www.youtube.com/watch?v=LabqeJEOQyL.

14. Dennis O'Connor, "What Is the Invisible Web? How Can You Search It? Why Would You Want To?" *21st Century Information Fluency*, last modified 2006, http://21cif.com/tutorials/micro/mm/invisible.

15. Domagoj Pavlčšić, *Bing vs. Google*, accessed April 14, 2013, http://www.bing-vs-google.com.

16. Asgeir S. Nilsen, *Twingine*, last modified 2005, http://www.twingine.no.

17. "Alerts," *Google*, accessed April 14, 2013, http://www.google.com/alerts.

18. *Prismatic*, accessed April 14, 2013, http://getprismatic.com.

19. *Feedly Reader*, accessed April 14, 2013, http://www.feedly.com.

20. *FeedDemon*, accessed April 14, 2013, http://feeddemon.com.

21. *FeedReader*, accessed April 14, 2013, http://www.feedreader.com.

22. *Beta Scrible*, accessed April 14, 2013, http://www.scrible.com.

23. *Diigo*, accessed April 14, 2013, http://www.diigo.com.

24. *Delicious*, accessed April 14, 2013, https://delicious.com.

25. *Pinterest*, accessed April 14, 2013, http://pinterest.com.

26. *Storify*, accessed April 14, 2013, http://storify.com.

27. *Scoop.it*, accessed April 14, 2013, http://www.scoop.it.

28. Greg Finn, "Pinning the Competition: Pinterest's Four-Digit Growth Is Tops of 2012,"*Marketing Land*, last modified December 4, 2012, http://marketingland.com/pinning-the-competition-pinterests-four-digit-growth-is-tops-of-2012-27769.

29. "Here Are the Basics of Getting Started on Pinterest," *Pinterest*, accessed April 14, 2013, http://about.pinterest.com/basics.

30. Dennis O'Connor, "21st Century Information Fluency: Learning to Find, Evaluate and Use Digital Information Effectively, Efficiently and Ethically," *Scoop.it*, accessed April 14, 2013, http://www.scoop.it/t/21st-century-information-fluency.

31. Carl Heine, *21st Century Information Fluency*, last modified April 16, 2013, http://21cif.com.

32. Joyce Valenza, "Joyce Valenza: Teacher-Librarian, Learner, Blogger," *Scoop.it*, accessed April 14, 2013, http://www.scoop.it/u/joyce-valenza#curatedTopicsTabSelected.

33. Buffy Hamilton, "Curation for Learning: How People Are Curating, Utilizing, and Sharing Information," *Scoop.it*, accessed April 14, 2013, http://www.scoop.it/t/curation-for-learning.

34. Howard Rheingold, "Crap Detection Mini-Course," *Howard Rheingold*, accessed April 14, 2013, http://rheingold.com/2013/crap-detection-mini-course.

35. Carl Heine, "The Four Factor Fair Use Test," *21st Century Information Fluency*, accessed April 14, 2013, http://21cif.com/rkitp/curriculum/v1n8/quickpick_v1n8.html.

36. Noam Chomsky, "Noam Chomsky: The Purpose of Education," *Learning without Frontiers*, last modified February 1, 2012, http://www.learningwithoutfrontiers.com/2012/02/noam-chomsky-the-purpose-of-education.

37. For more on how Common Core Standards relate to the Information Fluency Model, see Carl Heine, "Common Core State Standards Mapped to the Information Fluency Model,"

21st Century Information Fluency, last modified January 1, 2013, https://21cif.com/resources/difcore/ccss-dif.html.

38. Carl Heine, "Who Is the Author? An Interactive MicroModule Companion," *21st Century Information Fluency*, accessed April 14, 2013, http://21cif.com/rkitp/challenge/evaluation/author.swf.

39. Carl Heine, "Who Is the Publisher? An Interactive MicroModule Companion," *21st Century Information Fluency*, accessed April 14, 2013, http://21cif.com/rkitp/challenge/evaluation/publisher.swf.

40. Carl Heine, "Plagiarism I: An Interactive MicroModule Companion," *21st Century Information Fluency*, accessed April 14, 2013, http://21cif.com/rkitp/challenge/v1n8/plagiarism.swf.

41. Carl Heine, "Online Citation Wizards," *21st Century Information Fluency*, last modified February 12, 2013, http://21cif.com/tools/cite.

42. See note 41.

43. Carl Heine, "Self-Guided Assessment and Tutorial Packages," *21st Century Information Fluency*, last modified January 1, 2013, http://21cif.com/selfguided.html.

44. "Resources," *Stanford University, Stanford ASEE*, accessed April 14, 2013, http://www.stanford.edu/group/asee/cgi-bin/wiki/index.php/Resources.

45. "What Is DASH?" *Digital Access to Scholarship at Harvard*, accessed April 14, 2013, http://dash.harvard.edu.

46. "MITOpenCourseware," *Massachusetts Institute of Technology*, accessed April 14, 2013, http://ocw.mit.edu/index.htm.

47. "Digital Berkeley: Making Open Educational Resources," *Townsend Humanities Lab*, accessed April 14, 2013, http://townsendlab.berkeley.edu/digital-berkeley-making-open-educational-resources.

48. "The Future of Work," *Apollo Research Institute*, accessed 14 April 2013, http://apolloresearchinstitute.com/sites/default/files/future_of_work_report_final.pdf.

49. David Barr, "Rubrics: Dispositions," *21st Century Information Fluency*, accessed April 14, 2013, http://21cif.com/resources/difcore/index.html#dispositions.

Epilogue:
Looking Back

In a world of exponential digital information growth, teaching did not keep pace. Instead of systematic information-fluency training, twenty-first-century schools imposed filters and prohibitions. Instead of teaching students how to search for, evaluate, and cite information, teachers did the searching for the students, substituting Web quests and safe sites in place of the real thing. While students were not completely denied access to the Internet, their experience was, consistently, not with the real Internet. How well were learners, insulated in this way, prepared to query, browse, evaluate, and use what they find online?

By the time students reached college, most were mediocre searchers and careless consumers of information, ignorant of the need to evaluate and confused about how to avoid plagiarism. There wasn't a single study that suggested otherwise. While many good reasons existed to safeguard students, walling off portions of the Internet didn't prepare them to live without walls when they left school. Students remained poorly equipped to work with more than a handful of databases, to find information efficiently, and to avoid being scammed.

Hopefully, when future generations look back on the early part of the twenty-first century, this is not the history they will see. In large measure, it is the story being played out in our time and contains more fact than fiction. Unless current practices change, there is no reason to believe that the majority of teachers, students, and citizens will be any more information fluent in a decade than they are today. Search engines and software cannot completely make up for a lack of critical skills.

GOING FORWARD

This book asserts that most students are self-taught searchers—which is also true in the case of teachers. Self-taught strategies tend to work well enough when challenges are easy. The success rate dips to 50 percent or lower when hard-to-retrieve information is targeted, including academic-level research.[1] Moreover, investigative techniques are not intuitive; they need to be taught. Teachers who don't know how to fact check, search the Deep Web, or find elusive publication dates and backlinked secondary sources in order to evaluate the credibility of information are ill-equipped to pass those skills along to their students. Professional development in this area is sorely needed, made more challenging by the fact that teachers tend to overrate their skills. Exposing educators to intermediate and advanced querying and browsing, using unfamiliar databases, and tracking down elusive information for the purpose of evaluation and citation is strongly encouraged.

To some extent, Common Core State Standards represent a positive step forward. The standards directly embrace information-fluency competencies. Nonetheless, without a way to assess research competencies, reading and writing—competencies that are currently measured—will continue to demand the lion's share of attention. Teachers tasked with improving scores in language acquisition, reading, and writing will have precious little time left to devote to information gathering from digital sources, evaluating its worth, and teaching ethical use. While information-fluency instruction can be used directly and indirectly to reinforce reading, writing, and speaking in language arts, social studies, and science courses, this use has yet to be pioneered in many classes.

The approach recommended throughout this book involves blending search challenges with other instruction. Sufficient explanation is provided in the model lessons for teachers to become fluent searchers and investigators. Lead teachers and curriculum specialists may use these materials as a foundation for professional-development experiences. Reading about methods is not enough, however; it takes hands-on practice to become fluent and form lasting habits of mind. Still, embedded instruction doesn't have to take significant time away from other learning activities. Challenges can be assigned outside of class time. Existing lessons can be tailored to include elements of digital research, giving students authentic opportunities to do college-ready work. This is the future of information-fluency instruction.

The vision of an information-fluent society is attainable, but it will never be realized with better search algorithms alone. Software can help, but there will never be a substitute for informed, ethical consumption of information based on trust—not the blind trust that is a characteristic of the early-twenty-first-century online experience but trust that is earned by fact checking, community dialogue, and critical thinking.

NOTE

1. Lana Ivanitskaya, Irene O'Boyle, and Anne Casey, "Health Information Literacy and Competencies of Information Age Students: Results from the Interactive Online Research Readiness Self-Assessment (RRSA)," *Journal of Medical Internet Research*, 8, no. 2 (2006), accessed April 30, 2013, http://www.ncbi.nlm.nih.gov/pmc/articles/PMC1550696.

Appendix:
Model Lessons and
Instructional Resources

LESSON 1-1: EARTH'S FASTEST ANIMAL

- Query optimization, pp. 5–6, 41
- Fact checking and triangulation, pp. 7–8

Information Fluency Competencies

- Identify key concepts in a research question
- Create effective and efficient search queries
- Select digital search tools based on their effectiveness and efficiency
- Evaluate the quality of a search result to determine the reliability of its content

Common Core State Standards

- RL.3-12.1, RL.6-12.2, RL.3-12.4
- RI.3-12.1, RI.6-12.2, RI.3-12.4, RI.3.5, RI.6-12.6, RI.9-10.8, RI.6-8.9
- L.3-12.1, L.3-12.2, L.3-12.4, L.3-12.5, L.3-12.6
- W.3-12.7, W.3-12.8
- WHST.6-12.7, WHST.6-12.8

Method
- Search challenge

Resource
- Query Checklist

LESSON 1-2: CHINA'S GREAT WALL

- Query optimization, pp. 10–11, 13–14

Information Fluency Competencies

- Identify key concepts in a research question
- Create effective and efficient search queries
- Select digital collections based on their characteristics
- Select and apply appropriate search strategies to effectively and efficiently locate reliable digital information related to their academic learning goal(s)

Common Core State Standards

- RL.3-12.1, RL.6-12.2, RL.3-12.4
- RI.3-12.1, RI.6-12.2, RI.3-12.4, RI.3.5, RI.6-12.6, RI.9-10.8, RI.6-8.9
- L.3-12.1, L.3-12.2, L.3-12.4, L.3-12.5, L.3-12.6
- W.3-12.7, W.3-12.8
- WHST.6-12.7, WHST.6-12.8

Method

- Keyword game

Resource

- Keyword Challenge

LESSON 3-1: PERSPECTIVES ON POVERTY

- Query optimization, pp. 43–45, 47–48

Information Fluency Competencies

- Identify key concepts in a research question
- Create effective and efficient search queries
- Select digital search tools based on their effectiveness and efficiency

Common Core State Standards

- RL.3-12.1, RL.6-12.2, RL.3-12.4
- RI.3-12.1, RI.6-12.2, RI.3-12.4, RI.3.5, RI.6-12.6, RI.9-10.8, RI.6-8.9

- L.3-12.1, L.3-12.2, L.3-12.4, L.3-12.5, L.3-12.6
- W.3-12.7, W.3-12.8
- WHST.6-12.7, WHST.6-12.8

Method

- Think-aloud

Resource

- Query Checklist

LESSON 3-2: KEYWORD CHALLENGES

- Query optimization, pp. 45–46

Information Fluency Competencies

- Identify key concepts in a research question
- Create effective and efficient search queries
- Select digital search tools based on their effectiveness and efficiency

Common Core State Standards

- L.3-12.1, L.3-12.2, L.3-12.4, L.3-12.5, L.3-12.6
- W.3-12.7, W.3-12.8
- WHST.6-12.7, WHST.6-12.8

Method

- Learning games

Resources

- Keyword challenges (e.g., "Earthquake Challenge")

LESSON 3-3: MIDWEST PERSPECTIVES OF WAR

- Query screenshots, pp. 50–52

Information Fluency Competencies

- Identify key concepts in a research question
- Create effective and efficient search queries
- Select digital search tools based on their effectiveness and efficiency

Common Core State Standards

- RL.3-12.1, RL.6-12.2, RL.3-12.4
- RI.3-12.1, RI.6-12.2, RI.3-12.4, RI.3.5, RI.6-12.6, RI.9-10.8, RI.6-8.9
- L.3-12.1, L.3-12.2, L.3-12.4, L.3-12.5, L.3-12.6
- SL.3-12.1, SL.3-12.2, SL.3-12.3, SL.3-12.6
- W.3-12.7, W.3-12.8
- WHST.6-12.7, WHST.6-12.8

Method

- Group discussion, problem solving
- Simulated or live search

Resources

- JSTOR (or another proprietary search engine other than Google)
- Keystroke recorder software—may be available free of charge. For the IMSA study, a simulated JSTOR interface was created using Flash, and queries were saved in a database for analysis.

LESSON 4-1: SNOWSPORTS

- Better keywords, pp. 61–62

Information Fluency Competencies

- Identify key concepts in a research question
- Create effective and efficient search queries
- Select digital search tools based on their effectiveness and efficiency

Common Core State Standards

- RL.3-12.1, RL.6-12.2, RL.3-12.4
- L.3-12.1, L.3-12.2, L.3-12.4, L.3-12.5, L.3-12.6

- RI.3-12.1, RI.6-12.2, RI.3-12.4, RI.3.5, RI.6-12.6, RI.9-10.8, RI.6-8.9
- SL.3-12.1, SL.3-12.2, SL.3-12.3, SL.3-12.6
- W.3-12.7, W.3-12.8
- WHST.6-12.7, WHST.6-12.8

Method

- Game playing
- Group discussion

Resource

- "Snowsport Nym" Challenge

LESSON 4-2: PIRATES CHALLENGE

- Effective operators, pp. 62–63

Information Fluency Competencies

- Identify key concepts in a research question
- Create effective and efficient search queries
- Select digital search tools based on their effectiveness and efficiency

Common Core State Standards

- RL.3-12.1, RL.6-12.2, RL.3-12.4
- L.3-12.1, L.3-12.2, L.3-12.4, L.3-12.5, L.3-12.6
- RI.3-12.1, RI.6-12.2, RI.3-12.4, RI.3.5, RI.6-12.6, RI.9-10.8, RI.6-8.9
- SL.3-12.1, SL.3-12.2, SL.3-12.3, SL.3-12.6
- W.3-12.7, W.3-12.8
- WHST.6-12.7, WHST.6-12.8

Method

- Game playing
- Group discussion

Resource

- Pirates operator challenges

LESSON 4-3: PIRANHAS CHALLENGE

- Effective operators, pages 63–64

Information Fluency Competencies

- Identify key concepts in a research question
- Create effective and efficient search queries
- Select digital search tools based on their effectiveness and efficiency

Common Core State Standards

- RL.3-12.1, RL.6-12.2, RL.3-12.4
- L.3-12.1, L.3-12.2, L.3-12.4, L.3-12.5, L.3-12.6
- RI.3-12.1, RI.6-12.2, RI.3-12.4, RI.3.5, RI.6-12.6, RI.9-10.8, RI.6-8.9
- SL.3-12.1, SL.3-12.2, SL.3-12.3, SL.3-12.6
- W.3-12.7, W.3-12.8
- WHST.6-12.7, WHST.6-12.8

Method

- Game playing
- Group discussion

Resources

- Piranhas operator challenges

LESSON 4-4: *HOMELESS GUY* BLOG CHALLENGE

- Backlink investigation, pp. 64–66

Information Fluency Competencies

- Evaluate the quality of a search result to determine the reliability of its source

Common Core State Standards

- SL.3-12.1, SL.3-12.2, SL.3-12.3, SL.3-12.6
- RI.3-12.1, RI.6-12.2, RI.3-12.4, RI.6-12.6, RI.9-10.8, RI.6-8.9
- W.3-12.7, W.3-12.8
- WHST.6-12.7, WHST.6-12.8

Method

- Assessment challenge
- Group discussion

Resources

- "*Homeless Guy*" Challenge

LESSON 4-5: BROADWAY DATABASE CHALLENGE

- Deep Web searching, pp. 66–68

Information Fluency Competencies

- Identify key concepts in a research question
- Create effective and efficient search queries
- Select digital search tools based on their effectiveness and efficiency

Common Core State Standards

- RL.3-12.1, RL.6-12.2, RL.3-12.4
- L.3-12.1, L.3-12.2, L.3-12.4, L.3-12.5, L.3-12.6
- SL.3-12.1, SL.3-12.2, SL.3-12.3, SL.3-12.6
- W.3-12.7, W.3-12.8
- WHST.6-12.7, WHST.6-12.8

Method

- Assessment challenge (option: tag-team or group searching)
- Group debrief

Resources

- Broadway challenge

LESSON 4-6: KERMIT CHALLENGE

- Keyword identification, pp. 68–69

Information Fluency Competencies

- Identify key concepts in a research question
- Create effective and efficient search queries

Common Core State Standards

- RL.3-12.1, RL.6-12.2, RL.3-12.4
- L.3-12.1, L.3-12.2, L.3-12.4, L.3-12.5, L.3-12.6
- RI.3-12.1, RI.6-12.2, RI.3-12.4, RI.3.5, RI.6-12.6, RI.9-10.8, RI.6-8.9
- SL.3-12.1, SL.3-12.2, SL.3-12.3, SL.3-12.6
- W.3-12.7, W.3-12.8
- WHST.6-12.7, WHST.6-12.8

Method

- Word-generation game
- Group debrief

Resources

- Kermit challenge

LESSON 4-7: DMOZ.ORG CHALLENGE

- Effective browsing, pp. 68–69

Information Fluency Competencies

- Select and apply appropriate search strategies to effectively and efficiently locate reliable digital information related to their academic learning goal(s)

Common Core State Standards

- RL.3-12.1, RL.6-12.2, RL.3-12.4
- RI.3-12.1, RI.6-12.2, RI.3-12.4, RI.3.5, RI.6-12.6, RI.9-10.8, RI.6-8.9
- L.3-12.1, L.3-12.2, L.3-12.4, L.3-12.5, L.3-12.6
- SL.3-12.1, SL.3-12.2, SL.3-12.3, SL.3-12.6
- W.3-12.7, W.3-12.8
- WHST.6-12.7, WHST.6-12.8

Method

- Think-aloud or group browsing (crowd sourcing)
- Group discussion

Resources

- Soccer challenge
- Dmoz.org

LESSON 4-8: TOP TEN LIST

- Citation searching, pp. 71–72

Information Fluency Competencies

- Select and apply appropriate search strategies to effectively and efficiently locate reliable digital information related to their academic learning goal(s)
- Ethically use digital information

Common Core State Standards

- RL.3-12.1, RL.6-12.2, RL.3-12.4
- RI.3-12.1, RI.6-12.2, RI.3-12.4, RI.3.5, RI.6-12.6, RI.9-10.8, RI.6-8.9
- SL.3-12.1, SL.3-12.2, SL.3-12.3, SL.3-12.6
- W.3-12.7, W.3-12.8
- WHST.6-12.7, WHST.6-12.8

Method

- Search and display (anonymously)
- Group discussion

Resources

- Citation challenge (missing author and date)

LESSON 5-1: PACIFIC NORTHWEST TREE OCTOPUS

- Author investigation, pp. 85–87

Information Fluency Competencies

- Evaluate the quality of a search result to determine the reliability of its source

Common Core State Standards

- RL.3-12.1, RL.6-12.2, RL.3-12.4
- L.3-12.1, L.3-12.2, L.3-12.4, L.3-12.5, L.3-12.6

- RI.3-12.1, RI.6-12.2, RI.3-12.4, RI.3.5, RI.6-12.6, RI.9-10.8, RI.6-8.9
- SL.3-12.1, SL.3-12.2, SL.3-12.3, SL.3-12.6
- W.3-12.7, W.3-12.8
- WHST.6-12.7, WHST.6-12.8

Method

- Think-aloud investigation looking for red flags, however individual or group searching is recommended
- Group discussion

Resources

- Pacific Northwest tree octopus site

LESSON 5-2: PACIFIC NORTHWEST TREE OCTOPUS

- Publisher investigation, pp. 87

Information Fluency Competencies

- Evaluate the quality of a search result to determine the reliability of its source

Common Core State Standards

- RL.3-12.1, RL.6-12.2, RL.3-12.4
- L.3-12.1, L.3-12.2, L.3-12.4, L.3-12.5, L.3-12.6
- RI.3-12.1, RI.6-12.2, RI.3-12.4, RI.3.5, RI.6-12.6, RI.9-10.8, RI.6-8.9
- SL.3-12.1, SL.3-12.2, SL.3-12.3, SL.3-12.6
- W.3-12.7, W.3-12.8
- WHST.6-12.7, WHST.6-12.8

Method

- Think-aloud investigation looking for red flags, however individual or group searching is recommended

Resources

- Pacific Northwest tree octopus site
- Whois.net

LESSON 5-3: HARRY POTTER SORTING HAT TEST

- Publisher investigation, pp. 88–89

Information Fluency Competencies

- Evaluate the quality of a search result to determine the reliability of its source

Common Core State Standards

- RL.3-12.1, RL.6-12.2, RL.3-12.4
- L.3-12.1, L.3-12.2, L.3-12.4, L.3-12.5, L.3-12.6
- RI.3-12.1, RI.6-12.2, RI.3-12.4, RI.6-12.6, RI.9-10.8, RI.6-8.9
- SL.3-12.1, SL.3-12.2, SL.3-12.3, SL.3-12.6
- W.3-12.7, W.3-12.8
- WHST.6-12.7, WHST.6-12.8

Method

- Think-aloud investigation looking for red flags, however individual or group searching is recommended
- Group discussion

Resources

- Harry Potter Sorting Hat Personality Test
- Whois.net

LESSON 5-4: SPAM E-MAIL

- Fact-checking investigation, pp. 89–90

Information Fluency Competencies

- Evaluate the quality of a search result to determine the reliability of its content

Common Core State Standards

- RL.3-12.1, RL.6-12.2, RL.3-12.4
- L.3-12.1, L.3-12.2, L.3-12.4, L.3-12.5, L.3-12.6
- RI.3-12.1, RI.6-12.2, RI.3-12.4, RI.6-12.6, RI.9-10.8, RI.6-8.9

- SL.3-12.1, SL.3-12.2, SL.3-12.3, SL.3-12.6
- W.3-12.7, W.3-12.8
- WHST.6-12.7, WHST.6-12.8

Method

- Group game: "Find the Red Flags"
- Group discussion

Resources

- Ban Ki-moon fake e-mail

LESSON 5-5: HARRY POTTER SORTING HAT TEST

- Date investigation, p. 91

Information Fluency Competencies

- Evaluate the quality of a search result to determine the reliability of its content

Common Core State Standards

- RL.3-12.1, RL.6-12.2, RL.3-12.4
- RI.3-12.1, RI.6-12.2, RI.3-12.4, RI.6-12.6, RI.9-10.8, RI.6-8.9
- SL.3-12.1, SL.3-12.2, SL.3-12.3, SL.3-12.6

Method

- Page mapping to find the date
- Group discussion

Resources

- newmedz.com, see p. 91

LESSON 5-6: TEEN BRAIN, TEN HIKES

- Date investigations, p. 93

Information Fluency Competencies

- Evaluate the quality of a search result to determine the reliability of its content

Common Core State Standards

- RI.3-12.1, RI.6-12.2, RI.3-12.4, RI.3.5, RI.6-12.6, RI.9-10.8, RI.6-8.9
- SL.3-12.1, SL.3-12.2, SL.3-12.3, SL.3-12.6
- W.3-12.7, W.3-12.8
- WHST.6-12.7, WHST.6-12.8

Method

- Think-aloud or individual or group searching using "Page Info," Javascript, and page properties
- Group discussion

Resources

- "Myth of the Teen Brain" Challenge
- "Top Ten Hikes in Southern Arizona" Challenge
- Archive.org

LESSON 5-7: MARTIN LUTHER KING JR.

- Bias investigation, pp. 93–95

Information Fluency Competencies

- Evaluate the quality of a search result to determine the reliability of its content

Common Core State Standards

- RL.3-12.1, RL.6-12.2, RL.3-12.4
- L.3-12.1, L.3-12.2, L.3-12.4, L.3-12.5, L.3-12.6
- RI.3-12.1, RI.6-12.2, RI.3-12.4, RI.6-12.6, RI.9-10.8, RI.6-8.9
- SL.3-12.1, SL.3-12.2, SL.3-12.3, SL.3-12.6
- W.3-12.7, W.3-12.8
- WHST.6-12.7, WHST.6-12.8

Method

- Group discussion

Resources

- Martinlutherking.org

LESSON 5-8: MARTIN LUTHER KING JR.

- Secondary-source evaluations, pp. 95–97

Information Fluency Competencies

- Evaluate the quality of a search result to determine the reliability of its content

Common Core State Standards

- RL.3-12.1, RL.6-12.2, RL.3-12.4
- RI.3-12.1, RI.6-12.2, RI.3-12.4, RI.6-12.6, RI.9-10.8, RI.6-8.9
- SL.3-12.1, SL.3-12.2, SL.3-12.3, SL.3-12.6
- WHST.6-12.7, WHST.6-12.8

Method

- Group discussion

Resources

- List of secondary sources that link to martinlutherking.org

LESSON 6-1: GENOCHOICE

- Content evaluation, pp. 100–1

Information Fluency Competencies

- Evaluate the quality of a search result to determine the reliability of its content

Common Core State Standards

- RL.3-12.1, RL.6-12.2, RL.3-12.4
- RI.3-12.1, RI.6-12.2, RI.3-12.4, RI.3.5, RI.6-12.6, RI.9-10.8, RI.6-8.9

- SL.3-12.1, SL.3-12.2, SL.3-12.3, SL.3-12.6
- WHST.6-12.7, WHST.6-12.8

Method

- Compare two pages
- Group discussion

Resources

- Genochoice.com
- Genochoice.com/credits.shtml

LESSON 6-2: GENOCHOICE

- Finding red flags, pp. 101–5

Information Fluency Competencies

- Evaluate the quality of a search result to determine the reliability of its content
- Evaluate the quality of a search result to determine the reliability of its source

Common Core State Standards

- RL.3-12.1, RL.6-12.2, RL.3-12.4
- RI.3-12.1, RI.6-12.2, RI.3-12.4, RI.3.5, RI.6-12.6, RI.9-10.8, RI.6-8.9
- SL.3-12.1, SL.3-12.2, SL.3-12.3, SL.3-12.6
- WST.6-12.8
- RST.6-12.6

Method

- Think-aloud
- Individual searching
- Share findings, draw conclusions

Resources

- Genochoice.com
- Whiteboard

LESSON 6-3: GENOCHOICE

- Finding red flags, pp. 105–8

Information Fluency Competencies

- Evaluate the quality of a search result to determine the reliability of its content
- Evaluate the quality of a search result to determine the reliability of its source

Common Core State Standards

- RL.3-12.1, RL.6-12.2, RL.3-12.4
- RI.3-12.1, RI.6-12.2, RI.3-12.4, RI.3.5, RI.6-12.6, RI.9-10.8, RI.6-8.9
- SL.3-12.1, SL.3-12.2, SL.3-12.3, SL.3-12.6
- WST.6-12.8
- RST.6-12.6

Method

- Think-aloud demonstration
- Individuals search
- Share findings, discuss conclusions

Resources

- Genochoice.com
- Whiteboard

LESSON 6-4: GENOCHOICE

- Finding red flags, pp. 108–9

Information Fluency Competencies

- Evaluate the quality of a search result to determine the reliability of its content
- Evaluate the quality of a search result to determine the reliability of its source

Common Core State Standards

- RL.3-12.1, RL.6-12.2, RL.3-12.4
- RI.3-12.1, RI.6-12.2, RI.3-12.4, RI.3.5, RI.6-12.6, RI.9-10.8, RI.6-8.9
- SL.3-12.1, SL.3-12.2, SL.3-12.3, SL.3-12.6
- WST.6-12.8
- RST.6-12.6

Method

- Group fact checking and triangulation
- Jigsaw: Share findings, discuss conclusions

Resources

- Genochoice.com
- Digital projector

LESSON 6-5: GENOCHOICE

- Finding red flags, pp. 109–10

Information Fluency Competencies

- Evaluate the quality of a search result to determine the reliability of its source

Common Core State Standards

- RL.3-12.1, RL.6-12.2, RL.3-12.4
- RI.3-12.1, RI.6-12.2, RI.3-12.4, RI.3.5, RI.6-12.6, RI.9-10.8, RI.6-8.9
- SL.3-12.1, SL.3-12.2, SL.3-12.3, SL.3-12.6
- WHST.6-8.1, WHST.6-8.8

Method

- Think-aloud demonstration
- Homework: Backlinks investigation
- Discussion

Resources

- Genochoice.com
- Whiteboard

LESSON 6-6: GENOCHOICE

- Finding red flags, pp. 110–12

Information Fluency Competencies

- Evaluate the quality of a search result to determine the reliability of its content

Common Core State Standards

- RL.3-12.1, RL.6-12.2, RL.3-12.4
- RI.3-12.1, RI.6-12.2, RI.3-12.4, RI.3.5, RI.6-12.6, RI.9-10.8, RI.6-8.9
- SL.3-12.1, SL.3-12.2, SL.3-12.3, SL.3-12.6
- WST.6-12.8

Method

- Individual or group search challenge
- Share findings, discuss conclusions

Resources

- Genochoice.com
- Whiteboard

LESSON 7-1: PLAGIARISM DROPBOX

- Avoiding plagiarism, pp. 129–31

Information Fluency Competencies

- Ethically use digital information

Common Core State Standards

- RL.3-12.1, RL.6-12.2, RL.3-12.4
- RI.3-12.1, RI.6-12.2, RI.3-12.4, RI.3.5, RI.6-12.6, RI.9-10.8, RI.6-8.9
- L.3-12.1, L.3-12.2, L.3-12.4, L.3-12.5, L.3-12.6
- W.3-12.7, W.3-12.8
- WHST.6-12.7, WHST.6-12.8

Method

- Self-paced tutorial

Resources

- 21cif.com: Plagiarism DropBox (requires a license)

LESSON 7-2: APA CITATION WIZARD

- Citing information, pp. 132–34

Information Fluency Competencies

- Ethically use digital information

Common Core State Standards

- RL.3-12.1, RL.6-12.2, RL.3-12.4
- RI.3-12.1, RI.6-12.2, RI.3-12.4, RI.3.5, RI.6-12.6, RI.9-10.8, RI.6-8.9
- L.3-12.1, L.3-12.2, L.3-12.4, L.3-12.5, L.3-12.6
- W.3-12.7, W.3-12.8
- WHST.6-12.7, WHST.6-12.8

Method

- Demonstration
- Student practice

Resources

- 21cif.com: APA Citation Wizard
- 21cif.com: CSE Citation Wizard

LESSON 8-1: LIBRARY OF CONGRESS LESSON PLAN

- Unfamiliar search engine, pp. 140–43

Information Fluency Competencies

- Identify key concepts in a research question
- Create effective and efficient search queries
- Select digital search tools based on their effectiveness and efficiency

Common Core State Standards

- RL.3-12.1, RL.6-12.2, RL.3-12.4
- RI.3-12.1, RI.6-12.2, RI.3-12.4, RI.3.5, RI.6-12.6, RI.9-10.8, RI.6-8.9
- L.3-12.1, L.3-12.2, L.3-12.4, L.3-12.5, L.3-12.6
- W.3-12.7, W.3-12.8
- WHST.6-12.7, WHST.6-12.8

Method

- Individual or group querying
- Browsing (optional)

Resources

- Library of Congress lesson plan

LESSON 8-2: LIBRARY OF CONGRESS LESSON PLAN

- Image searching, pp. 143–45

Information Fluency Competencies

- Create effective and efficient search queries
- Select digital search tools based on their effectiveness and efficiency

Common Core State Standards

- RH.6-12.6, RH.6-12.7, RH.6-12.6.8
- RI.3-12.1, RI.6-12.2, RI.3-12.4, RI.3.5, RI.6-12.6, RI.9-10.8, RI.6-8.9
- WHST.6-12.6, WHST.6-12.7, WHST.6-12.8

Method

- Individual or group Google image searching

Resources

- Library of Congress lesson plan
- Google image search

LESSON 8-3: LIBRARY OF CONGRESS LESSON PLAN

- Secondary-source evaluation, pp. 145–47

Information Fluency Competencies

- Identify key concepts in a research question
- Create effective and efficient search queries
- Select digital search tools based on their effectiveness and efficiency
- Evaluate the quality of a search result to determine the reliability of its content

Common Core State Standards

- RI.3-12.1, RI.6-12.2, RI.3-12.4, RI.3.5, RI.6-12.6, RI.9-10.8, RI.6-8.9, RI.6-12.9, RI.6-12.10
- W.6-12.9, W.6-12.10
- SL.3-12.1, SL.3-12.2, SL.3-12.3, SL.3-12.6, SL.9-10

Method

- Searching for secondary sources
- Discussion

Resources

- Library of Congress lesson plan
- Google image search·

LESSON 9-1: SCOOP.IT

- Curation, pp. 165–68

Information Fluency Competencies

- Identify key concepts in a research question
- Create effective and efficient search queries
- Select digital search tools based on their effectiveness and efficiency
- Evaluate the quality of a search result to determine its usefulness in the search process
- Evaluate the quality of a search result to determine the reliability of its content
- Evaluate the quality of a search result to determine the reliability of its source
- Ethically use digital information

Common Core State Standards

- L.3-12.1, L.3-12.2, L.3-12.4, L.3-12.5, L.3-12.6
- RI.3-12.1, RI.6-12.2, RI.3-12.4, RI.3.5, RI.6-12.6, RI.9-10.8, RI.6-8.9
- W.3-12.7, W.3-12.8
- WHST.6-12.7, WHST.6-12.8
- RH.6-12.7, RH.6-12.8

Method

- Curation

Resources

- Curation template
- Scoop.it

Bibliography

12th Annual Healthcare Internet Conference. Orlando, Florida. Sponsored by Greystone
   .net. Staywell Communications in cooperation with the Forum for Healthcare Strategists.

21st Century Information Fluency. Accessed April 23, 2013. http://21cif.com.

"2012 Cost of Cyber Crime Study: United States." *Ponemon Institute.* October 2012, http://
   www.ponemon.org/local/upload/file/2012_US_Cost_of_Cyber_Crime_Study_FINAL
   6%20.pdf.

"About." *Creative Commons.* Accessed April 26, 2013. http://creativecommons.org/about.

"About | Biography." *VirgilWong.* Accessed March 30, 2013. http://virgilwong.com/bio.

"About the Licenses." *Creative Commons.* Accessed April 26, 2013. http://creativecommons
   .org/licenses.

"About the Pacific Northwest Tree Octopus." *WayBack Machine.* Last modified August 18,
   2000. http://web.archive.org/web/20000818130120/http://zapatopi.net/treeoctopus.html.

"Action Zone." *21st Century Information Fluency.* Last modified February 17, 2013. https://
   21cif.com/rkit/actionzone/index.html.

Ad Hoc Committee on Fair Use and Academic Freedom, International Communication
   Association. "Clipping Our Own Wings Copyright and Creativity in Communication
   Research." *Center for Social Media.* Last modified 2013. http://www.centerforsocialmedia.
   org/fair-use/related-materials/documents/clipping-our-own-wings-copyright-and-creativity
   -communication-r.

Adams, Douglas. *The Hitchhiker's Guide to the Galaxy, 25th Anniversary Edition.* New York:
   Del Rey Books, 2009.

Alcibar, Jon. "Notes on 'Power Searching with Google' Course, July 2012." *Google Docs.* Accessed January 30, 2013. https://docs.google.com/document/d/1DShfXSPP3GjDIAiSnOP
   qfCTUzc31l1FsT8voM65i2kI/edit.

"Alerts." *Google.* Accessed April 14, 2013. http://www.google.com/alerts.

Aufderheide, Patricia. "CCUMC Adopts Librarians' Code, Retires Previous Fair Use Guidelines." *Center for Social Media.* Last modified January 29, 2013. http://www.centerfor

socialmedia.org/blog/fair-use/ccumc-adopts-librarians%E2%80%99-code-retires-previous
-fair-use-guidelines.

"Avoiding Fake Web Sites." *Township High School District 214.* Accessed March 30, 2013. http://
www.d214.org/district_library/Fake_sites.aspx.

Axelrod, A. *Edison on Innovation: 102 Lessons in Creativity for Business and Beyond.* San Francisco: Jossey-Bass, 2008.

Barr, David. "Rubrics: Dispositions." *21st Century Information Fluency.* Accessed April 14,
2013. http://21cif.com/resources/difcore/index.html#dispositions.

Barr, David, Paula Garrett, Dan Balzer, Carl Heine, and Bob Houston. "Search Challenges
as Assessment Tools: A Collaboration between the Library and the 21st Century Information Fluency Project in Illinois." Paper presented at the Australia Library and Information
Association Biennial Conference, Perth, Australia, 2006, http://conferences.alia.org.au/
alia2006/Papers/David_Barr_and_Paula_Garrett.pdf.

Barr, David, Bob Houston, Carl Heine, Dennis O'Connor, and Dan Balzer. "Digital Information Fluency Model." *21st Century Information Fluency.* Last modified January 1, 2013.

Barron, Paul. "How Google Works: Are Search Engines Really Dumb and Why Should
Educators Care?" *Internet@Schools.* Last modified January 1, 2011. http://www.internet
atschools.com/Articles/PrintArticle.aspx?ArticleID=73090.

"The Beast as Saint." *Stormfront.* Last modified January 15, 2007. http://www.martinluther
king.org/thebeast.html.

Beta Scrible. Accessed April 14, 2013. http://scrible.com.

Brooks, Marta, and Jodi Allison-Bunnell. "Explorations in American Environment History."
Library of Congress. Accessed February 26, 2013. http://www.loc.gov/teachers/classroom
materials/lessons/explorations.

Burn-Murdoch, John. "UK Was World's Most Phished Country in 2012—Why Is It Being
Targeted?" *The Guardian.* Last modified February 27, 2013. http://www.guardian.co.uk/
news/datablog/2013/feb/27/uk-most-phishing-attacks-worldwide.

Carlson, Dick. "State Goal 5: Use the Language Arts to Acquire, Assess and Communicate
Information." Last modified October 10, 2007. http://www.isbe.net/ils/ela/pdf/goal5.pdf.

Carter, Jeffrey. "What's a Pain Point?" *Points and Figures.* Last modified April 27, 2012. http://
pointsandfigures.com/2012/04/27/whats-a-pain-point.

Center for Talent Development, Northwestern University. Online survey (unpublished).

Cheng, Jacqui. "Students Trust High Google Search Ranking Too Much." *Ars Technica.*
Accessed January 16, 2013. http://arstechnica.com/science/2010/07/alt-title-students
-place-too.

"China's Wall Less Great in View from Space." *NASA.* Last modified November 30, 2007.
http://www.nasa.gov/vision/space/workinginspace/great_wall.html.

Chomsky, Noam. "The Purpose of Education." *Learning without Frontiers.* Accessed February
1, 2013. http://www.learningwithoutfrontiers.com/2012/02/noam-chomsky-the-purpose
-of-education.

"Code of Best Practices in Fair Use." *Association of Research Libraries.* Accessed April 20, 2013.
http://www.arl.org/focus-areas/copyright-ip/fair-use/code-of-best-practices.

"The Code of Best Practices in Fair Use for Media Literacy Education." *Center for Social
Media.* Accessed April 20, 2013. http://www.centerforsocialmedia.org/fair-use/related
-materials/codes/code-best-practices-fair-use-media-literacy-education.

"Colby Personality Lab." *Colby.* Accessed March 17, 2013. http://www.colby.edu/psychology/
labs/personality/index.html.

Common Core State Standards for English Language Arts and Literacy in History/Social Studies, Science, and Technical Subjects. Washington, DC: National Governors Association Center for Best Practices and the Council of Chief State School Officers, 2012. http://www.core standards.org/assets/CCSSI_ELA%20Standards.pdf.

Coombs, Dan. Personal correspondence (e-mail). March 6, 2013.

"Copyright and Fair Use: Measuring Fair Use: The Four Factors." *Stanford University Libraries.* Last modified 2010. http://fairuse.stanford.edu/Copyright_and_Fair_Use_Overview/chapter9/9-b.html.

"Copyright and Fair Use in the UMUC Online or Face-to-Face Classroom." *University of Maryland University College.* Accessed April 20, 2013. http://www.umuc.edu/library/libhow/copyright.cfm#copyright_notincluded.

"Copyright Law of the United States of America and Related Laws Contained in Title 17 of the United States Code: Circular 92." *U.S. Copyright Office.* Accessed April 21, 2013. http://www.copyright.gov/title17/92chap1.html#106.

Corwith, Susan, and Carl Heine. "Improving 21st Century Information Fluency Skills." Presentation, Annual Convention of the National Association for Gifted Children, New Orleans, LA, November 3–5, 2011.

Creative Commons. Accessed April 20, 2013. http://creativecommons.org.

"Credits." *Genochoice.com.* Accessed March 30, 2013. http://www.genochoice.com/credits.shtml.

Csikszentmihalyi, Mihaly. *Finding Flow.* New York: Basic Books, 1998.

Cummings, Alex Sayf. *Democracy of Sound: Music Piracy and the Remaking of American Copyright in the Twentieth Century.* New York: Oxford University Press, 2013.

"D. B. Cooper." *Wikipedia.* Accessed March 14, 2013. https://en.wikipedia.org/wiki/D._B._Cooper.

Delicious. Accessed April 14, 2013. http://delicious.com.

Derstine, Robert. Personal correspondence (e-mail). March 6, 2013.

———. "Top Ten Things to Know As You Begin Your Career." Last modified June 4, 2012. http://web.archive.org/web/20120604165148/http://faculty.kutztown.edu/derstine/Top TenThingsToKnowToStartYourCareer.htm.

"Digital Berkeley: Making Open Educational Resources." *Townsend Humanities Lab.* Accessed April 14, 2013. http://townsendlab.berkeley.edu/digital-berkeley-making-open -educational-resources.

Diigo. Accessed April 14, 2013. http://diigo.com.

"Directories, Calendars, Research Guides, Encyclopedias and Hoaxes." *Online Public Relations.* Last modified December 22, 2012. http://www.online-pr.com/directory.htm.

DMOZ Open Directory Project. Accessed March 5, 2013. http://www.dmoz.org.

"Do Piranha's Have Fears?" *Answers.* Accessed February 23, 2013. http://wiki.answers.com/Q/Do_piranha's_have_fears.

"Doctor Finder." *American Medical Association.* Accessed March 30, 2103. https://extapps .ama-assn.org/doctorfinder/recaptcha.jsp.

Doctorow, Cory. "Using Clickfraud on Google Ads to Amass Shares of Google." *Boing Boing.* Last modified June 7, 2011. http://boingboing.net/2011/06/07/using-clickfraud-on.html.

"Documentary Filmmakers' Statement of Best Practices in Fair Use." *Center for Social Media, School of Communication, American University.* Accessed April 26, 2013. http://www .centerforsocialmedia.org/fair-use/best-practices/documentary/documentary-filmmakers -statement-best-practices-fair-use.

Duncan, Amanda, and Jennifer Varcoe. *Information Literacy Competency Standards for Students: A Measure of the Effectiveness of Information Literacy Initiatives in Higher Education.* Toronto: Higher Education Quality Council of Ontario, 2012.

Eisenberg, Mike, and Bob Berkowitz. "Introducing the Big6." Last modified January 28, 2012. http://big6.com/pages/lessons/presentations/big6-overview-2011.php.

"English Language Arts Standards: Grade 7: 8." *Common Core State Standards Initiative.* Accessed March 23, 2013. http://www.corestandards.org/ELA-Literacy/RI/7/8.

"English Language Arts Standards: Grade 9-10: 8." *Common Core State Standards Initiative.* Accessed March 31, 2013. http://www.corestandards.org/ELA-Literacy/W/9-10/8.

Epstein, Robert. "Myth of the Teen Brain." Last modified April 7, 2007. drrobertepstein.com/pdf/Epstein-THE_MYTH_OF_THE_TEEN_BRAIN-Scientific_American_Mind-4-07.pdf.

Evernote. Accessed January 20, 2013. http://evernote.com.

"Faculty: Virgil Wong." *The New School for Public Engagement.* Accessed March 30, 2013. http://www.newschool.edu/public-engagement/faculty-list/?id=87942.

FeedDemon. Accessed April 14, 2013. http://feeddemon.com.

Feedly Reader. Accessed April 14, 2013. http://feedly.com.

FeedReader. Accessed April 14, 2013. http://feedreader.com.

Finn, Greg. "Pinning the Competition: Pinterest's Four-Digit Growth Is Tops of 2012." *Marketing Land.* Last modified December 4, 2012. http://marketingland.com/pinning-the-competition-pinterests-four-digit-growth-is-tops-of-2012-27769.

"The Future of Work." *Apollo Research Institute.* Accessed April 14, 2013. http://apolloresearchinstitute.com/sites/default/files/future_of_work_report_final.pdf.

Gabrick, Robert, and Barbara Markham. "Thomas Edison, Electricity, and America." *Library of Congress.* Accessed March 1, 2013. http://www.loc.gov/teachers/classroommaterials/lessons/edison.

"Gallery of Hoax Websites: A–J." *Museum of Hoaxes.* Accessed March 30, 2013. http://www.museumofhoaxes.com/hoaxsites.html.

Garrett, Paula. "Search Challenges as Assessment Tools." PowerPoint presentation for the Australian Library and Information Association Biennial Convention, Perth, Australia, September 19–22, 2006.

GenoChoice. Accessed March 25, 2013. http://www.genochoice.com.

"Google Analytics." *Google.* Accessed January 25, 2013. http://www.google.com/analytics.

"Google Images." *Google.* https://www.google.com/imghp.

"Google Intuitive Search Answers Are SO weird . . ." *Facebook.* Accessed January 23, 2013. https://www.facebook.com/pages/Google-Intuitive-Search-Answers-are-SO-weird/204484611531.

"Google Patent Search." *Google.* Accessed March 1, 2013. https://www.google.com/?tbm=pts.

"Great Walls of Liar." *Snopes.com.* Last updated September 6, 2010. http://www.snopes.com/science/greatwall.asp.

Gross, Melissa, and Don Latham. "Undergraduate Perceptions of Information Literacy: Defining, Attaining, and Self-Assessing Skills." *College and Research Libraries* 70, no. 4 (July 2009): 336–50. Available at http://eduscapes.com/instruction/articles/gross.pdf.

Hakia. Accessed January 31, 2013. http://hakia.com.

Hamilton, Buffy J. "Curation for Learning: How People Are Curating, Utilizing, and Sharing Information." *Scoop.it.* Accessed April 19, 2013. http://www.scoop.it/t/curation-for-learning.

Hargittai, Eszter, Lindsay Fullerton, Ericka Menchen-Trevino, and Kristin Yates Thomas. "Trust Online: Young Adults' Evaluation of Web Content." *International Journal of Communication* (vol.) 4 (2010): 468–94.

Hargittai, Eszter, W. Russell Neuman, and Olivia Curry. "Taming the Information Tide: Perceptions of Information Overload in the American Home." *The Information Society* 28, no. 3 (2012): 161–73.

Heine, Carl. "Action Zone User's Guide to Keyword Challenges." *21st Century Information Fluency*. Last modified January 28, 2009. http://21cif.com/rkitp/curriculum/v1n3/use_flash_applications_v1n3.html.

———. "Citation Challenge." *21st Century Information Fluency*. Last modified August 8, 2012. http://searchwhys.com/posttest/exam-10.html.

———. "College Ready Research Skills." Presentation, Illinois School Library and Media Association. Annual Conference, St. Charles, IL, October 18–20, 2012.

———. "Common Core State Standards Mapped to the Information Fluency Model." Last modified January 1, 2013. https://21cif.com/resources/difcore/ccss-dif.html.

———. "DIF to CCSS Comparison." *21st Century Information Fluency*. Last modified October 15, 2012. https://21cif.com/resources/difcore/DIF-to-CCSS-Comparison.pdf.

———. "Evaluating Digital Information." *21st Century Information Fluency*. Last modified February 12, 2012. https://21cif.com/rkitp/features/v1n4/leadarticle_v1_n4.html.

———. "Fact Checking Spam." *Internet Search Challenge*. Last modified April 19, 2012. http://internetsearchchallenge.blogspot.com/2012/04/fact-checking-spam.html.

———. "The Four Factor Fair Use Test." *21st Century Information Fluency*. Accessed April 14, 2013. http://21cif.com/rkitp/curriculum/v1n8/quickpick_v1n8.html.

———. "Information Researcher." *21st Century Information Fluency*. Last modified May 30, 2012. http://searchwhys.com.

———. "Internet Search Challenge: Find the URL of a Website That Displays the Results of Soccer Matches between International Clubs Prior to 1888." *21st Century Information Fluency*. Last modified February 17, 2013. https://21cif.com/tutorials/challenge/SC001/SC_04.swf.

———. "Internet Search Challenge: Snowsport Challenge I." *21st Century Information Fluency*. Last modified December 28, 2007. https://21cif.com/rkitp/challenge/nyms/snowsports/Nyms_snowsport1.swf.

———. "Internet Search Challenge: What Is the Earliest Broadway Show for Which Both the Opening and Closing Dates Are Published?" *21st Century Information Fluency*. Last modified March 4, 2012. http://21cif.com/tutorials/challenge/SC001/SC_01.swf.

———. "Internet Search Challenge: What Toy Model a Construction Principle That Can Reduce Damage from Earthquakes?" *21st Century Information Fluency*. Last modified June 26, 2007. http://21cif.com/rkitp/challenge/v1n3/SC_earthquaketoy/SC_012.swf.

———. "Keyword Challenge." *21st Century Information Fluency*. Accessed January 20, 2013. https://21cif.com/rkitp/challenge/v1n3/Keyword_Challenge/KeywordChallenge.swf.

———. "Online Citation Wizards." *21st Century Information Fluency*. Last modified February 12, 2013. http://21cif.com/tools/cite.

———. "Metadata Search Wizard," *21st Century Information Fluency*, Last modified June 3, 2013, https://21cif.com/tools/evaluate/lastmodified.html.

———. "Optimal Query Checklist." *21st Century Information Fluency*. Last modified January 1, 2013. https://21cif.com/resources/curriculum/querychecklist.html.

———. "Pirates and Piranhas Users Guide." *21st Century Information Fluency.* Last modified January 28, 2009. https://21cif.com/rkitp/curriculum/v1n7/use_flash_applications_v1n7 .html.

———. "Plagiarism I: An Interactive MicroModule Companion." *21st Century Information Fluency.* Accessed April 14, 2013. http://21cif.com/rkitp/challenge/v1n8/plagiarism .swf.

———. "Plagiarism Dropbox." *21st Century Information Fluency.* Accessed April 23, 2013. http://searchwhys.com/plagiarism-dropbox-2.swf.

———. "Quick Reference Guide: Freshness." *21st Century Information Fluency.* Last modified June 30, 2012. http://searchwhys.com/CTD12/QR/freshness-1.html.

———. "Self-Guided Assessment and Tutorial Packages." *21st Century Information Fluency.* Last modified January 1, 2013. http://21cif.com/selfguided.html.

———. "Speculative and Investigative Searching." *21st Century Information Fluency.* Last modified January 28, 2009. https://21cif.com/rkitp/newRkit/gettingstarted/searchtypes.html.

———. "Taking Advantage of Operators." *21st Century Information Fluency.* Last modified January 20, 2010. https://21cif.com/rkitp/features/v1n7/leadarticle_v1n7.html.

———. "Teaching Research Skills Using the Internet." Presentation to the Illinois School Library Media Association Annual Conference, Arlington Heights, IL, October 5–6, 2005.

———. "Thinking Outside the Search Box (Confessions of a Search Challenge Designer)." *21st Century Information Fluency.* Last modified January 20, 2010. https://21cif.com/rkitp/ features/v1n9/outsidethebox.html.

———. "Tips from Google: What's Missing?" *Internet Search Challenge.* Last modified July 3, 2012. http://internetsearchchallenge.blogspot.com/2012/07/tips-from-google-whats -missing.html.

———. "Turning Questions into Queries." *21st Century Information Fluency.* Last modified January 1, 2013. https://21cif.com/resources/features/leadarticle_v1_n0.html.

———. "What Is the Date? An Interactive MicroModule Companion."*21st Century Information Fluency.* Accessed April 23, 2013. http://21cif.com/rkitp/challenge/evaluation/date .swf.

———. "Who Is the Author? An Interactive MicroModule Companion." *21st Century Information Fluency.* Accessed April 23, 2013. http://21cif.com/rkitp/challenge/evaluation/ author.swf.

———. "Who Is the Publisher? An Interactive MicroModule Companion." *21st Century Information Fluency.* Accessed April 23, 2013. http://21cif.com/rkitp/challenge/evaluation/ publisher.swf.

Heine, Carl, and Dennis O'Connor. "Final Report for the Center for Talent Development." Unpublished report, Chicago, IL, 2010.

———. "Final Report for the Center for Talent Development." Unpublished report, Chicago, IL, 2011.

———. "Final Report for the Center for Talent Development." Unpublished report, Chicago, IL, 2012.

———. "Information Fluency in the Classroom: Evaluation and Critical Thinking." Workshop presented at the annual conference of the International Society for Technology in Education, Philadelphia, PA, June 26–29, 2011, and San Diego, CA, June 24–27, 2012.

Help Save the Endangered Pacific Northwest Tree Octopus from Extinction! Accessed January 26, 2013. http://zapatopi.net/treeoctopus.

"Here Are the Basics of Getting Started on Pinterest." *Pinterest.* Accessed April 26, 2013. http://about.pinterest.com/basics.

Hess, Diana. "Discussion in Social Studies: Is It Worth the Trouble?" *Social Education* 68 no. 2 (2004): 151–55.

The Homeless Guy. Accessed March 5, 2013. http://thehomelessguy.blogspot.com.

"INFOMINE: Scholarly Internet Resource Collections." *The Regents of the University of California.* Accessed April 30, 2013. http://infomine.ucr.edu.

"Information Literacy Competency Standards for Higher Education." *American Library Association.* Accessed December 15, 2012. http://www.ala.org/acrl/standards/informationlit eracycompetency.

Internet Broadway Database. Accessed March 3, 2013. http://www.ibdb.com.

"ISTE Model Lesson: Lesson 1: 'Think Aloud' Demonstration." *21st Century Information Fluency.* Last modified January 1, 2013. http://21cif.com/iste-lesson-1.html.

"ISTE Model Lesson: Lesson 2: 'Teamwork or Jigsaw' Method." *21st Century Information Fluency.* Last modified January 1, 2013. http://21cif.com/iste-lesson-2.html.

"ISTE Model Lesson: Lesson 3: 'Flipped Discussion' Method." *21st Century Information Fluency.* Last modified January 1, 2013. http://21cif.com/iste-lesson-3.html.

"ISTE Model Lesson: Lesson 4: 'Search Challenge' Method." *21st Century Information Fluency.* Last modified January 1, 2013. http://21cif.com/iste-lesson-4.html.

Ivanitskaya, Lana, Irene O'Boyle, and Anne Casey. "Health Information Literacy and Competencies of Information Age Students: Results from the Interactive Online Research Readiness Self-Assessment (RRSA)." *Journal of Medical Internet Research* 8, no. 2 (2006). Accessed April 30, 2013. http://www.jmir.org/2006/2/e6/.

Kida, Thomas. *Don't Believe Everything You Think: The 6 Basic Mistakes We Make in Thinking.* Amherst, NY: Prometheus, 2006.

King, Jan, and Rena Nisbet. "Out of the Dust: Visions of Dust Bowl History." *Library of Congress.* Accessed February 27, 2013. http://www.loc.gov/teachers/classroommaterials/lessons/dust.

Krane, Beth. "Researchers Find Kids Need Better Online Academic Skills." *University of Connecticut.* Last modified November 13, 2006. http://advance.uconn.edu/2006/061113/ 06111308.htm.

LeClair, Dave. "3 Video Games That Actually Made Me Laugh Out Loud [MUO Gaming]." *MakeUseOf.* Last modified March 27, 2012. http://www.makeuseof.com/tag/3-video -games-laugh-loud-muo-gaming.

Lengel, James G. "Teaching with Technology: Copy, Right?" *Power to Learn.* Last modified January 22, 2008. http://www.powertolearn.com/articles/teaching_with_technology/ article.shtml?ID=67.

Lessig, Lawrence. *Remix: Making Art and Commerce Thrive in the Hybrid Economy.* New York: Penguin Press, 2008.

Levy, Steven. "Has Google Popped the Filter Bubble?" *Wired.* Last modified January 10, 2012. http://www.wired.com/business/2012/01/google-filter-bubble.

Maass, Peter, and Megha Rajagoplan. "Does Cybercrime Really Cost $1 Trillion?" *ProPublica.* Last modified August 1, 2012. http://www.propublica.org/article/does-cybercrime-really -cost-1-trillion.

"Many See Those in 'Poverty' as Not So Poor." *Rasmussen Reports.* Last modified August 19, 2011. http://www.rasmussenreports.com/public_content/lifestyle/general_lifestyle/ august_2011/many_see_those_in_poverty_as_not_so_poor.

"Media Advisory: Schools Facing Learning Crisis Spawned by Internet." *PRWeb.* Last modified January 28, 2011. http://www.prweb.com/releases/2011/01/prweb5010934.htm.

"MITOpenCourseware." *Massachusetts Institute of Technology.* Accessed April 14, 2013. http:// ocw.mit.edu/index.htm.

Miranda Hope: Home. Accessed March 30, 2013. http://mirandahopemusic.com.

"Mission and History." *Library of Congress, American Memory.* Accessed February 26, 2013. http://memory.loc.gov/ammem/about/index.html.

Mori, Masahiro. "The Uncanny Valley." *Energy* 7, no. 4 (1970): 33–35. Trans. Karl F. Mac-Dorman and Takashi Minato. *Android Science.* Last modified September 19, 2005. http://www.androidscience.com/theuncannyvalley/proceedings2005/uncannyvalley.html.

"Narrative Medicine Rounds: Virgil Wong." *Columbia University, School of Continuing Education.* Accessed March 30, 2013. http://ce.columbia.edu/narrative-medicine/events/narrative-medicine-rounds-virgil-wong.

New York State Physician Profile. Accessed March 30, 2013. http://www.nydoctorprofile.com.

NewMedz. Accessed March 19, 2013. http://newmedz.com.

Nielsen, Jakob. "Search: Visible and Simple." *Nielsen Norman Group*, Last modified May 13, 2001. http://www.nngroup.com/articles/search-visible-and-simple.

Nilsen, Asgeir S. *Twingine.* Last modified 2005. http://www.twingine.no.

O'Connor, Dennis. "21st Century Information Fluency: Learning to Find, Evaluate and Use Digital Information Effectively, Efficiently and Ethically." *Scoop.it.* Accessed April 26, 2013. http://www.scoop.it/t/21st-century-information-fluency.

———. Online course forum (unpublished).

———. "What Is the Invisible Web? How Can You Search It? Why Would You Want To?" *21st Century Information Fluency.* Last modified 2006. http://21cif.com/tutorials/micro/mm/invisible.

Ong, Josh. "Internet Crimes Cost China over $46 Billion in 2012, Report Claims." *The Next Web.* Last modified January 29, 2013. http://thenextweb.com/asia/2013/01/29/china-suffered-46-4b-in-internet-crime-related-losses-in-2012-report.

Pariser, Eli. *The Filter Bubble: How the New Personalized Web Is Changing What We Read and How We Think.* London: Penguin, 2011.

———. "Filter Bubble, Meet Upworthy." *The Filter Bubble.* Last modified March 26, 2012. http://www.thefilterbubble.com.

———. "TED Talk." *The Filter Bubble.* Accessed March 21, 2013. http://www.thefilterbubble.com/ted-talk.

Pavlešić, Domagoj. *Bing vs. Google.* Accessed April 14, 2013. http://www.bing-vs-google.com.

"PersonalityLab.org." *PsychCentral.* Accessed March 17, 2013. http://psychcentral.com/resources/detailed/4617.html.

Pinterest. Accessed April 14, 2013. http://pinterest.com.

Piper, Paul S. "Better Read That Again: Web Hoaxes and Misinformation." *Searcher.* Last modified September 2000. http://www.infotoday.com/searcher/sep00/piper.htm.

POP! The First Male Pregnancy. Accessed March 30, 2013. http://www.malepregnancy.com.

Preatner, Elizabeth. "home.mov." *GenoChoice.* Accessed April 5, 2013. http://www.genochoice.com/quicktime/home.shtml.

Prensky, Marc. "Digital Natives, Digital Immigrants." *On the Horizon* 9, no. 5 (October 2001). Accessed February 5, 2013. http://www.marcprensky.com/writing/Prensky%20-%20Digital%20Natives,%20Digital%20Immigrants%20-%20Part1.pdf.

Prismatic. Accessed April 14, 2013. http://getprismatic.com.

"Privacy and My Location." *Google.* Accessed January 31, 2013. http://support.google.com/maps/bin/answer.py?hl=en&answer=153807.

"Public Opinion and Attitudes." *The Stanford Center on Poverty and Inequality.* Accessed January 31, 2013. https://www.stanford.edu/group/scspi/issue_public_opinion_attitudes.html.

Purcell, Kristen, Joanna Brenner, and Lee Rainie. "Search Engine Use 2012." *Pew Internet*. Last modified March 9, 2012. http://pewinternet.org/Reports/2012/Search-Engine-Use-2012/Main-findings/Search-engine-use-over-time.aspx.

Purcell, Kristen, Lee Rainie, Alan Heaps, Judy Buchanan, Linda Friedrich, Amanda Jacklin, Clara Chen, and Kathryn Zickuhr. *How Teens Do Research in the Digital World*. Washington, DC: Pew Research Center, 2012. http://www.pewinternet.org/~/media/Files/Reports/2012/ PIP_TeacherSurveyReportWithMethodology110112.pdf.

"Recast Copyright Law for the Digital Era: It's Time to Regain Public Respect with Laws That Make Sense." *Dominican University*. http://gslis.dom.edu/newsevents/news/call-action-recast-copyright-law-digital-era.

Rector, Robert, and Rachel Sheffield. "Understanding Poverty in the United States: Surprising Facts about America's Poor." *The Heritage Foundation*. Last modified September 13, 2012. http://www.heritage.org/research/reports/2011/09/understanding-poverty-in-the-united-states-surprising-facts-about-americas-poor.

"Red Flag (Signal)." *Wikipedia*. Accessed March 13, 2013. https://en.wikipedia.org/wiki/Red_flag_(signal).

"Resources." *Stanford University, Stanford ASEE*. Accessed April 14, 2013. http://www.stanford.edu/group/asee/cgi-bin/wiki/index.php/Resources.

Rheingold, Howard. "Crap Detection Mini-Course." *Howard Rheingold*. Accessed April 14, 2013. http://rheingold.com/2013/crap-detection-mini-course.

"RIAA v. The People: Five Years Later." *Electronic Frontier Foundation*. Last modified September 30, 2008. https://www.eff.org/wp/riaa-v-people-five-years-later.

Richtel, Matt. "A Silicon Valley School That Doesn't Compute." *New York Times*. Last modified October 22, 2011. http://www.nytimes.com/2011/10/23/technology/at-waldorf-school-in-silicon-valley-technology-can-wait.html.

Rosenbaum, Steven. *Curation Nation: How to Win in a World Where Consumers Are Creators*. New York: McGraw Hill, 2011.

———. "Innovate: Curation!" *YouTube*. Last modified June 6, 2011. http://www.youtube.com/watch?v=iASluLoKQbo.

Roush, Wade. "In Defense of the Endangered Tree Octopus, and Other Web Myths." *Xconomy*. Last modified August 8, 2008. http://www.xconomy.com/national/2008/08/08/in-defense-of-the-endangered-tree-octopus-and-other-web-myths.

"S.487: Technology, Education, and Copyright Harmonization Act of 2001."*Library of Congress*. Last modified September 25, 2002. http://www.gpo.gov/fdsys/pkg/BILLS-107s487es/pdf/BILLS-107s487es.pdf.

"SCC English." *The English Department of St. Columba's College*. Accessed January 20, 2013. http://www.sccenglish.ie.

SchemeHater. "Malinformation." *Urban Dictionary*. Last modified April 20, 2009. http://www.urbandictionary.com/define.php?term=Malinformation.

Scoop.it. Accessed April 14, 2013. http://www.scoop.it.

Scott, Thomas, and Michael O'Sullivan. "Analyzing Student Search Strategies: Making a Case for Integrating Information Literacy Skills into the Curriculum." *Teacher Librarian* 33, no. 1 (October 2005) page 21.

"Section 107. Limitations on Exclusive Rights: Fair Use." *U.S. Copyright Office*. Accessed April 14, 2013. http://www.copyright.gov/title17/92chap1.html#107.

Shepperd, James, Wendi Malone, and Kate Sweeny. "Exploring Causes of the Self-Serving Bias." *Social and Personality Psychology Compass* 2, no. 2 (2008): 895–908.

Shirky, Clay. "Web 2.0 Expo NY: It's Not Information Overload. It's Filter Failure." *YouTube*. September 19, 2008. http://www.youtube.com/watch?v=LabqeJEOQyI.

Siegler, M. G. "Eric Schmidt: Every 2 Days We Create as Much Information as We Did up to 2003." *TechCrunch*. Last modified August 4, 2010. http://techcrunch.com/ 2010/08/04/ schmidt-data.

"The Size of the World Wide Web (The Internet)." *WorldWideWebSize.com*. Accessed January 24, 2013. http://www.worldwidewebsize.com.

Slobogin, Kathy. "Survey: Many Students Say Cheating's OK." *CNN*. Last modified April 5, 2002. http://articles.cnn.com/2002-04-05/us/highschool.cheating_1_plagiarism-cheating -students.

Smith, Kevin, and Lorene Stone. "Rags, Riches, and Bootstraps: Beliefs about the Causes of Wealth and Poverty." *The Sociological Quarterly* 30, no. 1 (Spring 1989): 93–107.

Storify. Accessed April 14, 2013. http://storify.com.

TED: Ideas Worth Spreading. Accessed April 14, 2013. http://www.ted.com/talks.

"TED Conversations: Topics." *TED*. Accessed April 14, 2013. http://www.ted.com/conversa-tions/topics/communication.

"Top: Sports: Soccer: Statistics." *DMOZ Open Directory Project*. Accessed March 5, 2013. http://www.dmoz.org/Sports/Soccer/Statistics.

"Topic: RYT Hospital." *Snopes.com*. Accessed March 30, 2103. http://msgboard.snopes.com/ message/ultimatebb.php?/ubb/get_topic/f/81/t/001144.html.

"Tor: Overview." *Tor*. Accessed March 21, 2013. https://www.torproject.org/about/overview .html.en.

"Trademarks Home." *The United States Patent and Trademark Office*. Accessed March 30, 2013. http://www.uspto.gov/trademarks.

Trail, Mary Ann, and Amy Hadley. "Faculty-Librarian Collaboration to Teach Informa-tion Literacy in an Online Environment." Last updated November 20–21, 2009. *Faculty Resource Network*. http://www.nyu.edu/frn/publications/challenge.as.opportunity/Trail .Hadley.html.

Turnitin. Accessed April 23, 2013. http://turnitin.com.

The United States Patent and Trademark Office. http://www.uspto.gov/patents/process/search/ index.jsp.

"Useful Links." *Pasadena City College*. Accessed January 20, 2013. http://www.pasadena.edu/ studentservices/lac/links.cfm.

"Using Hashtags on Twitter." *Twitter*. Accessed April 30, 2013. https://support.twitter.com/ articles/49309-what-are-hashtags-symbols.

Valenza, Joyce. "Joyce Valenza: Teacher-Librarian, Learner, Blogger." *Scoop.it*. Accessed April 14, 2013. http://www.scoop.it/u/joyce-valenza#curatedTopicsTabSelected.

"View." *Thesaurus.com*. Accessed January 30, 2013. http://thesaurus.com/browse/view.

"Virgil Wong and the Medical Avatar at TED." *YouTube*. Last modified March 28, 2012. http://www.youtube.com/watch?feature=player_embedded&v=ePlB2W66zWc.

"What Does Copyright Protect?" *U.S. Copyright Office*. Last modified June 4, 2012. http:// www.copyright.gov/help/faq/faq-protect.html.

"What Is DASH?" *Digital Access to Scholarship at Harvard*. Accessed April 14, 2013. http:// dash.harvard.edu.

"What Is the Earliest Broadway Show for Which Both the Opening and Closing Dates Were Published?" *Answers*. Accessed March 2, 2013. http://wiki.answers.com/Q/What_is_the_

earliest_Broadway_show_for_which_both_the_opening_and_closing_dates_were_published.

"Which Toy Demonstrates a Construction Principle That Can Reduce Damage from an Earthquake?" *Answers.* Accessed February 15, 2013. http://wiki.answers.com/Q/Which_toy_demonstrates_a_construction_principle_that_can_reduce_damage_from_an_earthquake.

"White Paper: The Plagiarism Spectrum." *Turnitin.* Accessed January 21, 2013. http://pages .turnitin.com/rs/iparadigms/images/Turnitin_WhitePaper_PlagiarismSpectrum.pdf.

"Who Is Lyle Zapato?" *Zapato Productions Intradimensional.* Last modified June 2, 2004. http://zapatopi.nct/zapato.

"WHOIS Information for Personality.org." *Whois.net.* Accessed March 17, 2013. http://www .whois.net/whois/personalitylab.org.

Wikipedia. Accessed April 30, 2013. http://www.wikipedia.org.

"Yahoo! Directory." *Yahoo!* Accessed April 30, 2013. http://dir.yahoo.com.

Index

About the Authors

Carl Heine's career in education spans over 30 years, including assignments at College of DuPage and currently, the Illinois Mathematics and Science Academy (IMSA), where he is director of CoolHub and the TALENT entrepreneurial program. In 2004, Carl joined the team of IMSA's 21st Century Information Fluency Project, later becoming its director. In 2008, he and Dennis O'Connor assumed ownership of the project and established it as an independent business. Carl's chief contributions include authoring curriculum, designing assessments, and programming online game applications. Carl earned his doctorate in education at the University of Chicago, studying the effects of instructional practices on motivation (flow) and mathematical achievement. His passion is creating multimedia applications for learning, synthesizing a range of prior work experiences as a teacher, freelance author, curriculum developer, composer, set designer, stage director, and web animator.

Dennis O'Connor has 39 years of teaching experience. This includes 25 years as k-12 classroom teacher, language arts and computer coordinator and professional development specialist. His classroom work led to recognition as a MilKen National Educator in 1995. Since the turn of the century, he has worked as an online teacher and instructional designer for the University of Wisconsin-Stout and the Illinois Mathematics and Science Academy (IMSA).

Dennis earned an MS in Online Teaching and Learning from California State University East Bay and a MEd in Technology Integration and Instructional Design from Western Governors University. He enjoys curating digital information on a variety of topics and creating online learning environments.